ST DITKA
LONG LIVE DA COACH!!

2004/12/14
2004/10
POLICE
2807

EXIT WOUNDS

SOLDIERS' STORIES - LIFE AFTER IRAQ AND AFGHANISTAN

PHOTOGRAPHS AND INTERVIEWS BY JIM LOMMASSON
INTRODUCTION BY JONATHAN SHAY, M.D., PH.D

With Photographs and Words by Veterans of the Iraq and Afghanistan Wars

Schiffer Publishing Ltd®
4880 Lower Valley Road • Atglen, PA 19310

Library of Congress Control Number: 2015931628

Type set in Impact/Zurich BT

ISBN: 978-0-7643-4893-8
Printed in China

Published by Schiffer Publishing, Ltd.
4880 Lower Valley Road
Atglen, PA 19310
Phone: (610) 593-1777; Fax: (610) 593-2002
E-mail: Info@schifferbooks.com

For our complete selection of fine books on this and related subjects,
please visit our website at www.schifferbooks.com. You may also write for a free catalog.

This book may be purchased from the publisher. Please try your bookstore first.

We are always looking for people to write books on new and related subjects.
If you have an idea for a book, please contact us at proposals@schifferbooks.com.

Schiffer Publishing's titles are available at special discounts for bulk purchases for sales promotions or premiums.
Special editions, including personalized covers, corporate imprints, and excerpts can be created in large quantities
for special needs. For more information, contact the publisher.

Acknowledgments

Thank you to my family: Vern, Irene, Cindy, Harold, and Zora.

Thank you to all of my friends. My sincere gratitude. In alphabetical order: Garrett Anderson, Christopher Arendt, Zemula Barr, Brendan Bannon, Nick Benas, Eddie Black, Woodrow and Susan Blettel, Steve Bloch, Blue Sky Gallery, Robert Britt, Ruth Ann Brown, Baher Butti, Mariya Cables, Joe Callan, Michael Campbell, Joe Cantrell, Clinton Carroll, Lily Casura, Jan David Critchfield, Scott Dawson, "Penny Dex", Chanan Suarez Diaz, Alexa Dilworth, Daniel Donovan, "John Doe," Virginia Dodier, Joe Dunn, Megan Driscol, Margo Ellis, Vincent Emanuele, Ryan Endicott, Lucia Enriquez, John Oswald Fett IV, Mike Francis, Arturo Franco, John Gattuso, Mary Geddry, Davis Gorsek, Myla Haider, Jerome Hart, Mandy Martin Hartman, Stewart and Lynda Harvey, Alison Heppner, Sally Heppner, Blair Holt, Grandmother Violet Hortdorf, Allen Huck, Khieem Jackson, Phillip (Vinnie) V. Jacques, Dahr Jamail, Malia Jensen, Edward Ted Jewell, Ann Jones, Andrea Joseph, Joni Kabana, Scott Kaney, Grace Kim, Governor John Kitzhaber, Sergio Kochergin, Evan M. Knappenberger, Ian LaVallee, Seth Manzel, Rick Lawson, Jim Leisy, Carol Levine, Benji Lewis, Lelyn Masters, Shawn McKenzie, Michael Meade and Mosaic, Jake Meeks, Claudia Menza, "Michael William Michaels," Nicole Mitchell, Luis Carlos Montalvan, Corey Moore, Tamika Faye Moore, Philip Nannery, Sophia Oldencamp, The Odysseus Project, Oregon Humanities, Tim O'Brein, Alex Paul, Cheri Beddel Peters, Mary Ann Puls, Regional Arts and Culture Council, Christopher Rauschenberg, Jenny Richardson, Prudence Roberts, Laura Russell, Jonathan Sanford, James Schumock, Dennis Seals, Dr. Jonathan Shay, Dan Shea, Joshua Simpson, Maya Raven Skye, Donna and Jerry Slepack, Cameron Smith, Stephen Sparks, Janet Stein, Pete Stone, Jennifer Stoots, Julie Sullivan, Anthony Swofford, Dr. Edward Tick, Terry Toedtemieer, Ehren Tool, Heather Wakehouse, Jeremiah "Miah" Washburn, Jonathan Wei, Ciana Mae Wells, Mark Wexler, Lamarris Williams, Lucas Wilson, Ash and Seres Woolson, Colonel Mary A. Wright, Carol Yarrow, and Millicent Zimdars. And to all of my nieces and nephews, and everyone who has helped with this book and exhibition.

Dedicated to the soldiers and their families, and the victims of all wars.
Thank you for your stories.
I hope we listen.

I wouldn't wish war on my worst enemy.

– John Oswald Fett, U.S. Marine Corps

Exit Wound

Forensic pathology: the "goodbye" lesion that a bullet or other projectile causes when leaving the body; exit wounds are often larger than the entrance wound.

Contents

The soldier, above all others, prays for peace,
for it is the soldier who must suffer and bear
the deepest wounds and scars of war.

— General Douglas MacArthur

America is not at war. The Marine Corps is at war; America is at the mall.

Despite more than a decade of occupation and armed conflict, there is one reality show American viewers are not offered. War. Barely one percent of the American population has actively participated as a member of the U.S. military in the conflicts in Iraq and Afghanistan. As one high-ranking officer explained, "Never have so few fought for so many."

During the Vietnam war, the nightly news carried graphic footage and images of the aftermath of heated battles. Today, our news is little more than sound bites and short clips of dust settling over rubble.

The American public is spared—or perhaps deprived—of the emotional jolt of viewing the images of flag-draped coffins landing at Dover Air Force Base, and our media is so sanitized that the frustrated author of that handwritten note scrawled on a wall in Ramadi (quoted above) might almost be able to forgive us our inattention.

During the Battle of the Bulge—the bloodiest battle that U.S. forces experienced in World War II—a young, decorated American soldier stationed with his combat battalion in France grew weary of sleeping in wet and muddy foxholes next to the corpses of his friends and eating rancid food. He left his regiment without orders or permission and hiked into German-occupied Nancy, France, where he rested, and where his fair hair and blue eyes allowed him to swim in the municipal pool. A sign read, "Nur Offizier" (Officers Only). Two weeks later, the AWOL soldier worked his way back through enemy territory to resume his position on the front lines. The soldier had already been awarded three purple hearts and a bronze star, but this did not sway his superiors from arresting him. The soldier resumed his combat duties for the remainder of the war; then he was court-martialed for taking his unauthorized vacation. The soldier was my father.

As I was growing up in the '50s and '60s, the stories he told were generic, and agreed with the choppy newsreels and movies I was raised on. The few stories he told seemed to support the nobility of serving your country as a soldier and that it was right to serve your country and fight in a war.

When I approached the age of eighteen in 1968, the Vietnam War was raging and my dad was dead set against sending me to war. He said, "The one thing that I learned from volunteering into the Army was to never volunteer for anything." I got enough subtle messages over the years that maybe war wasn't all it was cracked up to be.

It was more than sixty years after the Battle of the Bulge before my father began to tell me his painful stories of war. His walker rattled and his feet barely cleared the cracks in the sidewalk as we ambled around our North Portland neighborhood, where we had lived most of our lives. The walks were long, even though the distances were short. The war had always been with him privately, but at the end of his life he was finally ready to purge those long-buried experiences and his halting reminiscences revealed a darker side of war.

It's clear to me now that the man who gave me everything he was capable of did his best to spare me—and everyone else—the reality of war. Despite all he experienced, and the pain he kept buried, he was a loving, generous father. My father's revelations gave me an idea about doing a soldiers' oral history of the current wars in Iraq and Afghanistan.

As the mother of a twice-deployed Marine said:

> Before we as a people send our youth into war, we have a responsibility and an obligation to fully understand the enormity of what it is we ask them to do. We are asking them to die. We are sending them into horrible situations in which they face horrible decisions and partake in horrible acts. To truly honor the warrior, every patriotic American must bear witness to their stories and their pain.

"To save your world, you asked this man to die: Would this man, could he see you now, ask why?" – W.H. Auden, epitaph for the tomb of an unknown soldier.

In the words of General William Tecumseh Sherman, "War is hell."

We know from historic literature and epic poems like the *Iliad* and the *Odyssey* that Sherman's words have always been, and will always be, true. If it can be held that we are individually the sum of our experiences, and our society is the sum of its individuals, then we must accept responsibility or we are little more than rear echelon motherfuckers (REMF) who, in the words of retired Marine Lt. Gen. Greg Newbold, "never had to carry out these missions or bury the results."

My first interviews began in 2007. My approach to interviewing was to ask basic questions about where and when the Veterans were born, when they joined the military, what rank, and what job. My primary questions were about their return from war and reintegration into civilian society, yet most of those interviewed quickly shifted from homecoming to sharing their wartime experiences. All soldiers felt a strong need to contextualize how the war affected their ability to reintegrate into civilian society. Eventually, I learned to shut up and just listen. The interviews all took their own organic path. They are profound stories of men and women who have been asked to do the unimaginable.

The soldiers I interviewed and photographed have been intimately forthcoming about their experiences. They taught me what it is to descend into hell and then try to find a way home. Many of the details of my father's experience are lost with him, but as I chronicle the lives of today's young soldiers, their stories are his story. Listen closely to what they have to say, so that you never wonder if they might ask you "why?" Sixty years is too long to keep a secret.

Foreword

Dr. Jonathan Shay wrote *Achilles in Vietnam: Combat Trauma and the Undoing of Character* and *Odysseus in America: Combat Trauma and the Trials of Homecoming*.

We need more books like this!

Lommasson has brought together his considerable artistry as a photographer with first-person narratives, their voices entrusted to him by a broad cross section of Iraq and Afghan War veterans—men and women. Not all are psychologically or morally injured—some are doing quite well, thank you. As such, the book embodies the social process that artists—at least since Homer—have mediated: the communalization of war experience, sometimes physically and/or psychologically traumatic war experience.

"Somebody listened. Somebody cared." These were the words of one of my patients, a 101st Airborne Veteran of Vietnam, describing the beneficial effect of seeing and hearing his own narrative in the shared social space. Such narrative is greatly thickened by the visual arts, such as photography. This same 101st AB trooper angrily demanded that Larry Burrows's great war photo "Reaching Out"[1] be enlarged to 18 feet by 24 feet and be placed behind the Speaker's rostrum in the U.S. House of Representatives for the Congressmen to contemplate as they made decisions that affect military matters.[1]

The full circle of communalization of trauma is accomplished when a Veteran feels safe and empowered enough to tell his or her story; a hearer feels safe and empowered enough to listen, to remember, and to repeat the story—safe enough to retell the story with enough comprehension and heart that the Veteran can say, as my patient did, "Somebody listened. Somebody cared." The circle has completed. The artist can mediate any part of the circle of communalization.

No hearer-reteller can understand *everything* about the experience, unless "he was there," and maybe not even then. Sometimes, the artist is the firsthand Veteran-teller, but more often the artist is the hearer-reteller. After all, Homer was neither witness to nor participant in the Trojan War, centuries prior to composition of the great epics the *Iliad* and the *Odyssey*. But the poet(s) who composed these giant songs had, without question, "seen the elephant" themselves or had listened with both head and heart to those who had. Ancient Greece was constantly at war—one lost war away from annihilation—to a degree that we can barely imagine. Athens was engaged on six fronts during the year that Aeschylus produced the *Oresteia* trilogy in the theater. Every male citizen in that audience was a soldier or warship crew, or both as naval infantry. No exceptions!

Psychological and moral injury from war has been with us since the beginning of the human species. This is not to bless this human practice—no one abominates war with loathing fiercer than those who have been in it—but I mention this to emphasize that the usual march through "Nostalgia" (17th C.), "Soldier's Heart" (19th C.), Shell Shock (early 20th c.), War Neurosis (mid-20th C.) and Post-Traumatic Stress Disorder (PTSD, late 20th C.) is *not* the history of the phenomena of psychological and moral injury from war, but rather, is the history of the *medicalization* of these phenomenon. Prior to its medicalization, it was understood, I believe, mainly in religious, supernatural, and magical terms, which is where historians should look for footprints—not in medical texts.

Just as many have passed through battle without physical injury, some who travel the length of war's "valley of the shadow of death" escape psychological and moral injury—but no one emerges unchanged.

The little, long-term, intensive VA outpatient program, for which I was the psychiatrist for twenty plus years, had the slogan: "Recovery happens only in community." Nothing is more important to the formation of community than its stock of images and stories. This book brings the faces and the voices of today's Veterans to you, the reader. Look and listen. They are us. As Aristotle said, a *philos*—Greek for military comrade, family member, and fellow citizen—is "another myself." *All* of the varied veterans and service members in this book are *us*.

Jonathan Shay, MD, PhD
Massachusetts, USA

[1] ...which I was fortunate to get as the cover art for my first book, *Achilles in Vietnam: Combat Trauma and the Undoing of Character*. To see this image, Google "Larry Burrows Reaching Out."

2004/11/08

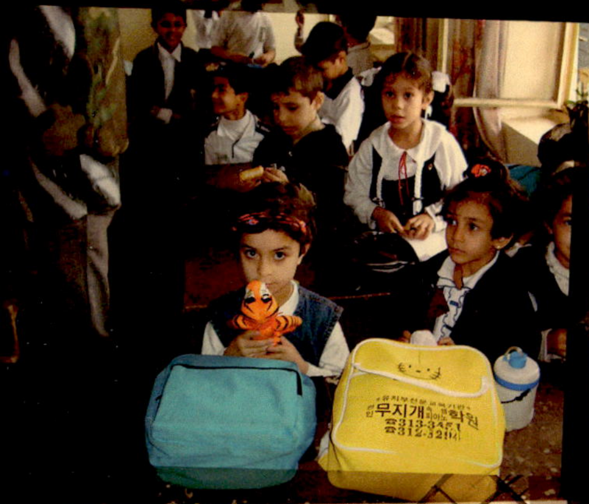

2004/11/08

يرفع الله الذين آمنوا
2004/11/

An Open Letter from a Marine

by Eddie Black

True peace is not merely the absence of tension; it is the presence of justice.

– Dr. Martin Luther King, Jr., *Stride Toward Freedom: The Montgomery Story* (Harper Brothers, 1958)

Dear Reader:

Please allow me a moment of your heart and mind's openness. I ask for your suspension of personal beliefs, your politics, your philosophy, and your ideas of membership in various groups. Open yourself to me. Please.

What is a hero? The term is used loosely and, at times, cheaply. Yet, if I were to ask you to think and tell me who your heroes are, whom would you say? Are they people of character, people of virtue, people who lived a life of purpose beyond their own? I will assert that a hero is all of these things and is also one of action—we are what we do. Heroes are people of character that exemplify virtues for reasons beyond themselves. There are many types of heroes who live lives of inspiration with generative stories that elevate our hearts, should we pause in attention.

There is, however, another type of hero that seems to typify all that we consider heroic or villainous. Upon these human beings we drape meanings and archetypes of dramatic proportions, projecting onto them all of our greatest hopes and all of our greatest fears. We admire their valor, virtue, courage, and self-sacrifice against

impossible odds; and we detest and cry out against their ferocity, violence, and great propensity for destruction. These complex beings, rarely seen for what they are—human—are Veterans in our armed services.

Whether termed Post-Traumatic Stress Disorder (PTSD), Combat Stress Injury, or viewed as the human heart coming to terms with what it has experienced, there are many reasons for these wounds suffered by our Veterans. Some were not in combat, but, instead, they escorted flag-draped coffins back to the states. Others were surgical techs operating on yet another roadside bomb victim. Some, after weeks of heavy patrols, might have taken an R&R break for a day, only to find out a buddy was killed on a patrol "in their stead" that day. The sense of guilt carried is overwhelming. Others, like myself, find that to fight a war within a civilian population is heartbreaking beyond words. Within tragic situations there are, at times, only tragic choices. Yet, let there be no mistake; the chief purpose of the soldier is war: it is to kill. In the end, that is what it all boils down to. The actions of this hero, apart from others, are chiefly to end another human life.

Nietzsche warned of looking into the abyss; it looks back. Many are the smug civilians who have never looked and are ignorantly confident this void is not within their own hearts. Veterans know better. Some are horrified at the depth of that abyss of death within their hearts. Some have sought to cut off this knowledge with alcohol, risk-taking, picking fights, and shutting off all emotions. Yet, in doing so, they also cut off their knowledge of love, for the muscles that strike out are the muscles that can also embrace. Love is a soulful desire to embrace the qualities of something and to let it enter into your soul. In that crucible of the soul, one comes to a crossroad to open one's self to the ferocity needed to win at war. Gore-stained Ares with Eris (strife) and Phobos (fear) walk our ranks. It is telling that an ancient sacrifice to fierce and aggressive Ares was the small and innocent symbol of a puppy. This love of death alters who we are. It changes us, fundamentally, in the mortar of our soul. And within is the great paradox and complexity that this person who craves war also loves and will die for their fellow comrades, family, or country.

There are many reasons to go to war: economics, religion, politics, a "just cause," protection against danger, and more. There are unjust wars fought justly, just wars fought without merit, and many shades and combinations of the two. Rarely, in going to war, are there only a black and white. Yet, down in the "mud and the blood" things become just that: to live or die. We learn to fight and learn it well, for if we do not, we die—or far worse, our buddy dies. In this stark, bare-teethed reality, the soldier learns to follow Homer's declaration in *The Iliad*: "To meet destruction or to come through: these are the terms of war."[1] As William Manchester, a Marine veteran of the Pacific theater in WWII, wrote: "No man in battle is really sane. The mind-set of the soldier on the battlefield is a highly disturbed mind, and this is an epidemic insanity which afflicts everybody there, and those not afflicted by it die very quickly."[2] U.S. Marine Pvt. Elton Mackin wrote in the WWI book *Suddenly We Didn't Want to Die* of the complete

realization of being in a life and death struggle of war: "A flush of shame relieved the scared whiteness of his face. It robbed him of what little strength remained. At that moment boyhood lay behind him forever and, back of a small mound of earth, a disciplined soldier faced the long slope ahead, determined to do his part."[3] In other words, to live in such a fierce, kill-or-be-killed world, one must foster growth of a deep and primal part of the human soul that kills. This is no easy task, for humans are supremely and innately social and cradled in a modern belief of frailty. The fabric of our way of thinking, of our emotional landscape, and of our processing and learning skills is due to the fundamental nature of what it means to be human . . .

. . . part of a community.

Richard Gabriel, former intelligence officer in the Pentagon's Directorate of Foreign Intelligence and expert on combat psychiatry, noted: "There is no such thing as getting used to combat . . . studies of World War II soldiers revealed that 2 percent did not collapse. But these men were already mad, for most of them were aggressive psychopathic personalities before they entered battle. It is only the sane who break down."[4] It is cruelly ironic that combat veterans know that it is within our human condition to be the most vile, brutish animal on the planet (our species was responsible for Auschwitz), yet many of us forget that other human traits, such as forgiveness, compassion, and love, apply to ourselves as well. We know intimately the breadth of the human heart, and yet we do not allow ourselves forgiveness. We see ourselves as that overly simple definition of what the Self is: we are what we do . . .

. . . and we are killers.

We go off to war with a flurry of noise and celebration, with "freedom packages" of toothpaste and letter-writing gear, American flags everywhere, and rock-n-roll music blaring over loudspeakers. For others, there is a solemn ceremony with family and friends—proud, nervous, and scared—in the wings, watching their "heroes" leave for distant Troy. And at Troy, we fight and we fight well. We become very good at patrolling streets where every quarter mile is another roll of the dice for a possible roadside bomb. Every speeding, erratic moving car (and they are all so) is a possible car bomb. One must be on constant guard against an enemy that will use any means necessary to kill you that blends into an environment packed with decent families and smiling children. We do so with the fear, the dread, and the supremely heartbreaking anguish that our actions are—in part or in whole, directly or indirectly—responsible for the death of a father, a mother, or a child. Again, sometimes the only choices open to us are tragic, reflecting a tragic situation. The weightiness of this "situation" is obscenely unknown by the very nation that has so easily sent us off to war.

And we wonder, in the private chambers of our heart, what "hero" can do as we have done. By holding ourselves up with tortured judgment, we forget that we too are characters within a tragic play. In a military culture that is so fundamentally unselfish—where brother sacrifices for brother, sister for sister—we hold onto our injuries ourselves. The Purple Heart is given out for physical injuries, but life-altering injuries of the mind are not considered "real" in our culture. We happy few—we warrior stoics who live by the dictum "do or die"—do not know how to classify our own combat stress injuries of the heart and mind. Our myths, as complex as they are, do not give us healing, but instead twist our hearts more. For we know heroes are not weak.

As Jonathan Shay noted in *Odysseus in America*, it is common for soldiers to consider their own pain unworthy compared to that of others by placing one's self in a "hierarchy of suffering" to one's own disadvantage. What are our sufferings compared to those in Vietnam? What are theirs compared to those who slogged through "The Frozen Chosin" of Korea? What are those compared to the "Bataan Death March" in WWII? What are those compared to the unending trench warfare of WWI? What are those compared to the slaughter of the Civil War?

And if you are that veteran asking this, I ask you, "Who are you to not acknowledge the sacrifice of your own suffering? Do you think that every soldier before you did not try to live up to 'the code' (the demands and the mythic ideal of warriors) that came before? Do you think that those from an earlier war did not look upon their latter brethren with hearts of understanding and compassion?" The look in the eyes of vets of wars past as they welcomed me home from Iraq was supremely humbling to me. These men are giants to me, and they opened their arms to welcome me home. None understand as well as we.

There is a photograph taken in Iraq that shows graffiti written on a wall where some marines are bunked. It reads, "America is not at war. The Marine Corps is at war; America is at the mall." Right now, at this moment, some patrol is walking down a dark street on foot; they have no lights turned on, and most are not wearing night vision because it doesn't work as well with city lights all around. These soldiers are looking for roadside bombs. They are looking for wires, looking in holes, and kicking over piles of rubble. Instructors tell us, "Never kick a pile of rocks," yet, after doing many route clearances like this for hours, one tires quickly of being overly cautious and just starts kicking over rocks. In another area, a convoy is heading through ambush alley. It is the only route through the area, and there are craters along the road the size of Volkswagens—evidence of past ambushes. In a building, a team is searching for the enemy, and a team member is killed while entering a room. Along a marshy road, a bomb explosion hits a Humvee, killing two inside. In a tight alley with no maneuvering room, RPG teams and automatic fire ambush another patrol. To get out of the alley, and to live, is to shoot back. After yelling and hesitating as much as he can before being killed, the gunner fires back, killing a kid nearby. Unable to bear this grief, he is shipped home the following week. In another area, a patrol is providing security at the scene of a car bomb that blew up in front of a hospital. The body parts are the size of grapes. Tell me, dear reader, what did you do today?

We are coming home to a country that is at the mall. As Odysseus sat in the Phaeacian court and told his tale, it was all entertainment to those around him. We find that we do not want to tell our stories to people who are incapable of hearing us with their hearts. To listen with heart is to set aside your judgment, your biases, and your moral superiority, offering us only your love and space. Please do not ask us if we've killed anybody. This is the number one question posed to us, and it reflects the morbid curiosity of those wanting to be entertained. Do our jumpy movements at loud noises, our constant scanning down alleyways as we drive by, our growing and confusing anger when going to a crowded store, and our uncomfortable nature at a 4th of July celebration seem like entertainment, something to be pitied? For us it is neither. Yet, for lack of the "red badge of courage," the wounds in our hearts and minds are viewed as not real or not as important as physical wounds, and we keep silent.

Yet, recovery happens only in community, and two people (a vet and a therapist) are not a community. The absence of a disorder is not the presence of well being. It takes a nation to send troops off to war; it takes a nation to bring them back. I came upon an interesting study that noted the very low prevalence of PTSD in Finnish war vets when they fought off a Russian invasion. It is suggested that the community of the country—of all of their citizens—gave a shared meaning to all through their struggles. Our veterans are willing to take the fight away from home but, in return, we are still separated from our families and churches, our towns and businesses, and our children who do not share in our war. And, again, we cannot, do not, and will not bring upon others the burdens that we've shouldered. It isn't who we are. Were we to want to bridge that gap—with a wife, a mother, or father—how could we contaminate the hearts of our loved ones with such as we've known? How can we tell those who love us the things we've done, the choices we've made? If those around us are ignorant of the abyss within, it is a blessed ignorance we are loathe to kill, as we've done to ourselves. And if we do not, how can we ask for simple acceptance if they know not what secrets we keep in our hearts?

Do not ask us if we've killed, but ask us our stories and let us tell them truthfully as we would to a trusted friend: with honesty. We are not the mythic symbols of heroes or villains. We are humans who have done both valiant and reprehensible acts, and many in between. Instead of being heroes, look at us as your brothers and sisters, mothers and fathers, your sons and daughters. Bring us into your communities and welcome us home—all of us; there are still veterans waiting forty-five years for a welcome home. Listen to our stories with your heart. Allow us the right to weep as Achilles wept for Patroclus. Allow us our confusion and anger. Let us feel that we are part of your community, our community. It takes more than a yellow ribbon on a car. The next veteran you see—of any war—go up to him or her and offer a hug or a handshake.

And to my comrades in arms, remember that you are both the most terrible thing to walk the earth, spreading death and misery like grain seed, but you are also the most beautiful and noble of souls as well. Know that I love you. What an amazing and heart-wrenching burden you volunteer to carry. Yet, remember that if you are what you do, then you must act in order to obtain peace. You must do the work. You must allow yourself forgiveness. You must allow yourself closeness with others. To have trust in relationships, you must trust. You must allow yourself the work and pain it takes to grow and heal wounds. Allow yourself the right to weep, not only for Patroclus, but also for you. We will go into any fight, yet we are afraid to display our own sufferings. If you would be a hero, defined as one who acts and never gives in, who lives for a higher purpose, then do not give yourself to resignation and self-medication. Peace isn't the absence of tension or the absence of a disorder, but the presence of justice, a thriving human spirit. Do not turn your back on the needs at

hand. Be heroic for yourself, your fellow soldiers and Marines, and your loved ones. Tell your story, reach out, get help, and deal with your own experiences. And when you begin to recover, find a brother in arms and help him in return.

Semper Fi

50 Soldiers' Stories

Lucas Wilson pheasant hunting in Maupin, Oregon. He lives in Hermiston, Oregon. On his second day in Iraq, Wilson was hit by an RPG and lost his left leg just above the knee. He spent almost a year recovering at Walter Reed Army Medical Center. Luke said, "At Walter Reed, if your amputation is below the knee, the 'real amputees' don't consider you one of them!"

Lucas Wilson

Growing up, my whole dream was to be in the Army. That's all I ever wanted to do, was be in the Army and lead men into combat. I got 30 seconds of my dream. I'd give my other leg to live it again.

Ever since I was three, when I was in the grocery store and I'd see someone come up in uniform, I'd be like, "Mommy! G.I. Joe, G.I. Joe!" I think it was part G.I. Joe and probably some movies. I'm not exactly sure what it was but, to me, that was the most honorable profession there was. I joined the National Guard February 17, 1997. I actually had to go find the recruiter to join.

The military trains you that you, as an individual soldier, are one of the best soldiers in the world; with all the training and everything, you're one of the best soldiers in the world. But as a group—either as your squad, or as your platoon, or whatever size element it is—you're better. Your job within that element is to protect the guys to your right and to your left. So when I got wounded and I left, I wasn't protecting the guys to my right and left after that.

I'm a "true member of the amputee club." The "true members of the amputee club" are above-knee. The ones that want in but only have pretty much just a scratch are the below-the-knee guys.

At Walter Reed, you're watching everything unfold on the news. I know the news ain't totally accurate. They like to report the bad things that are going on—that sells. You keep hearing about all these soldiers being killed in Fallujah, Najaf, and Baghdad. These were all places that the Oregon National Guard guys were. I just really felt nervous about it and felt real guilty for not being there with them. Every time our battalion lost someone, I sent a card to every family while I was at Walter Reed.

I went to the reunion at the Salem, Oregon, National Guard Armory. I pulled up in the truck in a handicapped spot there—I got my little blue sticker. I just sat there about twenty, thirty minutes, just watching the guys. I saw a lot of guys I knew and I just sat there, me and my dog Buddy in the truck. I couldn't get the nerve to get up and go out. I finally did. When I came around the corner of the building, that's when they all started recognizing me and they just dog-piled me. It was great seeing those guys. I don't know, I just sat there, not knowing what their reaction would be: would they hate me because I left them? I was nervous.

I feel like I'm getting better every day. I'm helping soldiers now, which helps me heal. Like I said, if you talk to the wife, she'll have a different answer. We showed the documentary *This is War* in Salem.[1] It was the very first premiere we ever did of it, and this lady holds her hand up and we call on her. I think it was her son or son-in-law that had just gotten back from Iraq. He's different now than when he deployed. She wanted to know if that happened to any of us. I'm not sure who answered first, but then I took the mic, and I was like, "Well, I'll tell you that I'm the same person now that I was before I deployed, but if you want the truth or the real answer, better talk to my wife." The whole crowd started laughing. But it's pretty much the truth.

We were in Wal-Mart. and I had my two-year-old Lauren—she's like "Daddy's Little Shadow"—in the cart. I've got this Army shirt that I wear, and she loves that shirt. She'll sit there and go, "Ar-my, Ar-my." I got her an Army shirt—it's that digital camo—and it says "Army" across it. Underneath in small letters it says, "Can you see me now?" She loves that shirt. We're in Wal-Mart, and she's sitting in the cart and someone came in in uniform. She immediately jumps up and goes, "Daddy, Daddy! Ar-my! Ar-my!" It totally surprised me. I was so proud of her . . . I was so proud of her.

If I can help somebody else, that's a good thing. At the same time, those guys are helping me, too. That's just the way it works with Wounded Warrior Project.

Lucas Wilson (L) at the Sportsman's Pub 'n Grub Cafe in Wamic, Oregon, after a day of pheasant hunting with his son.

Ash Woolson

The convoy hit this kid and then, um, killed this girl and two goats. I went out with the Civil Affairs and we paid 'em off, we paid off the family. We paid the going rate of a goat and the going rate of a daughter. The going rate of a goat was twice that of a daughter. I think they got, like, $2,000 for the whole package. It was horrible.

I didn't tell my family before I joined. They didn't like it at all. They were antiwar and anti-military. My dad didn't go to Vietnam; he evaded the draft. My family offered me their life savings, they said, "Hey, don't go. Just get out of here." But at the time, I felt as a lot of people have felt, "well, there's something that needs to happen." I didn't agree about the U.S. going in by itself, but I thought there was an action that needed to happen and so I wasn't completely against it.

I did National Guard because I didn't want to be deployed. Okay, what's more honorable than the National Guard? Your first thing is to protect the state from natural disasters. I'd do that anyway. I'd do that now. And they paid for one hundred percent tuition. It was a ticket into college and it wasn't a hard price to pay. They don't teach you that the National Guard was in Vietnam; they don't teach you that the National Guard has been deployed several times. It's a gamble.

Then, when I was in Iraq, I just didn't question myself, because you can't—there's no point. You would just drive yourself insane if every single day you thought what you were doing was the worst thing in the world. The thing is, I don't think I ever did anything horrible in Iraq, but the part that gets me is just being part of the machine; it's like I was used as part of this machine that did these horrible things, that's doing these horrible things.

This is a typical mission. We just kind of go out; you have three or four guys and a 50-caliber gun. It was just ridiculous how open we were. At the time, we were working with Civil Affairs, which goes into small towns and tries to communicate with the kids and build relationships with the locals. We bring 'em the medic and we do the whole town. But you can't say, "We're going to be back on this and this date and bring you medicine."

At the time, in 2003, in a lot of the towns the kids were great. They didn't hate us then, we hadn't pissed them off. This is when our mission was first completed. President Bush came out and told us, "Mission accomplished." The first thing their government pushed for was that we leave, and we just didn't. I think it was a turning point for the citizens, for Iraqis. They expected us to come in and save them from Saddam and, hopefully, just leave. That was their idea, that's why they were so welcoming, but then we just never left.

I remember one Civil Affairs convoy (actually, I saw this from both sides); the convoy hit this kid and then, um, killed this girl and two goats. Not my vehicle—it was a different vehicle. We were told not to stop, so they just ran her over. Because it was close to a town, I went out with Civil Affairs and we paid 'em off, we paid off the family. We paid the going rate of a goat and the going rate of a daughter. The going rate of a goat was twice that of a daughter. I think they got, like, $2,000 for the whole package. It was horrible.

Probably one of the most painful things is that people will ask you how many people you killed, like that's a badge of honor. Like you're not a vet unless you killed someone. So I was struggling with the idea that I wasn't a vet. I was thinking about my grandpa, who's a vet. He's a real vet; he was in World War II. He crawled through the field to grab some guy in a land-mine detector with half a leg, under fire. We look at those wars totally differently. They were quick and they were won quick. High death tolls, but it was over quickly. Over before you knew it. It's hard to put myself in the same category as my grandpa. I just went and did my job.

The thing is, if you're a veteran and you speak out against the war, you're a phony soldier—you're a traitor, you know?

In 2008, Ash walked 1,000 miles with ten other people from Hiroshima to Nagasaki over a period of seventy-two days to bring attention to Article 9 of the Japanese Constitution, the "No War Clause." More than 7,000 people came out to walk a portion of the distance to show their support. Ash and his group of peace-walkers would stage events, play guitar, and talk about peace at train stations and private homes. They eventually arrived in Makuhari on May 4, where 15,000 others had come for the conference. Ash reports in his blog for the Peace Walk that his journey has only strengthened his desire to devote himself to "waging peace."

Ash Woolson and his daughter Finn. Finn was two when I met Ash in 2008. Ash lives with his wife, Sarah; daughter, Finn; and son, Leaf, in Driftless, Wisconsin, on the Kyrie Hill's Berry Farm, since 2011. He is a working artist with a master's degree from Ohio State University. Ash also co-chairs the art committee at the National Veterans Art Museum in Chicago, Illinois.

Luis Carlos Montalvan with his service dog, Tuesday, at the Cathedral Church of Saint John the Divine in New York City, near his apartment.

Captain Luis Carlos Montalvan

I'm a seventeen-year veteran and former Captain in the U.S. Army. It has been three years since getting out. It has been a journey.

The following is an excerpt from *Until Tuesday: A Wounded Warrior and the Golden Retriever Who Saved Him*

Before Tuesday, I couldn't work. Before Tuesday, I couldn't sleep. I drank whole bottles of rum in one sitting to escape, but still lay in bed, unable to shut my eyes. And every time I did, I saw terrible things: a murderous assailant, a dead child. After one grueling therapy session I went to a coffee shop, opened my laptop, and saw the face of a suicide bomber from Sinjar, Iraq. A platoon of Iraqi soldiers partnered with our regiment had placed their rest tent too close to their vehicle checkpoint and the bomber had blown several of them apart. When I arrived, the tent was still smoldering, sirens were blaring, and body parts were everywhere. I was stepping over a severed arm toward the blown-out frame of the suicide car when I saw the bomber. Not his body, which was obliterated. Not his head, which had been decapitated and pulverized. I saw his face, shorn clean by the blast, lying quietly on the ground in the middle of hell like a children's mask. The eye sockets were empty, but the rest was there: eyebrows, nose, lips, even his beard.

I buried that face in my mind for three years, but once it resurfaced in therapy I couldn't escape it. I saw it on my computer screen. I saw it on the television in the corner of the coffee shop. I left, but caught glimpses of it in every window I passed. I hurried to the subway station, pushing myself along with my cane. I reeled wildly into the first subway car and collapsed beside the door. I was sweating wildly and I could smell my stink, that funky mix of adrenaline and fear. I felt badly for the impeccably dressed black woman beside me, but I couldn't speak. I couldn't lift my eyes. I tried not to move. I closed my eyes, but the suicide bomber's severed face—so evil and yet so calm—was imprinted on my eyelids. I sloshed wildly as the train caromed down the track, my head drumming and my stomach lurching, until finally, as the hydrogen bomb of a migraine exploded, I hurled myself out of my seat, threw open the emergency door and, hunched over in the crevice between two subway cars, vomited onto the track, my life exploding out of me once again in a thousand little pieces.

I didn't pick myself up—not for real anyway—until Tuesday. I didn't start to put the pieces together, and hold them together, until this beautiful golden retriever, trained for two years to change the life of someone like me, became inseparable from my side. Tuesday gave me freedom, even from my worst fears, and by doing so he gave me back my life.

I was baptized Catholic and went to Catholic school for a number of years, and went to church regularly growing up. I haven't been a perfect Catholic, but having faith and spirituality was important to me, particularly during my time in Iraq. After Iraq, during the period of rehabilitation and recuperation, which is ongoing, going to a spiritual place like St. Johns Cathedral has been meaningful to me. It has allowed me to reflect on things and give me a sense of peace and hope, and of faith in the future.

Luis says that Tuesday watches his back, reducing his hyper-vigilance and PTSD. He says, "Tuesday and I go to the Cathedral nearly every day. We're grateful it's so close to our apartment. We spend most of our time there praying and meditating at the military chapel. Our prayers always include our friends, family, and veterans (and their families), as well as all people with disabilities and those struggling with hardship. With blessings to all."

Edward Jewell in his home in Washington, DC.

Edward Jewell

The only questions were exactly how many of us would go and when. In a quiet, almost chilling voice, he said it would be all of us and we would leave tomorrow. A loud gasp of disbelief burst from the group and some people started to cry.

Thinking Back, February 2014.

I served in the U.S. Navy as a doctor from 1981 to 2004. I was a participant in "Operation Iraqi Freedom"—the official name of the invasion of Iraq—in the spring of 2003. I kept a diary while at sea. My writing was subsequently included in a book titled *Operation Homecoming*, sponsored by the National Endowment of the Arts and published in 2006.[1] *Operation Homecoming* is an anthology of writings by service members who participated in the wars in Iraq and Afghanistan. Several of the contributors have become professional writers. I have since retired from the Navy, but the war memories stay with me. Anyone who has been in a war will tell you they never retired from the experience. A day does not go by where I do not have some thought, flashback, recollection, mental image, etc., of what occurred. The war ended for me eleven years ago, but it feels like a much more recent event. I am writing about the war with a decade of reflection. *Operation Homecoming* is still in print, and I hope people are still interested, but I felt it was time to write something new.

Like all career military people, I moved around a lot. My final duty assignment was at National Naval Medical Center, Bethesda, MD, the flagship of Navy medicine. Approximately one-third of the active duty at Bethesda carry collateral duty on the USNS (United States Naval Ship) *Comfort*, one of two floating hospitals in operation in the Navy. The *Comfort* is home-ported in Baltimore, mostly doing nothing, but is maintained in a ready state by a skeleton crew of Navy and civilian mariners. If a military or natural crisis occurs somewhere in the world, the ship may be activated. When this occurs, the medical staff at Bethesda assigned to the hospital ship are alerted and may be deployed, often on short notice. The medical crew assigned to the ship are known collectively as the MTF (military treatment facility). I was a crewmember in the MTF.

In the fall of 2002, the American military began preparations for war with Iraq. The political rhetoric was increasingly rancorous. In spite of near-unanimous condemnation worldwide, it was clear by Christmas that President George W. Bush was determined to invade Iraq. The stated reason was to remove the evil dictator Saddam Hussein because of alleged hidden stockpiles of chemical weapons. In January 2003, the *Comfort* was mobilized. The MTF would be sent later, and only if needed. The ship is a converted tanker. It trudged slowly across the vast sea, finally reaching the Indian Ocean. Here, the ship and its small nominal crew rested, awaiting further instructions. Meanwhile, back home in Bethesda, Maryland, MTF personnel were nervously preparing for deployment, getting their affairs in order in the event of a lengthy ordeal. The preparations were unsettling. There was no timeline on when, or even if, we would deploy, how long we would be gone, where exactly we were going, what we would do when got there, and whether there would be any method to communicate with folks back home. We were to pack our battle uniforms and sufficient toiletries to last a long, long time in only one duffel bag—no suitcases—and were not to bring PCs. We sat through grim training on the Geneva Convention and biological and chemical weapon injuries. We were immunized against all known and several non-existent communicable diseases. The shots included anthrax immunizations of unproven efficacy and not FDA approved; a series of six progressively more painful shots in the triceps that produce a swelling like an angry red egg. We were as ready as we could be. My bloated duffel bag was positioned by the front door of my house so I could grab it on the run. Then nothing happened. An enormous force of U.S. military was already pre-positioned in the Middle East and the U.S. awaited the go ahead signal. Diplomatic discussions continued. It seemed unlikely, but maybe there would be no war after all. We waited. And waited. And waited.

Finally, one day in early March 2003, the full MTF crew was summoned to the auditorium for a meeting with the Admiral in charge of the hospital. Of course, it was our mobilization orders; we knew that. The only questions we had were exactly how many of us would go, and when. In a quiet, almost chilling voice, he said it would be all of us and we would leave tomorrow. A loud gasp of disbelief burst from the group and some people started to cry. We were dismissed, and were to report back to the hospital early the next morning. I spent a sad and sleepless night with my girlfriend—now wife—Clara, and reported next day as ordered. The MTF mustered as a group for departure. Following a perfunctory rah-rah pep talk, we were paraded through the hospital to buses, passing through a gauntlet of well-wishing fellow Bethesda staff who were not going with us. The buses zoomed off to the airport, escorted by a phalanx of Maryland state troopers who cleared the highway ahead of us. No one spoke a word during the ride, as we were all lost in our private thoughts. The trip to BWI—normally an hour in traffic—took twenty minutes. The buses drove directly onto the tarmac, stopping to discharge us right at the doorways of the airplanes. The carriers were commercial airliners—mostly United—brightly decorated in patriotic regalia. My request to garner frequent flier miles was politely declined by the flight crew. The flight was a very pleasant experience and seemed incongruous, since we were headed to war. I got a sleeper seat (first time ever) and they fed us often. Unfortunately, no cocktails (surely the Navy had told United not to serve us alcohol). Reality first hit me in the gut as we flew over the Arabian Peninsula, which I recognized from the air by its unmistakable shape. The liner landed in Bahrain. The *Comfort* was anchored a few miles off shore. We were transported to the *Comfort* by a rickety ferryboat. Twenty-four hours after leaving home we were onboard, excited, scared, fatigued, and in disbelief—whatever—at least relieved the long build up and travel were behind us. What would the future hold?

The MFT arrived in theater with no firm assignment. There were treatment facilities established on the ground (known as "in the sand") at various locations in the general area. There are hospitals at the U.S. military facilities overseas, some small and others quite large. The process of triaging, treating, and transporting war casualties—known as "medical regulating"—is a complex administrative process. Providing medical care has great PR value, and inevitably politicking and inter-service rivalries become factors as the services vie for the limelight. We really did not know what we were going to do. We were told to, well, wait and see what happens.

The war began on March 19th, with the much-ballyhooed "Shock and Awe" assault on Iraq. The *Comfort* began to take on casualties immediately. The vast majority of the casualties were Iraqis, mostly soldiers captured by American soldiers and Marines. This became the pattern for the rest of the war. The American casualties were stabilized in theater and transported to the big Army medical center in Landshul, Germany. Injured enemy prisoners of war (EPWs) were brought to us. Patients were brought to us by helicopter, twelve to fifteen per bird. The landing zone was a few decks directly above the casualty receiving area ("cas rec"), where newly-arrived patients enter the ship. The big helos produce a deafening, violent rumble that causes the entire cas rec space to shake. We were rarely given any advanced word on expected incoming helos, nor how many patients were aboard. The days settled into a steady, exhausting routine. We worked from 8 a.m. until 10 p.m. every day, with a lunch and dinner break. I was one of four radiologists. We took one day "off work" out of every four days. Of course, you couldn't go anywhere, and we were not allowed to sleep during the day (no reason ever provided), so you were never really off duty. There were a few distractions to enjoy (TV lounge with twenty-four hour movies, a surprisingly good little library, a gym, free hair cuts, dally over a meal, etc.). I used to hide in the chapel and listen to music on headphones until I was discovered by one of the chaplains.

We became accustomed to the horrible injuries we saw; hopefully not hardened to the suffering, but at least more comfortable in seeing so many badly traumatized people. Some days, we received as many as fifty new patients. *Comfort* thus became a floating POW hospital. There was real concern that the patients would rise up and overwhelm the nursing staff on the ward, so we got a contingent of armed Marines to keep a constant eye on the Iraqi prisoner/patients. They behaved. The patients remained on board until stable and were then transported elsewhere by helo. The "elsewhere" was POW camps somewhere, maybe Kuwait. The doctors and nurses were really never told the disposition of the patients. We also never knew their names, as the patients were ID'd as John Doe and a number. By the time I left the *Comfort* in late April, we had treated over 900 John Does (and a few Jane Does). Some were children—war orphans who either became separated from their families in the confusion of war or lost their parents due to battle injuries. Some of our nurses wanted to adopt them, but this was not allowed. To this day, I wonder what became of the people we treated. How was life as a POW? How many survived to live normal lives? Did they ever get home to Iraq? Did they ever see their family and friends again?

No doubt, some of the MTF members had to be disappointed in our assignment and would have preferred a more glamorous role, like caring for U.S. Marines. I never heard anybody grumble. Like the professional sailors and health care providers we were, everybody accepted our role in this war. I was very impressed with the unselfish and professional demeanor shown by all. By late April, the Iraqi Army had been thoroughly defeated. Saddam Hussein fled the capital and was on the run. His sons and closest military advisors were captured or dead. "Regime change" had been accomplished. U.S. military occupation of the country began. With so-called "organized combat" over, the *Comfort*'s role in the war came to an end. Most of the MTF were sent home by the first of May. The real war, the fight to control the country against the insurgents, would soon begin. This was a confusing, maddening war of ambushes and improvised explosive devices (IEDs)—homemade bombs in soda cans and toys that tore off legs on detonation—a war of unceasing, brutal guerilla fighting that would last for years with no conclusion.

My involvement in the war was very brief—only two months—yet it was the most intense and memorable part of my twenty-four-year career in the Navy. I was extremely proud of my shipmates and how well we performed in difficult circumstances. We patched up many very badly wounded Iraqis, and I hope that somehow this will help foster a positive image of America and Americans in the Arab world. Thinking back, did the U.S. do any good in Iraq? Yes, the evil Saddam is gone. So are uncounted thousands of Iraqis, innocents who perished in a war not of their making. The Pentagon has never published exact casualty figures, but estimates are in the hundreds of thousands. Iraq has not recovered physically. Much of the infrastructure has not been rebuilt. Suicide bombings continue nearly daily. There is no social or political stability, only relentless fear and violence. Was this massive, destructive, destabilizing war the only way to rid the world of Saddam? How about the alleged chemical weapons? The war was prompted by the belief that Iraq had vast stockpiles of such weapons. Not a single canister of poison was found by U.S. troops. None. How do we explain that? How could our leaders not admit ineptitude and failure in their decision-making? How will future Iraqis understand what happened in their country and how will they feel about the U.S.? Did our efforts there serve only to foment hatred and resentment toward the U.S.? I can only hope Iraq will find a peaceful way to rebuild itself.

Edward Jewell, MD, CDR, MC, USN (ret)

Mandy Martin with daughter, Katrina, in 2008. Mandy struggled with leaving five-year-old Katrina to go to war in 2003.

Mandy Martin

I wish I did not have all these stories, I wish I did not have all these fucking stories, but I do.

I Don't Know

Katrina's 5. Mom's 25.
Mom's going to war—soon, too soon, not soon enough.
I don't know. We are watching *We Were Soldiers*. She says, "Mommy, that's war."
"Oh, Sweetie, don't worry, Momma's just driving trucks."
January 15th, no sleep. Making love to him for the last time—maybe—could be—maybe not—I don't know. Kisses.
So many kisses, tears, I love yous. I miss you right now! I'm not even gone and I miss you right now!
Don't let go of me. I can't get close enough.
Tighter.
I turned off the alarm. Who needs it. It's January 16th, 4:00 AM. I am in the shower with him. He brushes my hair.
I put it up according to military regulation.
Brown T-shirt, DCU bottoms. Tuck in, cinch the belt. Wool socks, tan boots, DCU top. IDENTIFICATION TAGS! For just in case.
Maybe, could be—maybe not—I don't know.
How does a mother say goodbye to her five-year-old child? What kind of goodbye is it? Is it the last goodbye?
Maybe, could be, maybe not—I don't know.
So kiss her while she sleeps, pat her strawberry blond hair, one last take-it-all-in glance.
Turn around—don't look back—keep going and walk out the door. For the last time?
Maybe—could be—maybe not—I don't know.

Mandy Martin reads her poem *I Don't Know*, which she wrote in a week-long retreat with storyteller Michael Meade and the Voices of Veterans, Voices of War workshop.

Mandy Martin

Every veteran has a different story. Everybody has a different homecoming, and everybody has a different result of how the war has affected them. There is one single string that ties us all together—it's military service. But all the rest of it is our own individual take on it.

I was born June 12, 1976, a Bicentennial baby. I was born and raised in Coquille, Oregon, and joined the military in 1994. I joined the active duty Army. I knew when I was twelve years old that I was going to join the military. My uncle Chuck, my aunt Carrie, and their family had moved in with us after he got out of the military. I was raised by my grandmother; my grandfather died when I was a young age. There's nothing in Coquille, Oregon, except flipping burgers and painting doughnuts, or working in the logging industry. That wasn't really on my agenda. School wasn't an option for us, because we simply couldn't afford it, and I couldn't continue living with Grandma because we were living on Social Security. There was just no way. The military was my only option: I couldn't wait, I could not wait, I *could not wait*. I graduated from high school on June 5, 1994. I turned 18 on June 12th, and on June 27th, I was on the bus to leave for the military. I wasn't playing. I knew when I was twelve what I was going to do and I did it. I served nearly ten years in the military between active duty and reserve. The dates for active duty were June 1994 through June 1998, and then 1999 through 2004. I was in Iraq from March 2003 through May 2004. This May I'll have been home ten years.

I worked in a Chinook helicopter unit. I served two different roles at two different times within that deployment: I was working the supply aspect in the motor pool and then I moved over to the supply force, the Chinook helicopters. We had fourteen Chinook helicopters in our unit. My unit was Alpha Company 5/159 Aviation Battalion.

I think that the very beginning of my deployment was probably the most surreal because there was so much unknown. At every single little drop of a dime it seemed like we were jumping into our chemical suits because we didn't know how Saddam Hussein was going to fight this battle. Everything forced us to don our chemical suits all of the time. It was constant. After a while we kind of got away from that, but we always ended up in our bunkers because there were so many mortars coming in all of the time. It's strange how, throughout time, as the mortars were coming in, you could feel them rattling in your chest; they were so close that you could feel them rattling. The change went from fear to just straight-up aggravation. The mortars became a nuisance. We had become so accustomed to heightened awareness that heightened awareness became our normal.

The coolest thing that happened while I was in Iraq was when Saddam Hussein was captured. I walked in to the brigade headquarters early Sunday morning and I hadn't seen it on the news because, at the unit level, we didn't have television. They had televisions and laptops. I saw it on the news and thought, "Oh my God. He was captured. He was captured last night." News trickled down to all of us and I remember being so excited about that. I was so happy for the Iraqi people that this man was captured, and hopefully—the fear and the torture, and all of those things that they had been exposed to—hopefully, all this was over. But that excitement only lasted for fifteen or twenty minutes, because I then realized that this didn't mean anything for us. We were still there. We had no idea how long we were going to be there. I ended up being in-country for fourteen months. I was hoping that it would be a sign, a symbol of the end.

When we left, everybody was very much pro-war. Everybody was in support of us going in-country. By the time we had come back, attitudes had shifted quite a bit. We kept hearing that this war wasn't going to turn into a Vietnam, it wasn't going to be a twenty-year war, a ten-year war; it wasn't even going to be a five-year war [sighs]. Here we are ten years later, and we're in Afghanistan, but it's still the same war [sighs].

When I came home, I took over every single aspect of every single thing that could possibly have anything to do with my existence and my family's existence. I took over everything. My family told me—and others around me were telling me—how different I was. I was very angry all the time. My temper was extremely, extremely short, and I just felt like I needed to be going and moving and doing all of the time. If I wasn't moving, going, and doing then I was just absolutely asleep, completely, totally. "All I want to do is sleep and I don't want to touch, see, hear, or think of anything."

Sometimes sleep was really hard. I had chatter going on in my mind all of the time. I couldn't shut that. The only thing that really shut anything up was drinking, because then the only thing I had to focus on at that point was the party. My relationships were getting difficult because of my changes. When we came back, we were all told over and over and over again, "Things will be different. You are a different person. You can't swim a river without getting wet. Going to a combat zone will change an individual." Whenever people were telling me that I was different, that I was angry, that I drank too much, that I was mean, or whatever, I always thought it was everybody else that was the problem. I thought, "You just don't want to accept the fact that I'm different, maybe you are the problem and not me." Panic attacks became a reality. Drinking became a reality. I remember at one point, when I was trying to sneak around the side of my friend's house because there was a big party going on—sneaking around the side of the house from the back to take a couple of hits of some marijuana—I heard my daughter in the background. She couldn't see me, but I heard my daughter say, "Oh, Mom's drunk again. I can tell." She was seven or eight at that point. That sticks with me.

My work was an important part of my homecoming. I worked as a secretary at the Portland VA Medical Center for five years. Then, a year and a half after I came back from Iraq, I went to the Portland Vet Center. I stayed there for a couple of years doing outreach, traveling throughout parts of the state. Then I moved to Military OneSource. I began doing outreach for the OneSource program all throughout the state, and that's how I really got involved with the Oregon National Guard leadership, as well as family programs around the state. That was a wonderful stepping stone for me to start seeing things—not just from a boots on the ground level, but also from a program level. It was while there that I received a phone call from somebody approaching me about potentially working at VA headquarters in Washington, DC, working in the Congressional Affairs office. In that time working for Military OneSource, the Oregon Department of Veterans Affairs named me Outstanding Woman Veteran of Oregon. I was on the Governor's Task Force for Women Veterans' Health in Oregon. I had gotten to know so many people and learn so much about military sexual trauma—so many different things. I went to DC in 2011. I've been here for three and a half years. I am involved in Congressional communications for the Department of Veterans Affairs. I walk the halls of Capitol Hill.

Mandy is a Congressional Communications Officer for the U.S. Department of Veterans Affairs in Washington, DC.

I'm not doing very well at my current job [laughs]. I miss my one-on-one outreach. The only thing that I can do is try as hard as I can every day to realize that I'm now in a position where I'm not helping singular individual veterans, but that there's a bigger picture. I really am that person who says, "Hi, I'm Mandy, what can I do for you?" or, "What are you willing to let me do for you?"

I think that veterans are getting more comfortable with the idea of counseling and involving the entire family. I think that is working. Getting the communities involved is working. I know this is a terrible way to say it, but shoving care down their throats is working. I think the VA is much more accessible than it ever has been. But I think there are still a lot of people who don't want to come to the VA and that's absolutely okay. I think communities really are embracing and wanting to help.

I'm encouraging people, as much as I can, to go to school; if you don't know what else to do, go to school. Take advantage of the GI Bill. It's there. It's an awesome deal. Do it, do it, do it. A couple of months ago a guy came up to me named Jonathan Stanford and said, "Mandy, I listened to you and I decided to go to school. I'm going to a state university and I'm interning and guess what? I am now the speechwriter for Congresswoman Darlene Hooley. Thank you very much." That veteran became the president of the Portland State University Student Veterans Association, then student body president, and now works for U.S. Senator Wyden full-time as a liaison and assistant for Veterans in Senator Wyden's office. He's a phenomenal dude—all because of a presentation that he happened to pay attention to.

Every veteran has a different story. Everybody has a different homecoming, and everybody has a different result of how the war has affected them. There is one single string that ties us all together—military service. But all the rest of it is our own individual take on it. Things happen—unbelievable, unthinkable things—that you would never be able to create in your own mind. Some of this stuff is so outlandish that it has to be the truth, because it's so ridiculous.

Never ever stop the support that this country provides for veterans. I'm deathly afraid this awesome support that the government has for veterans is going to die because of budget cuts. I am deathly afraid of that. Politicians don't kiss babies anymore, they hug veterans. They shake the hands of veterans now because that is the great political move. At the State of the Union Address, at the very end, the most powerful part was when this wonderful man, with the help of his father, stood up and waved at the president. Don't let support for that individual die. That's what I don't want to happen.

Veterans and community bond at a Voices of Veterans, Voices of War event. Organizer Michael Meade says, "Using ideas from traditional initiation practices, Mosaic will create a 'community of veterans' and encourage an artful expression of their need for welcome and understanding. Healing only happens where and when the burdens of war can be shared by the greater community. A public gathering allows citizens to become compassionate witnesses to the stories of war and the necessity of supporting a conscious and genuine return."

Major Khieem Jackson with his dog, Sasha, on his day off. Major Jackson is currently the Deputy Director for the Marine Corps Office of Legislative Affairs to the U.S. House of Representatives. Jackson explains his job: "If I had a bumper sticker, it would say our job is to educate and inform the U.S. Congress of the priorities and the mission of the United States Marine Corps as the nation's premier force in readiness."

Khieem Jackson

I think that for all of the right reasons, we as Americans would be willing to use our military to support the appropriate causes at the appropriate time. I don't think that any of us wants to be duped.

I'm a major in the Marine Corps. I'm a helicopter pilot. Most of our missions were convoy escort missions, but we did do some kinetic engagement type missions—that's shooting, being shot at, so there's force on force type stuff. We provided helicopter operations or aviation operations support of the ground units. Sometimes they took the form of medevac support, where we would typically escort an Army helicopter to move wounded or injured to a hospital or a facility. We did escort missions, and then sometimes we did ground escort missions, so you'd have a lot of infantry supply lines or infantry convoys going.

I think that everything I've gone through helped me do my job, but I never had a kind of moral conflict with helping the Iraqi people, because my Christian sensibilities agreed with at least the surface rhetoric of our administration, that we need to help the Iraqi people and they've been oppressed, etc., etc. So I was onboard with that. What I wasn't onboard with was the fact that I felt that we were duped. I don't think that was really the mission. I think there were some economic issues at play. The same folks that engineered this war were the same folks that engineered the Gulf War: Bremer, Wolfowitz, Rumsfeld, Bush, Sr., etc.

I think, at the end of the day, they understood that a geopolitical foothold in that region allows us to be able to project military force, or U.S. projection, around the world. I mean that's fine; I have no problem with that. What I had a problem with is, "Just tell us." I mean, we're going to go fight the war anyway whether we want to or not, and no Marine has a problem with doing what they are trained to do. That is why I joined, but I just felt we were being duped.

Interestingly enough, for the greater part of my entire experience there during '04-'05 in Iraq, my major battle wasn't even with the Iraqis. My battle tended to be with my own team, a few key-placed squadron mates. I spent a lot of my emotional energy and a lot of my time worrying about my own teammates and not so much the enemy. I knew how to deal with the enemy.

Ninety percent of the people you get along with, and it's great, but that well-placed ten percent? If you are not in that sphere, it might not be as easy as it should be. So I found myself in years prior, but particularly during that time, fighting fights from within, making sure that I got assigned the appropriate missions, where I was the section leader and not blackballed. I think a lot of that came out of my own sociopolitical views, that quite frequently are in contrast with what I think the views are of a very conservative Marine Corps. So I think, to a large degree, those unfortunately came to a head during a wartime situation.

I've learned to keep Ky Jackson separate from Major Jackson. When I was in Iraq during '08, I was a staff officer. We had lots of viewing screens where I worked. We were watching the concession speeches of Sarah Palin and John McCain and a lot of people were disappointed. However, when it came time to view the speech that Barack Obama was going to give for winning the presidency, they turned off the TVs. I kept my mouth shut. I did my job, but I was very disappointed to see they didn't want to see their new Commander in Chief make his speech. So those types of incidents forced me to keep Major Jackson very separate from Ky Jackson.

So anyway, I spent most of my time—emotional time—not focused on the enemy, or not perceiving the Iraqis as the enemy, but perceiving my own squadron as the enemy.

"I have five gold stars tattooed on my shoulder. That's five fucking brothers of mine who were killed by these people. It's been a pretty fucked up period in my life lately. My brigade is shipping out to Iraq again and it's fucking tearing me up. It's killing me, being stuck here and not going, knowing that my friends are going to face the hell of war and I won't be there with them. Sometimes being left behind is a fate worse than bearing the scars that war produces on the body and soul. I pray to God I don't have to tattoo anymore fucking stars." Excerpt from Miah Washburn's monologue for *The Telling Project*.

Jeremiah "Miah" Washburn

The thought of them leaving—if something happens to them and I'm home, retired? That's going to kill me. So I made sure that I would not be in that position again.

I go by Miah. I was born in 1974, in Weed, California. I'm in the Oregon Army National Guard now. I did four years in the Marine Corps to start my military career. I was in the Marine Corps from '93 to '97. Got out, came home, and joined the National Guard.

My first duty station was Guantanamo Bay, Cuba. I did a year down there. Then I did riverine war operations on gunboats deployed to Central America. Did some training in Panama and so forth after Operation Just Cause.

In February 2003, my battalion was activated for the invasion of Iraq. I ended up getting over to Kuwait five days before the end of offensive operations. About two months later, my company was sent north to Iraq, because the insurgency was starting up. We ended up making a lot of patrols; route clearance operations, getting to know the locals and trying to gauge what the atmosphere in our sector was. We really didn't do a lot the first tour. We got mortared a couple times, and there were a couple minor little firefights—I don't even want to call them firefights, they were more like fire spats. That was it. Went back to Kuwait, finished with a security force mission, and then headed home. In August, I volunteered to go back because our second battalion was over there. I got there just as we were leaving. They'd started taking a lot of casualties and they'd put in a request for replacements, so I'd volunteered to go in the first wave of replacements.

I'm at Portland State University now. I'm basically just doing all of my degree requirements. I'm taking a class called "On Democracy." I'm taking a philosophy class and a physics class to fulfill degree requirements. Actually, I felt more anxiety walking around campus and getting registered than I ever felt on any patrol I ever did. Portland State has a traditional image of being anti-war, anti-military. In fact, when we moved our office from the Extended Studies building up to Sixth and Clay, the next day we had a sign hung on our door by this group called "Queers Against Imperialism" or something, with a bunch of goose-stepping soldiers with their heads missing, saying, "ROTC at Portland State? What's that all about?" Basically, it was a denigration. It was funny, because at the same time I was involved in my first term in school, I had also just been accepted to *The Telling Project*.

I didn't volunteer for *The Telling Project*, I got "volun-told" to go interview for it. My boss had been nagging me, just jokingly it seemed, for about three weeks. "Hey, they're doing the Telling here at PSU, you should go interview, you got all these stories." He was convinced he was going to make me the next Charles Bronson and all this. "We can use it as a recruiting tool—'Go see our instructor, he's on stage.'" And I kept saying, "No, I'm not gonna—no one's gonna want to hear my stories," and all that stuff. He sent an email to Jake Meeks. I get a phone call in my office the next day, with Jake going, "Hey man, you know, your boss said you wanted to come down and interview for the Telling," I was like, "Oh, he did, did he?" The way they got me down there was by telling me, "Oh, we're just looking for stories. We've already got the cast set." So I was like, "Okay, sure, I'll give you some stories." At the end of my four-hour initial interview, Max Reiner was like, "Hey, we really want you to do this play, if you can." So I said, "All right, I think that was kind of my boss's intent anyway." So I got involved with *The Telling Project*. I had two monologues initially; the last monologue of the play wasn't even in the script.

They had written "Miah's monologue" in parentheses at the bottom, but I didn't have one yet. So the first few run-throughs I thought, "God, the second monologue's pretty powerful as far as showing the paradox of waiting to die and how funny things can be while you're doing it." But I wasn't really happy with it. I didn't think it conveyed what I thought I would want to convey to an audience if I were standing in front of them, talking about my experience of war. About a month later, Max did a phone interview with me and wanted me to talk about what it was like coming home. I had a really crappy day. I still get a little bit weirded out around Middle Eastern people, especially when they're in groups, and I'd had run-ins with that—nothing confrontational, but just the whole association. So I got home after rehearsal that day and he called me, and that whole monologue just came out. The first time I performed it, there were only two smokers in the cast of eight of us. I did my last monologue. Everybody except Joe went outside, bummed a cigarette, and started smoking. It was amazing.

I was actually performing it and there was an emotional engagement for me at that point. I started crying. All of a sudden I started talking about hate, talking about all kinds of stuff—my kids—then just breaking down and crying. Brian Friend—who's also going out there at the end—we're outside smoking and he's like, "Wow, man. Where the hell did that come from?"

That whole last act, everybody's story, there's something about it. I guess listening to all the other stories, all the other final wrap-ups—something clicked. You know, when Jake's telling his story about looking down the barrel of a 50-cal, asking his squad leader, "Hey, should I light these guys up?" I'm like, "Dude, I've been there. Lots of times." Being able to visualize what those guys are talking about, saying, "God, that was me. What the hell have I done?" So that last monologue, I just—it was really emotional for me. The downside of that, though, was we continued rehearsing, and every time we'd run through the whole script, and I had to do it again. And then we'd do it again. After doing that twice a day each time we rehearsed, I would go home literally just like a vegetable, 'cause I was just exhausted and drained from it. It got to the point when we were getting ready to do the show, and we had a final rehearsal, a technical. Max and John intentionally stopped the rehearsal right when they got to my monologue. They knew it was getting harder and harder for me to stay in it. Which is good, because it progressively got worse from the Friday show. I broke down a little bit. Saturday, a little more. Sunday, we were able to see the audience, and I saw my family sitting in the front row. They had never heard any of the stuff that I had said. They were all sitting there, tears running down their faces, and when I got to that last monologue I lost it to the point where I couldn't get the words out, so I had to pause for a minute and then carry on. I guess for theatrical effect it was more powerful on Sunday, but it became so exhausting. I didn't know how the hell I was going to do this in front of government officials and Hollywood people.

I could feel people responding. When I started doing my thing I could hear laughs and chuckles, and then sniffling, and then sobbing. I could hear all of that. That was the hardest performance that I had done, because I thought it was over. I didn't want to do it ever again, and then we were told, "Hey, we got a chance to go to D.C. and do it." So it was like all right, fine. I didn't think it would be as hard as it was.

When we did *Telling: D.C.*, I was doing my thing, I didn't notice anyone behind me, but there were families from service people who'd been killed, and there were vets from Iraq and Afghanistan, and VIPs. They were sitting behind us. Out in the audience there were a lot of cadets from the Naval Academy, other vets, and civilian members of the community. It was by far the largest single audience, which was great. I was actually kind of excited about that.

There was a representative from U.S. Senator Ron Wyden's (Oregon) office. I think he was overseas. The representative from his office couldn't speak at the end, she was crying. She came up to see us and just couldn't talk. U.S. Senator Jeff Merkley (Oregon) was there at the beginning when Michelle Obama took their picture. Michelle went backstage with everybody in the cast and crew, except for me—I wasn't allowed to be back with Michelle Obama, because I'm a felon. Yeah . . . yeah, I just thought it was funny. I'm a felon. I was sent to war three times and I'm not good enough to meet the wife of the man who has the power to send me again. But, whatever.

It got progressively worse as rehearsals went on. Just thinking about that stuff again, you know—and the part that really gets me every time is the part where I talk about my kids. How am I going to raise them to not see things the way I do? So yeah, it was really hard on me to do this one. I broke down pretty good on stage. At the end of it, when it was over, all I wanted to do was get off stage and leave. As soon as they started tearing the stage down they opened up this big door back stage so they could take the risers out, and I just took off. I just took off and went outside and smoked. I just wanted everyone to leave me alone for a while. The audience was really receptive. Everyone came up to us—half of the cadets that talked to me were crying about it, you know, they said, "I can't believe it, this was really great," and all, and a lot of the vets were like, "Hey," you know, "yeah." It's hard stuff to talk about, especially your personal feelings about the people over there, but you know—yeah, that's what I feel. One of my own personal fears about that part in particular—addressing my feelings or opinions of Middle Eastern culture and so forth—is that people are going to hear it and just think, "Man, this guy is an asshole. He just hates. That's all he is. He's just full of hatred." I'm not. I always had the concern that people were going to hear that. I don't want people to think that. Other vets say, "Hey—that's shit that we don't talk about, but thanks for saying it." It was vindication, or at least validation that I'm not the only one that feels like that.

I don't have any "Support the Troops" magnets on my car. I'm training our future officers. I think I'm supporting a hell of a lot of troops just by training those four guys. Each one of them is going to lead thirty soldiers in combat. By training them and doing the best I can, that's 120 soldiers—that's a company that I know will have good leadership.

There's this great thing that I heard a few years ago: "America's not at war. The American military is at war. America is at the mall." I *love* that, because it's so perfect—it's such a perfect description as to the actual mentality of the people of this country. One, they don't care about the war. Two, they don't hear anything about it, so it's not even in their mind. Three, they're pro-troops, but insomuch as they say, "I support the troops, I'm really all about the troops." "Well, really, what do you do?" "Well, I've got this yellow ribbon on my car." That's about the extent of it. And four, they're against the troops. That's a huge minority. It's a hell of a lot better than what the Vietnam vets got when they came home. If you really support the troops, vote people into office that can get us over there with enough equipment, enough troops, enough supplies, and enough resources to do what we need to do to end that war. Don't elect these morons—a junior Senator from Illinois that has no legislative, or no real experience in politics, and you're going to put him in charge of our military? Give me a break. That's where I think supporting the troops—if you're sincere about that, start voting for people that have a clue. We haven't had that kind of representation in a long time.

Ethnically, I'm part Iranian, but I don't define myself like that. The only issue that I have, the part I can't get away from, is that my biological father, grandmother, and aunts all are that, so I don't define myself like that. People ask, "What are you?" I say, "I'm American."

My father was a student here when the revolution took place in 1979. Then the rest of my family on that side came over; they had to flee. My grandfather was the minister of agriculture for the Shah, which I thought was all bullshit, until I saw newspaper clippings and stuff and was like, "Wow." My grandma's got a coronation video of Shah Pahlevi, and there's Grandma and Grandpa right there. I was like, "Son of a bitch." Yeah. They had to leave. In fact, my grandfather went back in the mid-1980s and they arrested him at the airport, shot him and hanged him outside.

It's shameful for me. I hate being Persian, or having any Middle Eastern ancestry. I think more than anything else it's an associative hatred, just because my mother and father got divorced when I was five 'cause my father beat my mom and me, basically from birth to five. They eventually got divorced. I didn't see him again until I was fifteen. Just hearing Persians, when they talk about how great Persians are and how we're better than Arabs, I think, "Oh, you're better than Arabs, yet you're Muslim. Isn't that a religion invented by an Arab? How superior can you really be?" It's just—there's so much lying and deception that are part of that culture, just in social interactions. I don't even talk to that side of my family anymore. I haven't been able to since I got home. After seeing the area of Afghanistan I was in when I first got over there. It was in Herat, which is the northwestern province of Afghanistan. It borders Iran. A lot of those guys still see themselves as Persian. If that's the case, I hate Persian culture, because it's just filthy. I have a hard time accepting that or feeling good about it. I hate the fact that I feel the way I do towards people of Middle Eastern descent. But if I could end all of this by killing every single Muslim on the face of the planet, I would shoot my grandmother and aunt myself. But luckily, that's a decision not up to me. Yeah, it's hard to reconcile the fact that I've got the same blood coursing through my veins as these bastards that I have to fight and who killed my friends. It's hard to deal with, and then I have to look in the mirror every morning when I wake up and brush my teeth and shave, and I see that asshole that shot at me, or that guy that was standing on the road when the IED went off. Looking in the mirror and seeing that every morning . . . you learn how to hate yourself. That's been something I'm constantly having to deal with. If I had any symptoms of PTSD, self-loathing might be one of them, based on that alone, which is stupid, because I know that race is more or less a social construct, there's no such thing as race. But, you know, I still can't help it. It's not ethnic-driven . . . I hate that culture. I hate Islam. Because I see what it is. I'm a rational man, I'm an educated man. I know biologically and sociologically that this makes no sense.

After going there, I seriously think those people are stupid to choose to buy into something that would set them back 2000 years. It's a pathetic culture, where you can dehumanize a woman because, "Well, she's just a woman." They can sit there and just simultaneously put down homosexuality, but they're all screwing each other. The whole "Women are for children, boys are for pleasure"—I mean, that's sick culture. And it's acceptable to them; they don't see anything wrong with it. You know, I mean, honestly . . . "Are you people just genetically retarded?" That can't be it, because I'm not and I'm half-Iranian ethnically. They'll sit there and smile at you and lie to your fucking face, and then at night come out and try to kill you.

About six months ago, I was kicking around the idea of retiring because we'd heard that we might be deploying to Afghanistan. As the first Sergeant of the company (I spent a year and a half training this company to be what I believe is the best infantry company in our battalion), I didn't feel right saying, "All right, have fun storming the castle. I'm out." So I'll go. We're going to be in-country later this year (2014), and we'll be back next summer. The thought of them leaving—if something happens to them and I'm home, retired? That's going to kill me. So I made sure that I would not be in that position again.

Arturo Franco served in Kosovo, Afghanistan, and Iraq. Arturo spends his days bunkered in his near-empty apartment, playing Xbox video games like *Call of Duty 4: Modern Warfare* with other gamer vets who speak to one another on headsets while they fight a virtual enemy.

Arturo Franco

They had everything to live for: family, wife, kids. I had none of that, so why didn't God take me?

When I went to Afghanistan, I was confident, well trained, and believed in what I was fighting for. The whole idea of war didn't fully hit me till about a month in-country. In Afghanistan, we mostly pulled guard and ran observation points. It was no picnic.

What will haunt me for the rest of my life is when we took prisoners of war. I had so much hatred for them. I didn't care if they lived or died. I will not go into details for fear of the law, but things still haunt me. I remember pulling guard on an insurgent that was about to be turned over to the local warlords. He was flex-cuffed and shaking so badly. I gave him a smoke and started small talk. At some point, I did a little hand gesture to tell him that he was about to get his head cut off, then I took the smoke from him and said some hateful words. Things like that still bother me.

After Afghanistan, and after I left Fort Bragg, I remember standing in the unemployment line, and my company commander called and asked if I wanted to come back and go to Iraq with them. I said no. A few months later, two very good friends were killed. To this day, I feel like I could have changed things if I went.

I went to Iraq in October 2004, and was assigned to 2-162 INF—a National Guard unit out of Oregon. We stayed in Baghdad, not too far from the Green Zone. I was a machine gunner on a Humvee. As a gunner, you are the most valuable person on that truck. The insurgents know if they take out the gunner, then the truck will be almost helpless. Every time we went out, I was constantly on alert for a million things: people, trash on the side of the road, cars, overpasses. At times it was overwhelming.

The worst night was when we were doing route clearance and I was in the lead vehicle. I was using a night vision device and I saw two figures in a three-story building. I took my eyes away and that's when it happened. An improvised explosive device went off ten feet from me. I saw in slow motion my friends get blown across the street. We lost a Sergeant that night. He didn't die, but he had enough shrapnel in his foot to go home. All hell broke loose. Machine gun fire was coming from all directions, and rocket-propelled grenades were firing at us. It was intense. I wish I could say that was all that happened, but I would be lying. A lot of ugly things happened over there: too many to list in one place.

I did not like fighting in Iraq. I did not believe in why we were there. I went because I felt I owed my friends that were killed over there. They had everything to live for: family, wife, kids. I had none of that, so why didn't God take me? What I did over there and in Afghanistan I am not proud of. It's funny that I had to actually experience it to know it was wrong. Don't think of me as a monster. I followed the rules of war. I helped people and felt sorry for people.

The side effects I have from my experiences have caused problems. I need counseling and pills to function properly in society. I hope people that read this will have a better understanding of what we went through over there and what we go through when we get home. Just because we are no longer in war doesn't mean we can forget about it overnight. It's something that is going to stay with us for a lifetime. We don't want handouts or special treatment. All we want is for people to understand us, to give us the respect we deserve.

It was really hard for me to write this, to remember all this stuff. Thank you to all who I served with. There will be none that can take your place. You are friends and brothers that I love for eternity. Take care.

Trying to get a counselor is easy, but after that, they just toss you away until an incident happens. If I call the Veterans Administration and say, "I need to see somebody," they say, "Well, come in to the emergency room." Within twelve, fifteen hours I could see somebody. But after that, it's not like I have a counselor I see once a week; they just kind of put me into the pile again until something else happens and they bring my file up.

Arturo holds his best friend in front of an American Flag that was given to him by his battle buddies before he separated from the military.

Chanan Suarez Diaz in the stairwell of his apartment in Seattle, Washington. Chanan started the Seattle chapter of Iraq Vets Against the War.

Chanan Suarez Diaz

I remember falling forward; my ears were ringing and, luckily, my gunner was inside. That's when the RPG hit. It hit the rear behind me; the shrapnel hit my back. At that point my body was in shock and I didn't really feel anything, and I was like, "Hey, is everyone okay?" All of a sudden I felt something trickle down my back. It was blood. I remember patting my vehicle commander, "I'm hit."

I was in college at that time and I wanted something new. I also wanted more military experience, to get involved in the medical field, and to travel. I didn't want to burden my mother with expenses for college, and I just wanted to be independent. The funny thing is, my family was not for it at all. My mom was against it from the beginning. She said, "Well, if you want to do this, then you need to do this on your own." So out to boot camp I went. From there, I went to hospital corps school. After that I was stationed in Okinawa for two years and I worked on the Med-Surgical floor. It was one of the best experiences in my life. I loved it. After that I basically had a choice between going with the blue side Navy on a ship or going with the Marine Corps. I remember in Corps school, we had what we call green side corpsmen as instructors. It's a very honorable thing to be a hospital corpsman with the Marine Corps because they have such a long legacy of saving lives, plus I viewed it as a huge challenge. I was scared, but I thought, "Ya know what? I'll challenge myself and go through it."

I was assigned to 2nd battalion 5th Marines out of the 1st Marine division. The 2/5 [2nd Battalion 5th Marines] is the most decorated battalion. I went with the Marines and was stationed with a weapons company in Iraq. I was one Corpsman in charge of twenty-seven guys. We deployed to Iraq in September '04. The majority of the Marines that I went to Iraq with were in the initial invasion; they would tell me stories and stuff, but it wasn't real. Until I got there.

I was in Al Ramadi; it's part of the Sunni Triangle. One moment that sticks in my mind was when our commanding officer got the whole company together in front of the barracks the day before we left for Iraq. He said this really patriotic motto, "We're there to help the Iraqis," and he said, "Look to your left, look to your right. Ya know, not everyone here is going to come back." That really stuck with me. I thought, "Wow, this is pretty real."

When I first arrived with the 2/5, I was there for a month, and then I deployed with my Marines. One thing about the Marines is that they can be pretty much assholes. They didn't know me and they didn't know my experience. I was "the new doc," so I had to prove myself. There were one or two Marines out of my platoon that actually talked to me and were nice. The rest were kind of like "whatever," and didn't really help me much.

I was always against "Don't Ask, Don't Tell," and I've seen what it's done to good service members who happen to be gay or lesbian. I had friends in Okinawa who went through witch hunts because their command, Captain, or whatever was some prick, right wing evangelical Christian who could make your life a living hell. I had a friend who was investigated for being gay because his roommate was very homophobic, and all of us were part of the investigation. People were scared that they're going to kick you out. So then, everything you've worked for, just because of who you are, they can kick you out. Then you don't get your benefits, you don't get this and that. And luckily, my friend didn't get kicked out. One of our other friends got kicked out; it's a horrible feeling to be singled out that way.

I've had a couple situations in the military where I had guys come up and harass, like, "Oh, are you a faggot," blah, blah, blah. I would almost get into fights, or get threats like blackmail. In Okinawa there was this dude. We shared the same bathroom, but we had our own living spaces. I had a couple friends over, we were hanging out, and all happened to be gay. (And that's another thing—the rumor mill—you know, if you really want to screw someone over, just start a rumor and it just goes like wildfire.) This dude threatened me and said, "I don't know what you guys did last night, but it seemed like you guys had all these orgies and I saw a condom in the bathroom." It was a completely insane lie. I confronted him because I heard the rumor and I knew who it was from. I confronted him in the laundry room and I said, "Why are you saying this?" As soon as I confronted him, he backed down and was like, "Oh, I have proof," and I said, "Show me," and of course it was bullshit. So I've had that before. In my platoon, the snipers were a couple of undercover Nazis, but straight up Nazis. They knew I was gay, or they assumed I was gay. I'm a person of color, and I'm Jewish. You know, everything they hate, I represent.

My platoon was more mature than the rest. It was more open, in the sense that people expressed themselves more and we had political debates. I remember one particular night in Iraq when we occupied this guy's home, and this young Iraqi guy that I was talking to—it was like two, three o'clock in the morning—he said that he was a medical student, but he had to come to Ramadi to take care of his dad. I asked him, "How do you feel about us being here?" He spoke really good English and he said, "You are only here because of the oil," and at that moment I was like, "Oh, okay, that makes sense," and I brought that back to the Marines and discussed it. I remember one of my Marines saying, "Oh, that's radical leftist propaganda," and I thought, "Well, this is just an ordinary Iraqi who has made that connection." There were a couple other Iraqis that I spoke to who said they were glad that Saddam Hussein was gone, and they said that Saddam was a bad guy. But they said, "We had running water and electricity, and we could walk outside our homes and not be afraid to die."

The main discussion was, "What the hell are we doing here if people don't want us here?" That's how a lot of Marines felt. I remember being very conscious and telling my Marines, "Don't take it out on the Iraqi people." When we went out on missions, I would tell them, "Don't kill innocent people." A lot of innocent people were killed, and there was this one particular platoon that, after two of their Marine friends got killed, talked about killing innocent people. They would brag about it and everyone knew, but it was on the hush-hush.

I only saw the Mujahedeen in the flesh and in person twice. I saw a lot of death and destruction and innocent Iraqis killed. I knew some Arabic. I took it upon myself to learn as much as I could, and the Iraqis always felt comfortable coming towards me because I look Arab. We would go and bust into people's homes, but when I went and talked with them, they were some of the most hospitable people I'd ever met.

The second day we were there, convoying into Ramadi, was when reality hit. We were crossing the Euphrates and going into our base, Hurricane Point. I remember seeing the Iraqis and they were not happy at all. I had the sense that they knew there was a huge turnover of Marine units. We went into the downtown, and all of a sudden there were rocket-propelled grenades, small arms. I remember getting out of my Humvee and I got right next to a wall. I was just orienting where I could see and I didn't see anything and people were yelling. It was very chaotic, and I remember there was one point where it was just surreal and kind of like slow motion, and I thought to myself, "What the hell did I get myself into?" I was insane.

We are always out there, and we are a big target. One of the biggest things that killed a lot of Marines and Iraqis is just being in the wrong place at the wrong time. I can't remember how many countless IEDs I've been through and survived. I really think that it's surreal when you think about how many times you can die.

I was there for, like, six and a half months, and we lost a total of ten or eleven people. One was my second CO, who everyone really loved. He was a really good guy. He died from a suicide VBIED [Vehicle Born Improvised Explosive Device]. Every day we would get mortared. I was so anxiety ridden every day, twenty-four seven.

I was able to save two lives in Iraq: one was my platoon sergeant who is still in the Marine Corps. We used to make fun of him behind his back. We used to call him Burl; he's kind of like this country guy from who knows where. The day it happened we were in downtown Ramadi and we were doing a search of the city, searching different places and trying to push out the Mujahedeen to make them come out and engage. We got a tip that they were in that area. There's an alley that is called RPG Alley (for a reason), and my Staff sergeant had his driver park right in the middle of that alley. Then all of a sudden I heard a "shhhhh" and "boom." All of a sudden they yelled "Corpsmen up! Staff Sergeant's hit." While being shot at, you just act instantly. You don't have time to think. I ran to him and it was really shocking. He lost his right leg from mid-thigh down, and there was the stench of blood and burning flesh and metal, and all that. It was nasty. And he was laying on his back and calling, "Doc, Doc!" I went and I responded, "Staff Sergeant, I'm here." He said, "Okay," and that helped him feel better. I started working on him and put a tourniquet on. He was in the beginning stages of shock and we had to take him out of the kill zone. Marines were posted next to me as security and I just worked on him and gave him the IV, stopped the bleeding, morphine, and checked everything. We called in Urgent Surgical to get him the fuck out. It seemed like forever until they came. I was covered in blood, and I was talking to him to get his mind off it. We put him on the half-back Humvee and that was it. They took him away. I remember seeing his foot while I was putting on the tourniquet. I remember seeing his foot with his socks. The RPG blew off his boot and his socks. I remember seeing his foot, and seeing his toe with blonde hair on it, and I was like, "God!" It's just one of those things that record. Thank God he is alive. I was drenched in blood. Luckily, nothing happened to me or any of my other Marines that day. We went back to base, I changed my uniform, cleaned up, and then we went to this Army base across the Euphrates and had food. I was still in shock. That was my first experience. Up to that point, my Marines said they trusted me, but after that they loved me.

We used to get mortared almost every day. One particular day all of my Marines were inside the hooch where we stayed because we were on the night schedule. I was in the head and I was with my new platoon sergeant. We were basically shooting the shit in the bathroom and all of a sudden a mortar drops right behind the hooch. We dropped to the floor and a Marine came running inside, yelling, "Corpsmen up!" He had a piece of shrapnel stuck in his forehead and blood coming out. I thought, "Okay, this guy will be all right." I remember running outside and it was smoky and that burning flesh smell, and all I remember was seeing somebody I didn't know who was split open. The mortar hit him; it landed right behind him and it basically cut his back open, then he fell forward. I remember running in the back with my med pack. I saw another Marine and realized that I couldn't do anything—he was gone. But a friend of mine, Sabina, was inside the mortar pit and his right knee was blown out. His left deltoid was blown and he was going through shock, so I just picked him up and took him to the front of the hooch. Another corpsmen came and we started working on him right then and there, just to stabilize him. Luckily, the clinic was right down the street, but I wanted to make sure he was okay. To this day he is alive and well. I found out not too long after Sabina was evacuated that the person who died was a guy I knew. His name was Cliff. He always had a smile on his face and I remember asking him, "How can you smile in a place like this?" He said, "Well, I'm alive." He was eighteen years old, and he was gone. So before I got wounded all of that happened. And on a daily basis all of that was going on. You just become numb. You just shut down.

The day that I got wounded was February 26th of '05, and it was a day raid. My platoon hooked up with our HQ, so our CO was with us, and we occupied a huge house with five families in it. We were in there for hours, so we were just hanging out at the house. I remember having a beautiful conversation with this one particular Iraqi family. I gave them meds and stuff and they had two kids; I remember seeing one of them had an IV before in his arm. The kid had leukemia. He was a small kid. His mother said that he was dying and that he needed medication and they didn't have any more, and I obviously couldn't do anything. I gave them meds. This kid was eight years old—the most beautiful kid I've seen, and just happy and nice. Then a platoon got engaged in downtown Ramadi, and we were all "Okay, we've gotta go." We left the family, and it was within fifteen minutes from when I left that house to respond that I got hit. We went downtown and all I remember seeing is shattered glass, blood, and a dead Iraqi man on the sidewalk. This was the middle of the day, like eleven or noon, and I think it was a Sunday, so people were out, and they opened up around them. I was in the third vehicle at that time. They always used to switch me. They never kept me in the first vehicle or the last vehicle; they rotated me. They dismounted and went into the cemetery, and I remember just hanging out. I was behind the passenger vehicle commander and I remember looking out; I remember seeing this big, huge wall and the cemetery. All I remember is just this "shhhuuuuu" and "boom." It lifted my Humvee. I remember falling forward—my ears were ringing and luckily, my gunner was inside. That's when the RPG hit. It hit the rear behind me and the shrapnel hit my back. At that point my body was in shock, and I didn't really feel anything and I was like, "Hey, is everyone okay?" All of a sudden I felt something trickle down my back. It was blood. I remember patting my vehicle commander, "I'm hit." And he was just kind of like, "What Doc?" The pain just hit me and I said, "I'm fucking hit!" They all scrambled and pulled me out of the vehicle. I couldn't walk so they dragged me. They had me on my stomach. They took off my gear and checked to see if I had any exit wounds—I didn't. They started working on me. I was hearing bullets and all types of stuff, and I remember my Marine was so nervous that he messed up giving me the morphine shot. I never got morphine. I remember feeling the needle going in and I'm like, "I didn't get it." And I remember telling my gunny, "Gunny, I didn't get morphine and I'm in extreme pain." And he thought I was lying or I was out of it so he said, "No, Doc, you can't have more."

I was in pain. They flew me to Baghdad and that's where I had my first surgery. I had my second surgery in Landstuhl, Germany. Landstuhl was a horrible experience. After that they flew me to the states. Then I went home for a month in Miami to recuperate.

The Marines gave me a choice. They told me I could be medically discharged if I wanted to, but I was still very gung-ho. Well, gung-ho meaning I missed my Marines, so I decided to finish it.

When I got out, I moved to Seattle and just threw myself into activism. I joined IVAW [Iraq Veterans Against the War] while I was on active duty. Then I started exploring Socialism. I started the Seattle chapter of Iraq Vets Against the War and ran for president. They voted me in and I was president of the chapter for about two and a half years. I literally threw myself into the activism and social movement, the anti-war movement. I was obviously more radicalized.

PTSD really hit me when I got out, because I was out of the military and just trying to get back to some normalcy. It was really, really rough: nightmares, very anxious all the time, irritable. A lot of things angered me; I had a short fuse and I drank a lot. I just wasn't taking care of myself. When I was involved in the movement, I was so driven by it and I wasn't taking care of myself. I would drink at least a six to twelve pack a day. It was crazy. With all the work I put into the movement and stuff, I had a breaking point to where I just broke down emotionally. I had a PTSD breakdown that landed me in the VA. I just lost it. My ex was there and he witnessed it. So I went to the VA. I had to step back from the activism. I didn't go cold turkey. I gradually stepped back and went to therapy, and it helped a lot. I was put on medications and I kind of struggled with that. Sometimes I was like, yeah, this helps, and then there were other times where I just felt like a zombie. I just didn't feel right. But I can definitely say that I'm in a better place than I was a couple years ago. I'm not on any meds now—I just feel healthier—but it was a real struggle. It was affecting me and my personal relationships and everything.

There's a crisis going on right now in the world, especially in America, with our great recession. It's sad. And the anti-war movement completely collapsed with the election of Obama; the anti-war movement does not exist right now. There's a lot of disillusionment and of feeling powerless. Change doesn't happen overnight, and that's the thing that really keeps me going. It's going to be a long-term thing. We lack a sense of history in the movement. You don't have to be a history major, but at least know past struggles and know how they've risen and why some of them failed, and apply those now. We can't make the world a better place overnight. People don't necessarily understand that. We all want the quick fix. That's just not how it works. Dismantling this system that perpetuates war, poverty, and oppression—these things take time. I don't know what's going to be the situation that's going to ignite that spark.

I wasn't radical in Iraq. It was after Iraq that radicalized me.

Facebook post of November 10, 2014:

I was just awarded the Navy Commendation Medal with Valor for saving my platoon sergeant's life during combat, circa 04-05, Ar Ramadi, Iraq. One of the proudest moments of my life.

Former United States Army Ranger Michael Campbell on his farm in Sturgis, Mississippi. Michael left the Army after his best friend was killed in Iraq when their vehicle ran over an IED. Michael says: "You have your good days and your bad days. The day I lost my good friend was a very bad day. I think Cesare Pavese, one of my favorite Italian poets, says it best, simply in two sentences, 'We do not remember the days. But we remember the moments.' . . . To me, we're made of our memories."[1]

Michael Campbell

I don't know how you define a warrior or hero; ya know, I think there's just that defining moment in an individual's life when they don't question whether they can do it or not . . . they are already doing it.

My first experience was at my duty station at Ft. Bragg. I walked into the chow hall and they had two televisions. They had one I will never forget, it was playing Clint Eastwood's *Pale Rider*. I'm a huge Clint Eastwood fan. On the other one was *Yo MTV Raps*. There was a salad bar in each room and I'm standing there with my food tray. I just got my food. I'm looking at this and I'm like, wow. They really did have shit segregated. This is in North Carolina; it really was segregated and it appears to still be. The salad bars were segregated, the TVs were segregated, and one cafeteria's got two of everything? What the hell is that?

I went in and watched *Pale Rider*. I'm a big *Pale Rider* fan. There were two NCOs; they were both white and I kinda ate my food and I looked over at 'em and they kinda looked at me. I didn't say anything to them; I just looked back and continued watching *Pale Rider* and eating my food. I said to myself, "I'll do what I have to do if that's what the situation is, but I'm not, I'm not living like this. And I'm gonna make that very clear from the first meal I eat to the last."

On 9/11, I remember sitting at Ft. Bragg and the TVs came on—I believe it was 9:27 in the morning, if I remember right—and there it was. Oh my God, they actually tried something! And you know what I honestly thought to myself, one tower was smoking, and I said, "Holy crap, what happened?" They were announcing that a plane had flown into the tower, and about that time another plane hit the other tower. That's the moment that America was jolted. We all saw the first tower burning. "What is this? Is there a fire up there? What's going on?" And I remember thinking to myself, "Who are those sons-of-bitches?" I mean instantly it just came over me, I thought, "Who would dare?"

The twelve Saudis . . . we saw them on the news. I don't know how many television sets got busted at Ft. Bragg, but I suspect it was a lot of 'em, ya know? That's the way the environment was. I don't think there was a single soldier at Ft. Bragg who wasn't ready to pull somebody's head off and throw it in the ocean.

Later, I counted up to my first forty-eight combat missions in Afghanistan and then I quit counting. I guess you could say the first forty-eight were worth counting; the rest really weren't, and they were just the same old thing, just another number. Ya know, I guess I began getting numb to the experience; I didn't really think, contemplate, or philosophize anymore. It was just, "This happens, do this; this happens, do this; this happens, do that."

I had no concept of politics at that time. I didn't even know the difference between Democrats and Republicans. There's no politics in war.

I'm proud of my service at home and abroad. At Fort Bragg, we had a previous unit come home and four of their wives turned up dead in just a few days. The post was in an uproar. Whether they were cheating on their husbands during their deployment, I don't know. That's one reason husbands come home and murder their wives.

We wanted solutions. My best friend, Trevor, called them social issues. We wondered what we could do. You've got a lot of crazy men running around with weapons and a lot of testosterone. He said, "We gotta do something." I said, "You've got eighty-five thousand single male soldiers on Ft. Bragg. This is a big job, bro."

I said, "Well, give me some suggestions." And he kind of said, "We need counseling." I said, "Well, that's not gonna work at Ft. Bragg. Give me another option." And he said, "Well, 'education,' how about 'education'?" And I said, "Well, is there any way we can twist the 'education' word and then actually do counseling?" And he said, "Okay, how about we start with some basic, fundamental 'education' courses. We start with sociology, psychology, child development, that type of thing." I said, "That's good, I think that might work. We might be able to sell that." He said, "Okay, I'll make you a deal. I'll do all the logistics if you do all the talking." I was good at talking and he was good at doing. "That's perfect, I'll do it. C'mon, let's go see company commander."

We went into our company commander's office and he had a big pile of Article 15s of soldiers getting into trouble: court martials, DUIs, and spousal abuse. I said, "I think we've got a solution sir," and he said, "What? Let me have it. I'm tired of this shit. We gotta get some order here." So we propositioned him with our idea and he said, "I LIKE IT! It's good, good, good leadership there, boy!" He gave us a couple classrooms.

We thought, "Well okay, let's back up. Let's make sure these soldiers want to do this before we go there." So we put a survey out with two classes on it, and out of 112 soldiers in Bravo Company, ninety-six signed up for both classes. That blew us away.

After we got started, you could tell it was working. You could see the hope, you could see the camaraderie coming back, and you could see interactions beginning to take place between soldiers again. We began to see it coming back. Like, "This is working, this is working, these guys are gonna get frickin' four-point-ohs in Psychiatry!"

Unfortunately, part way through we got orders to redeploy. I rushed over to headquarters to talk to the Sergeant Majors and plead our case. "Hey, look, we've got four weeks of this class left. It takes four weeks to get a whole unit deployed. Send us last, bring us back last. We'll get the class done, they'll get the credits, we're gonna go over there anyway, and we're coming home anyway."

They didn't give a shit. So we went. The soldiers were furious. I mean, it was all we could do to keep them from lynching them. I begged and pleaded with all of 'em not to pull any shit or they'd never let us back in that classroom, and they listened.

Fourteen days later, we stepped off on our first combat mission from Camp Mercury, outside of Fallujah. We went into Fallujah and we struck an IED. Once the smoke cleared I found myself sitting by Trevor and I just could not believe that the some-bitches got this one! It just blew my mind. Out of all forty-five of us, you got this one. It's the one I need. I need this one.

It was a very, very traumatic situation. We'd run over an IED and it had blown Trevor's left leg off from the hip down, and of course everyone in the vehicle was injured. I mean, we had legs missing, we had arms missing, and we had hands missing. Guys' eyes and faces were bleeding and it was a mess. I don't know, there is a lot of time that I don't remember—I had a lot of blackouts, and I don't know what I was doing.

I spent the last few minutes with Trevor. It's something that I hope nobody ever has to go through. He was dying and he knew he was dying. He was kind of holding his intestines and everything in and he was bleeding to death and he knew it. And I just told him, "Listen, I don't know what to do, I don't even know what to do here." And he just pretty much told me, "Don't worry about it, this is the way it goes." He was one of the most selfless men I have ever met in my life. I mean, he didn't whimper for himself a bit. He just said, "This is what I want you to do, I want you to remember what we did." He was talking about the education initiative program that we had brought to Fort Bragg for the infantry soldiers just a few days before they decided to deploy us. "Don't forget what we did. Do not forget what we did." And I said, "I will not," and I haven't. I will never forget.

Guys would get wounded, a couple would get killed, more guys would get wounded, another one would get killed, vehicles would get destroyed, we'd get bombed some more, and then get more rocket attacks. We'd find some caches, we'd blow up their stuff, we'd apprehend a few POWs, and we'd interrogate them. I would hear a lot about these secret POW compounds overseas and we had one. That's what we had and, yeah, I won't lie, there were some unconventional tactics utilized. But I'll add this: they worked very damn well. They gave us information, they gave us munitions, and it saved lives. I sleep like a baby. So I like to tell everybody, "You don't want us tying that man to a tree and leaving him there for two or three days to find out where the caches are, but you do when it takes your son's legs off. You don't give a damn what it takes, you want 'em, you want 'em found—you do when it blinds your kid. They blew off one of my buddies' arms, I'm gonna tie 'em to a tree, and they are gonna tell me where they built 'em, where they put 'em, and who helped 'em. And we gonna catch them, too."

These are our own guys; this is our own flesh and blood. I have no problem kicking the crap out of an individual who is threatening to harm our folks or bring risk to us. We're just good ol' country boys and girls who are just out there trying to protect each other.

NOTE: In March 2011, I spent two and a half days with Michael and his wife Ryann at their farm in rural Sturgis, Mississippi. Michael and I talked long into the nights about his time at war. In those conversations, he told me about his struggle with the loss of his friend, Trevor. That experience ended his military career. I debated whether to include the story in this book. I'm not sure why—there are many difficult stories here. I decided to ask him how he felt about it. He sent me two e-mails:

> Jim,
> It has taken me nearly 10 years to be at peace with what happened. It still hurts; however, I am at peace with our losses and mistakes. However, thanks for asking.
>
> —Michael

Jim,
Let me elaborate. I recently sat down with a WWII veteran who ran across the beach of Normandy, dodging bullets and dragging his friends' bodies to and from the ships as the Germans killed them one by one. When I asked him what gave him the courage and strength to continue into the night, he said, "I saw how suppressive the German regime was to the people and I knew what would happen to us if we lost." Immediately, I understood why Trevor and I had gone to the lengths we went. We understood the misconception the nation would have of our fighters. We hoped that could be washed away by education. A Ranger with a masters degree in engineering is an engineer, not a killer.

When I consider our Republic, I see the similarities to ancient Roman times. Caesar and many others knew that Rome was a fragile concept. A mere whisper could bring her down. That whisper was not the enemy or the plague—it was public perception. Our public's positive perception of America is a fraction of what it was in the '40s. Now, when the President speaks of how great we are, our people disagree!

Our Republic is whispering that we do not need cohesion, patriotism, honor, or sacrifice, but they will soon see how wrong they are. There are actually people in this country that think sacrifice and pain are unnecessary. That scares the shit out of me. We are too fat and happy as a country and we need our souls and borders tested so that we can refresh that concept of Unity. The caged bird forgets how to fly, or was never taught.

Al Qaeda, the Taliban, or Jihad brotherhood would destroy our economy and the country that I love in an instant if they thought they could get it done. I have seen the hate in their eyes, and please, if you believe anything I say, believe this: they will be back, and it will be worse—we better stay in step!

—Michael

Shawn McKenzie and his grandmother, Violet Hortdorf, at her home in Aumsville, Oregon. McKenzie served with the Army infantry in Iraq and joined the Oregon National Guard after returning home. He is now an officer.

Shawn McKenzie

I went to the mall and was disgusted with American society. It's like you've landed on another planet. People in America just don't fully understand . . .

\

My grandfather was in the infantry in World War II, and my uncle was in the infantry in Vietnam. I joined the Army to be in the infantry. I'm pretty happy that I did join the Army. I met a lot of really great friends.

People usually compare football to combat. It's much more like when I played baseball. All of a sudden something's hit at you out of the blue. Actual combat—I think the way it worked out—was on average once a month. Small arms fire every once in a while. We were constantly out in our area of the city, and that also kept the violence down. We were going into these neighborhoods, surrounding them, searching all the areas.

You could tell when you're in a neighborhood where you were not well liked. The little kids wouldn't come up to you; they all gave you dirty looks. If we established relationships in the neighborhood, the trust went way up. They are much more afraid of the insurgents, because they don't want the insurgents to come to their home and kill them. Their big thing was, we took their country over. Then all of a sudden, there's no law and order. That's what gained the insurgency some promise, is that they could say, "I can protect your neighborhood. The Americans can't do that." Once we figured that out, things are progressively getting better.

While I was over there, I didn't think that much about it. Even when a friend of mine was killed, it never really sunk in. It wasn't until I got back. And then it was all this. My wife noticed that my anger level was much higher. I was almost disgusted with American society. People in America, they don't fully understand what's going on. The first job that I had, I worked for Farmers Insurance. At work, it was like death by a thousand cuts to talk to these people. People would ask me things like, "Have you ever killed anybody?"

I've been working at the Portland State University police. There are a couple of Vietnam veterans that work there, and one of the guys that served with me over in Iraq. For me, it's a lot less stressful because of the other people that are around. People wouldn't think that this would be because of all the students here. It doesn't really bother me.

Right when I came back, I was pretty angry. I went to the VA and talked to counselors 'cause what I was considering, which I ended up doing, was joining the National Guard. Being able to go and reconnect with people and putting the uniform on for a limited time, it eases the blow to everything. It's going back to something that I know, whereas being thrown back into the civilian world, it's a shock to the system.

I don't see me going back to the same person I was before. It's frustrating for my wife, because that's what she wants. She wanted me to go on medication. I'm like, "They don't make medication that fixes that. It's not like I can just go to the doctor, and he's going to write me a prescription, and all of a sudden I'm cured." But I think for a lot of people that don't understand it, that's what they think. But it doesn't really work that way.

My grandfather never really talked to his family about his experience. Most of the information about the combat experiences that he had I've gotten from books, and my grandmother telling me about how he acted, and how my uncle acted. And then my wife sitting down and telling me, "You know, you got some pretty significant issues with anger, I think you maybe need to get help." Those were the things that put me on that path.

Grandmother Violet Hortdorf

When Shawn was over there, it was a living hell every day of my life. Every day you picked up the paper, every day you lived, you didn't know what you were going to hear. I don't think [the public] understands how horrible it is over there. I don't think that's published enough. They need to tell what a hell those guys go through. Oh my, it might scare us a little bit, and might make people get mad and demand something be done. People need to be well informed, but they're not, and some people don't care. It's a shame that it has to be this way, but hey, that's the name of the game, I guess.

Christopher Arendt—homeless—at a friend's apartment on Christmas Day, 2008. Arendt served as a guard at Guantanamo Bay. After leaving the military, Chris traveled to meet former Guantanamo Bay detainees to apologize for his involvement in their detention.

Christopher Arendt

People look at the Nazi concentration camps and wonder how can you do something like that? It's really easy.

People look at the Nazi concentration camps and wonder how can you do something like that? It's really easy. It's a simple thing. You make one wrong decision and you spend the rest of your life explaining that decision. I've barely made any choices in my life, and then I ended working in a concentration camp. You wake up every day, put your boots on, and go to work at the concentration camp.

What I hate about myself over there is the callousness, the emptiness. I wish I was angrier while I was there. But it's impossible to keep yourself: the sane, the normal, the feeling. You figure, I'll feel later. Three years later, I'm still trying to do that.

I understood that something about life had changed; life had become something to be afraid of. One must defend one's self against life. Because that is what war does to us. We have to do all of those horrible things because we were born poor and unfortunate, and we are citizens of a nation run by psychopaths.

Camp Delta is on a cliff that overlooks the ocean. I had never been to the ocean before in my whole life. There have been a few times in the military when I've been so stricken by the juxtaposition of how awful what is happening inside the moment is, and how aesthetically beautiful it is at the same time. Seeing the first couple of detainees start preparing for prayer, and then at the same time the sun starting to come up over the cliff base, was probably one of the most confusing moments of my life.

We were told when we were deployed to use the term "detainee." It had to be "detainee." If it's "prisoner," then they would have to be prisoners of war, and they're subject to entirely different laws. If they're detainees, then they are subject to no law whatsoever, because there aren't laws for detainees.

In every window I saw a different way to go crazy; in every different pair of eyes that flashed around wildly, some of them soaking every bit of visual information they could get out of the hole where my face was, and some of them just laying catatonically on their bare metal slab, while some others paced the few paces they could, constantly turning inside of their cells, talking to themselves.

Oscar 12 wanted things. He yelled down the causeway "MP, MP, MP!" until I showed up in his hole. He told me he needed some toilet paper. I told him I would have to ask my Sergeant if it was OK. He got very angry very quickly, annoyed with my inability to command enough authority to go out to the back and get a few sheets of toilet paper. I tried to explain to him that the SOP says that detainees on Oscar Block were only allowed toilet paper at certain hours and in certain quantities. He became irate.

He started screaming and swearing in his hood English. He called me a bitch in several different ways and told me he would kill me if he could get out of the cell. I was pretty nervous. I kept shifting my eyes to the other end of the block, where my trainers were smoking cigarettes in the air-conditioned booth. I finally decided I would break the rules and just get the toilet paper, because I'd look like a total fucking douche showing up in the guard shack asking if it was OK to do this.

I have finally resigned my pride. I'm broken and I need help. I guess I'm not the only one. There are more of us who try to do it alone, and even more who refuse to admit they need the help. After two hours of filling out forms, I threw my soaked cigarettes on the sidewalk and walked home in the rain, my eyes fixed on the pavement, my head five years in the past, remembering how difficult it was to get that blood out of my only pair of battle dress uniforms.

Myla Haider

The personnel who would have investigated my rape at the time were friends and coworkers of the rapist, and I was an intern. He was a more senior investigator and his colleagues would have investigated the offense. So I knew at that time there was no sense in reporting it, because nothing good could come out of it.

I'm from Northern Michigan. I joined the Army in 1994. I served in Germany, Croatia, Korea, Afghanistan, and Iraq.

Leading up to the invasion, my job was to do a study of various threats, the culture in Iraq, and all the elements that were associated with the invasion. I did intelligence planning, planning for the mission, and intelligence briefings prior to going into Iraq.

I spent six years in the Army before I decided to become an agent with the U.S. Army Criminal Investigation Command. I had to do an internship in order to submit an application to be a criminal investigator. It was during that internship that the rape occurred. After my internship, I went to Hunter 1st Airborne Division, went to Afghanistan, went to Iraq, and I went to become a CID agent. After about a year of being an agent, I received a phone call that the person who attacked me was being investigated as a serial sex offender and my cooperation was requested for the investigation.

It was during that time that I noticed the attitude towards cases involving female victims was a very victim-blaming atmosphere, so when it actually happened to me, I knew that if I reported it, I would face some kind of negative ramification, and then the offender would not be convicted.

I cooperated with the investigation and the offender was not convicted of any of the sex-related offenses against several different women. He was not placed on a sex offender registry, and within two months of the trial my command began administrative discharge proceedings. So after nine and a half years my career was over within months of the trial.

When the investigator approached me to give a statement, I already knew at that time that giving a statement would end my career in the Army Criminal Investigation Command. CID is a very close-knit organization, regardless of the severity of the complaints. Complaints against other agents are generally discouraged and people who make complaints are considered almost to be betraying their own by making those complaints.

I was administratively discharged, and I spent five years after my discharge fighting with the Department of Defense to get my record corrected. In 20—five years after my discharge—I was finally awarded a medical retirement.

After I got back from Iraq, I got my bachelors degree in psychology, mainly because I was suffering from PTSD. Then I got my masters degree in counseling.

I have a private counseling practice now. People are able to talk to somebody who's actually been there, someone who understands. It's a way for people to to receive counseling assistance without having to worry about negative ramifications or stigma.

It's difficult when a person gets back to, and has to adjust into, a life where pop culture takes precedence over the fact that you've just come from some place where people are dying. And every day could be your day. Or it could be somebody else's day. You just get really accustomed to that idea.

I think the thing that I want people to know about returning veterans is that people don't always feel good about what they've done, and not everybody wants to be regarded as a hero. It's very difficult for me to handle, and I think people need to keep in mind that when they are thanking somebody for what they did over there, sometimes that involves killing a child. It comes with the job.

People are under constant threat and they're reacting the best way they can in the situation, but that does not always involve some heroic outcome; it doesn't always involve people feeling good about what they did. People will be struggling with the things they have done for the rest of their lives, really. The psychological damage and the kind of long term effects of this are really only beginning, and they will continue over generations. People just kind of need to consider that.

Jake Meeks in his student apartment. Jake says that his cat, Hondo, has acquired secondary PTSD.

Jake Meeks

For all you Americans out there, The Telling Project, where vets tell their stories on stage, changed the direction of my life.

My name is Jacob William Meeks. I'm twenty-eight years old. I grew up in the small town of Shoshoni, Wyoming. I served four years in the United States Army, 82nd Airborne Infantry, where I did missions in Kosovo and Afghanistan. That's who I am. It doesn't say much, does it?

I'm supposed to write about war. Well, I don't know that much about war. What I do know, I'd prefer not to. I was lucky in my experiences. I was tired, cold, hot, afraid, and angry. I hit the high point of many emotions, and those emotions stay with me today. I've seen ugliness in humanity. I understand that life is a fragile thing. I know what people are capable of. I understand what I'm capable of.

There's nothing I can say that hasn't been said before. War should be a last resort. Sometimes I believe it is necessary, but those times are few and far between. Our culture shouldn't view war and the military as a Rambo movie, because it's not. We should be allowed to express our emotions, our feelings; bottling them up inside is not healthy. Empathy is necessary, but so is respect: respect for feeling, respect for humanity, respect for each other. Those things can be found in chaotic situations like war, but they can also be destroyed by it.

That's what I know. It's not much, but it is mine, and I feel I earned the knowledge. Now, I spend my days trying to help others. Right now I'm trying to help vets. Soon I'll find another community where, hopefully, I can be of service. I do these things because I think it's the right thing to do. I also do them for my own peace of mind. Some things in my life have taken that peace of mind away, if I ever had it. Now I try to get it back.

In mid-2009, I faced a crossroads. I was offered a job with the Student Veterans of America to become their Executive Director out of Washington, DC. I could have been in charge of a small but growing non-profit, overseen its growth, done fund raising, and would have been able to rub elbows with political elites to make headway on veterans' issues. Instead, I decided to go to a small NGO (humanitarian organization) camp on the border between North and South Sudan, in a place called the Abyei area. I ran operations, procurement, logistics, fleet, security, human resources, and more for our various development programs. I was present for the first elections in the country and the referendum when South Sudan decided to split from the north. I met a lot of people and, hopefully, even helped a few along the way. Since then I have traveled to Guatemala, Libya, Jordan, and Lebanon, all in a work capacity. I have worked on a number of various development and emergency programs: from transporting food and non-food items, to contracting municipal water infrastructure projects, to agricultural projects, to a variety of other things. I have managed seventy staff at my peak, and I have to say it's been a humbling experience. I learn more about people and the world every day and I'm very thankful that this is the direction my feet took me.

Former Marine Benji Lewis at a skate park near his apartment. Benji begins his poem *First Kill*: "I see these empty streets sneezing with a dust cloud energy, purple hazy rippling cracks crawling incrementally and a third of the population is already gone. This was at a time where I destroyed a Mosque."

Benji Lewis

My resistance was a conscious decision to cease participation, in any way, in the continued maintenance and creation of empire through military intervention and global abuses of economic tyranny.

In October 2008, I announced at a Winter Soldier hearing in Portland, Oregon, that I was being considered for involuntary activation back into the Marine Corps for a third tour of duty as an infantry mortar man. The day after this announcement, I reported to Mobilization Command in Missouri, as ordered. I reported with the intention of exercising civil disobedience, in order to make a political point by refusing activation. The Marine Corps selected me for activation and, since that time, I have been publicly refusing service.

My resistance was a conscious decision to cease participation, in any way, in the continued maintenance and creation of empire through military intervention and global abuses of economic tyranny. That is, I resisted on ideological grounds. I think that in order for institutions to change their behavior, it is often necessary to work outside the framework of those institutions. I did this in one way, simply by no longer recognizing the military's sovereignty over my person, and also by speaking out and educating citizens about the practices of their military.

Resistance takes many forms and functions: from active civil disobediences, to the reservists who quietly ignore their activation orders and continue on with their lives. When a person is attempting to overthrow injustice or to increase human understanding, even the smallest forms of resistance, such as suspending judgment amidst the whims of mass culture, become ripples in the water to be proud of. I will continue the work of supporting and organizing for GI Resistance that I started, and continue to pursue the goal of peaceful justice. This is an important struggle that affects all society and it is far from over.

It has become clear that the institutionalized militarism within the U.S. has now had an immeasurable impact on us and the world. The fallout of this impact is still being assessed. Certainly, anti-U.S. sentiment has increased drastically in the world in response to a militaristic U.S. foreign policy and debilitating foreign investment practices. Predictably, the more the U.S. flexes its military and economic muscles, the more enemies are made. And clearly, if we are to address the growing violence around the world, we must begin investigating some of the inherent, unintended consequences of capitalism.

We have seen another generation of veterans come home damaged by their experiences, and the human consequence abroad has been far more severe. Our emphasis on institutionalized militarism as an integral part of our economy, with the military and military-related projects amassing more monetarily and materially than the rest of the world combined, is quickly bringing us and the globe to the brink of our own demise, not only financially, but also environmentally.

In order to pull ourselves out of this mess, we must first acknowledge it. As a society, we must take responsibility for our actions, intentional or unintentional. Only when we acknowledge our mistakes can we freely educate ourselves on issues and talk about the world in meaningful ways with the bridge of understanding. That is the path to peaceful and synergistic human relations. It can no longer be denied that America was formed and molded through the displacement of hundreds of advanced societies that had formerly held sovereignty over the continent. We still have not accepted responsibility for that, much less current world turmoil. A familiar example is the CIA's involvement in training the Mujahidin we are now combating in Afghanistan, another piece of evidence showing us how we helped create the global war on terror.

The events of 9/11 were horrible beyond doubt, but the amount of horror that has transpired since then has been worse still and, like many other acts of violence, could have been prevented. The U.S. has been the single biggest perpetrator of terrorism in the world in recent decades, through a variety of tactics. These tactics include economic sanctions, biased aid, imposed free trade agreements, self-exclusion, direct military intervention, and support of brutal dictators, among others—all this in the name of protecting vital U.S. interests. U.S. interests usually translate into the interests of those who would profit and acquire power, and that is very rarely the average American.

Scott Kaney and his son, Carter, in front of their home. Kaney served two deployments in Iraq and one tour in Afghanistan with the 1st Marine Regiment. Scott says that Carter, and his wife, Amber, saved his life. He says, "I thought I'd pass out when I saw my son. All those kids that I saw there had no family; most were dead."

Scott Kaney

My dreams would make a Stephen King movie like "Saw" look like child's play.

The honest reason why I joined was because I was filled with rage. I wanted to know how to direct my rage. I looked at the pattern of the way things went, and I figured it out: "We go to a conflict every ten years, so if I stay in long enough, I'm going to end up in a war." I was so mad at things that I was dealing with that I was like, "I want to do the hardest thing," which is join the Marine Corps. I needed the discipline.

Boot camp broke me of all that anger. Many days of push-ups. After that, I calmed down. It wasn't until after the second tour that the anger started getting out. After the third tour it was really bad, because Fallujah was like nothing I ever saw in my life. I had never seen such carnage. Nothing. It put in my mind what I always thought war would be like: like Normandy. That wasn't even like Normandy. I was just baffled. Of course, you're not baffled when you do it. It doesn't hit you until seven or eight months later.

I was back here and drinking a lot, trying to drown it all out. Waking up in the middle of the night, punching my pillow or punching my wall, screaming. I'm in the corner screaming and I don't realize it. My wife comes over to help me and I yell at her. Pacing through the house for an hour or two at night, I was putting weapons strategically so that if anyone broke in, I'd have a weapon at every possible point. I was really on edge.

It's definitely just what I saw. I can remember things in exact detail. I have dreams about 'em all the time. I'll be having a great dream, and then all of a sudden it turns into it again. Like a cat chewing up a carcass, or dogs tearing people apart. The stench of rotting corpses was just like, phew. I'm not really getting overly descriptive, that's just a touch of it.

We did a lot of humanitarian work. Kids loved us; they'd come up and shout, "American, American!" We always took candy bars when we came out for kids. This one kid reaches his hand out, and all of a sudden I look down and I see his arm and it's just totally broken. I mean completely. He was totally happy. I would be in pain—anybody would. If that kid would have gotten help from us, his family would have gotten killed. Here's all these kids, glowing with life and limitless potential, and their lifespan could be the next day, or the day after. It's really mind boggling. You don't have enough to give them. I guess that's why I want to work with youth. I came from a broken home, grew up all up and down the West Coast. My father was murdered. I had drugs and abuse my whole life. But what's funny is, I always looked to the positive. My whole life, I always looked to the positive.

Now all I can see is the negative. It feels like this is my punishment. Of all the good I wanted to do, it's the one thing I can't get out of my mind. It's just this frickin' curse that I have I'm trying to get over. I think if they had more veterans' counselors available, man, it would be huge. I know it's hard, but . . .

Man, getting out, I was just crushed. I was like, "Gosh, I'm supposed to feel great. I'm free." It was the opposite. What I was able to cling to was that I have a little boy and I have a wife. Over time, these deep problems have really crippled me from being there the way I know I should be. I know I'm not fulfilling my full potential because there's this monkey on my back, and it's like, "Dude, you just need to get over this, and you need to figure this out." That's my determination right there. I say that now, but then I'll go through this swing where it'll be like, "I don't want to deal with it today. I don't want to do anything. I don't want to think about anything." They gave me these two medications and they're like, "Just take this." It's not that I don't believe that medication is there to help you, but it's a man-made pill.

I know that I need to get my butt out. I have no interest in a lot of things. The things I do have interest in are my wife and my son and making memories with them.

Jan Critchfield (R) takes target practice with fellow Iraq vets at Seth Manzel's Fourth of July BBQ party. The vets told me that hearing fireworks around the neighborhood created anxiety. They decided to have their own fireworks show that night. Soldiers are good with explosives . . .

Jan Critchfield

What is a soldier when you wash the Hollywood away? What is a warrior when you dispel the mythology surrounding their nobility? Everyone needs to know the answer to that question. The voices of those who have relevant experiences must make their struggles known, for their own healing and for the dream of peace.

I did know better. That phrase sums up my current feelings about joining the Army shortly after turning seventeen. I've gone through all of the traditional stages of emotion—blame, shame, anger, whatever—but the conclusion that I keep turning towards is that I *did* know better.

My parents, a teacher, friends, parents of friends; many tried to convince me not to join—almost everyone who knew about my decision was against it.

The teacher pulled the angry teenager that I was aside for a chat. He attempted to communicate in the time between classes how ridiculous my decision was; that I would be told to do immoral things and that I had the potential to do much more with my life. I knew at that age that I was politically liberal, but I had also developed mistrust for what I saw as wishy-washy "hippie ideology," or youthful angst against previous generations. I had also fine-tuned the teenage art of dismissing elders.

An acquaintance of mine joined the Marine Reserves around the time I signed up. He got his deployment orders early. If he had deployed with his unit, he would have likely been running fuel with the initial push from Kuwait towards Baghdad. His reasons for deciding not to go were many, but the one that made the most sense to me at the time was that he thought it would be miserable to walk across the street with the guys in his unit, let alone the possibility that one of their ugly mugs might be the last thing he saw before bleeding out. He complained that his unit was full of cruel, misshapen idiots. He was among the first, nationwide, to refuse to deploy to Iraq. Instead of throwing him in jail, the Marines quietly out-processed him at a base near New Orleans. From what I heard, when he returned to Seattle, he spent a year of paperwork and hard partying with others who were being out-processed.

My father passed along a few stories about experiences in the draft Army during Vietnam. His last bit of wisdom before co-signing my enlistment paperwork was: "They will put you where they need you, you will do what they say." Just in case I thought I was signing up for the Boy Scouts. My brother was in the Boy Scouts, and they lit picnic benches on fire with stove fuel when the Scoutmaster wasn't around. I never had that much fun in the Army—except for the part with Everclear in South Carolina—but I can't remember much of that.

My father told stories about the basic training "fun" of pretending to kill the enemy; training in the San Francisco Bay area just in time for the Summer of '69, grabbing a guitar from his wall locker every weekend to go jam with the hippies in Golden Gate Park. He described to my brother and me the experience of being handcuffed to a bench after refusing orders to military police training, being told that he could either go to Vietnam or go to jail. Pulling drunk, angry grunts out of Saigon hotel rooms didn't have much luster for the thinking man in those days. Telling "The Man" that you played a music gig for socialists solved that problem. Such were the times.

My family has a history with the U.S. Army. My great grandfather—a Silver Star recipient—was deployed along the U.S.-Mexico border, and then to Europe with the rest of the doughboys. My father's father sums up his service with a tidy story: He was sitting in the barracks during basic training when someone walked in and asked if anyone knew how to play the trumpet. Instead of being sent to the Pacific Theater as an infantryman, he played in an Army band.

I joined almost as soon as I could, the fourth youngest in a basic training company of around 230. Foremost during this teenage confusion was my hope of not ending up in a cubicle; experiencing the world for myself, instead of through books and TV. I wanted fun, travel, and adventure. I wanted to escape high school and impress people. I wanted to be the hero by helping people and killing our enemies. I wanted to do something other than just be another angry teenager with nothing to say and a cheap beer in his hand.

That beautiful, stupid idea may have come to pass if I had spent my contract fighting forest fires. Instead, at the orders of the President, I was conscripted to active duty in support of Operation Saturate Iraq with Depleted Uranium. (War crimes? What, me worry?)

I joined pre-9/11. The country hadn't reached the nauseating panic of war hysteria; the nation was focused on Bosnia, Kosovo, and Bill Clinton's reproductive organs. My father's cautionary talks seemed inapplicable. I knew I would carry a rifle, but I thought it was unlikely that I would ever have a reason to use it.

Conversation one, during day one of life as an Army recruit (literally right after being issued our work uniforms), we ask each other why we joined. It was a natural topic for a chow hall table full of strangers and plenty of time to jaw, since we were still in the holding company, waiting to start training. Everyone gives their reason: I want to be a mechanic, I want to be a nurse, I want to be a journalist. Then the guy sitting directly across stares me in the eye and coughs up his reason: "I joined because the only legal way you can kill someone is either in the military or as a cop." He forgot dentist. All kidding aside, the moment you realize you have a four-alarm psycho sitting across from you is an interesting moment.

Welcome to the real world. Violence is what happens on TV until it happens right in front of you. Since this writing is already fully retrospective, it's safe to say that one of the trainees at that table should have reported the guy as a mental case. Whatever Psycho's case may have been, there's an acronym, YES, that some recruiters use to guide their prospects through the initial medical screening process. The acronym stands for Your Enlistment Stops. If you answer "yes" to any of the questions that the doctor asks you, your enlistment will stop. You will not get your bonus. You will not get the next plane to somewhere other than Bumhump, Wherever, USA. You will not get your citizenship.

I graduated from basic as one of the two best soldiers in the company, having demonstrated a superior level of proficiency in the skills we were taught. (I was soldier of the cycle and had to read a pre-written speech at graduation; the other guy won the Gauntlet Award for being a badass.) I finished high school with honors and a scholar/athlete award. I wasn't destined to be a cubicle drone if I didn't want to be one. People join for citizenship, people join for the college money, and people join for no reason at all. Boredom may even be a more common reason than love of country, if people were to be honest.

Now I'm sitting in my living room, reminiscing about what could have been, and I haven't even reached thirty. I have a criminal record, an unimpressive resume full of employment gaps, and few marketable skills. I'll get some sleep, get up, and go get a free hamburger for being a veteran. The next day, I'll kill a case of beer with a friend and see a school advisor about getting my life back on track, but not in that order, of course.

I'm not nearly as nihilistic as I was as a teenager, and I really wasn't that nihilistic as a teenager at all. The entire point I've been building up to here is that I knew better than to join the side of the executioners. I may have had a million bullshit reasons for joining the Army, and possibly the lamest of all was that all of my heroes at seventeen had served in their nation's military or somehow been deeply affected by war—Steinbeck, Capa, Camus—they all wrote about or photographed war. But there's one in that list that stands out very prominently, isn't there?

He was a man whose father had died serving France when he was very young. He was deemed unfit for military service (illness), but participated in the French Resistance, helping to publish the newsletter *Combat*. I had read *The Stranger*, *The Fall*, *The Myth of Sisyphus*, *The Rebel*, and *The Plague*—all of his major novels and essays—by the time I finished high school. He spent serious ink writing about never taking the side of the executioners by opposing the death penalty, even when applied to famous war criminals and murderers, but also by opposing more generally the political murders of Stalin and the terrorist tactics of Algerian revolutionaries. He applied this moral vantage to government-sponsored murder everywhere, but stopped short of saying France could not defend itself when threatened by the Nazis. In fact, he even advocated for the execution of Nazis and their French collaborators in letters published in *Combat* during the war.

My knowledge at seventeen of Camus's thoughts about killing was not as detailed as it is today, but his ideas and style have made an impact. Unfortunately, this impact didn't happen to help me connect the dots that I easily connect today: my teenage literary hero opposed slaughter for power and considered war to be an absurd human activity; my personal knowledge of the Army at the time was that I would be placed directly in these situations; and my sole reason for joining was to be placed in those situations because I was bored with life.

Again, my sole reason was basically to mistreat myself into sensing the world. I can't think of a better way of writing it: the reason I kept to myself, the strange reasoning in the back of my mind that I never shared with my parents or anyone else. It was no secret I wanted adventure, but that I myself objected to joining would have been a confusing thing to tell people as I put ink on the contract. My seventeen-year-old wisdom led me to ignore the warnings of my elders and knowledge of atrocities committed in every war since the beginning of time. I basically did it for the hell of it.

Fast forward a couple of years from signing that contract, and I'm in a latrine in Baghdad, thinking about how easy it would be to chamber a round and shoot myself. Fast forward a few more years and I'm beating my wife in a fit of rage and sitting out a few months in the county jail. Fast forward to now and I'm picking up the pieces of a wasted decade of life and seriously considering becoming an ex-patriot because of my personal disgust for this nation's somnambulism.

I just received a text from my mother, who is in bed with a head cold, and I asked her if she wants help making chicken soup. A few sentences ago, I silently hoped that she would never know about some of my experiences, but I believe other young people of the world need to know.

What is a soldier when you wash the Hollywood away? What is a warrior when you dispel the mythology surrounding their nobility? Everyone needs to know the answer to that question. The voices of those who have relevant experiences must make their struggles known, for their own healing and for the dream of peace.

Some of the USO entertainers that I interviewed in Iraq commented on how intelligent and articulate the soldiers they met were. Just to be clear, these guys were comedians and said everything with tongue firmly in cheek. But their expectations about what soldiers would be like—grunting Neanderthals with guns—speaks to the separation between public perception and reality. Our army is a business and its business is war. It is made up of honest, honorable men and women: brave soldiers who walk down a road full of artillery shells, cutting command detonation wires with a knife to clear the way for their comrades; medics who never fold under pressure until the job is done; and soldiers who are proud of their job and service to countrymen they will never meet. But keep in mind, they are accompanied by psychopaths and rapists: young soldiers who shoot dogs for fun; men who will offer you the opportunity to kill a child; men who rape and murder their female sisters-in-arms. And you can't tell them apart because they all walk the same walk and talk the same talk. Keep that in mind before you put ink on that contract.

Keep in mind that you may find yourself in a land you don't understand, doing bad things for questionable reasons. Then you'll come home and adjustment might come easy. But it might not. You may find yourself paralyzed by panic, pulling off to the side of the road, your head swimming and the world spinning. Then your girlfriend will call you and chew you out for not picking her up on time and she won't understand what's wrong with you. She'll complain about being kicked and choked in bed at night, and you won't remember doing it. You may do things to people you care about that will haunt you for years. You may see the bodies of the dead, shrunken and charred by fire, and you will never forget them. And unless you believe that our country can do no wrong by its citizens and the rest of the world, your sacrifices will seem in vain. Crack open that history textbook and find out for yourself.

I hope that on future Veterans Days the voices attempting to dissuade the young from fraternizing with state-sponsored terrorism will not be drowned out by the nauseating freak show that is puffed-up, chicken hawk patriotism.

Note: The following photographs were taken while Jan David Critchfield was deployed with the Army's 1st Cavalry Division to Baghdad, Iraq, in 2004. Although he was originally trained to be a filing clerk, he worked as a journalism "stringer" and wrote feel-good stories about the occupation that were published in 1st Cavalry Division newsletters, on Department of Defense websites, and by civilian news outlets in the Fort Hood area. A photograph taken during this deployment earned a second place Keith L. Ware journalism award (stand-alone photo category).

A patrolling First Armored Division soldier covers a corner while a curious boy hopes for a handout of candy. Photo: Jan Critchfield

A poor teenager sits on the rubble of a Baghdad housing project that was interrupted by the 2003 invasion. Many people in Baghdad went without shoes or sandals despite unsanitary conditions. Photo: Jan Critchfiied

A young student relaxes on a swing that was set up inside a Baghdad classroom. Photo: Jan Critchfield

Children from an orphanage peek through the gate of a former mental hospital that was converted into a retirement home during the occupation.
Photo: Jan Critchfield

Former Marine Margo Ellis in the Senate Rotunda in Washington, DC. Margo works for the Department of Veterans Affairs. She is a Congressional Liaison in the Office of Congressional and Legislative Affairs.

Margo Ellis

As the deployment progressed, we came to the realization that if we are going to end this war, we have to have women take over our mission. But Iraq has never had a female Iraqi security force. So I got the opportunity to do on-the-job training for the first female Iraqi security forces.

When I enlisted in the Marine Corps, I decided I wanted to be a tanker. Unfortunately, that job specialty is not open to women, so I changed paths and decided to become an engineer. "Engineer" in the Marine Corps is kind of code for either blowing stuff up or building stuff up. I was on the build stuff up side. I was a heavy equipment mechanic with an engineering platoon when I started, then worked my way up from being a mechanic to being an Engineer Chief.

I would definitely say it was a challenge being both a woman and African American in the jobs that I chose. I kind of did that on purpose. For the most part, I grew up in a white environment and assimilated, to a very large degree, to the point that people didn't think of me as black. Even people who had funny feelings about black folks didn't have those funny feelings about me. I saw it as kind of opportunity to help open the world, if you will. I just knew I'd be accepted. Unfortunately, I didn't realize how long it would take to gain that acceptance. The first job I picked was Engineer. When I showed up, my Gunny [Gunnery Sergeant] almost dropped dead because in seventeen years in the Marine Corps, he'd never seen a black woman in that job.

I was deployed to Iraq from 2007 to 2008. I went to Fallujah. It was the second part of the troop surge, so by the time I got there things were getting better, but we didn't realize it yet. When I went it was very, very nerve wracking, because all my friends who had come back from the previous deployment did not fare well. I was concerned I would end up in the same boat. I, however, totally lucked out and came in—as much as there's a good time to go—at the best time around that era.

Since women cannot serve in combat positions, I volunteered to be part of the Lionesses (lioness like a woman lion). It's now called Female Engagement Teams.

We realize that in Iraq we were actually creating more enemies than we were making friends by having our guys search their women, especially in public. So we tried to turn back the clock on that and started embedding women with the infantry platoons to search women. I was a part of that effort. It was really interesting, because I was one of the female searchers who would actually go out for a week at a time with the guys. When I first got there, it was so bad we had to actually shut traffic off in Fallujah. We wouldn't let people drive their cars in or out because so many people were devastated by roadside bombs that it was just too easy to carry contraband.

Coming home was tough. I think it's tough, initially, for everybody. The first six months you just can't sleep well. I don't know anybody who can. But it's over time that most people acclimate and they are okay. In fact, Secretary of Veterans Affairs General Shinseki has started to make a distinction between what he calls PTS, which is Post-Traumatic Stress (when you come home and have feelings of anxiety and are not able to sleep), as opposed to PTSD (which is the disorder when you don't get over it).

There was the psychological stuff, but it was also about trying to get a job. Jobs are something they have been talking a lot about lately here in Congress. If you are a combat medic and you have been driving Humvees as a first line of defense ambulance person in the worst possible areas in the world, you can't come home and become an EMT because you are not certified. That's why some folks, especially Iraq and Afghanistan Veterans of America, have submitted a legislative proposal to Congress which essentially says: "We're spending millions of dollars training folks to do work, and then they can't get work when they get out of the military. We are really wasting our tax dollars."

Nick Breslin, Evan Knappenberger, Azadeh Breslin, Finn, Ash Woolson, and Sarah Kyrie at Ash and Sarah's house in Bellingham, Washington, in 2008. The house functions as an informal sanctuary for fellow vets.

Evan M. Knappenberger

Thank you for your service, unless you're for peace—in which case you should just shut the fuck up.

The Soldier as a Gesture

My friend, Hannah, was in her early thirties when the dot-com company she managed went bankrupt. Later that year her primary long-term relationship ended. Devastated by these dual blows, Hannah left the corporate world, burned her art collection, sold her various properties, and joined the U.S. Army, where we met at Fort Hood. Well-educated and armed with a sharp intellect, Hannah was a master of words in her native Korean and in English. She had quite the rebellious streak in her. One of my favorite stories from the Army is how she repeatedly refused to be promoted to Sergeant, planting in my mind the idea of an intentional culture of under-indoctrination. When the first Sergeant tried to trick Hannah into getting promoted, she made a gesture of dismissal in front of the whole company, shrugging off both his criticism and the unwanted responsibility of being a non-commissioned officer. That one potent gesture of dismissal destroyed—for me and for the other volunteer enlisted personnel who witnessed it—the artificial ethos of the professional soldier. It was a contra-salute, and it struck me right in the gut.

Before the war irrevocably marred our lives, Hannah and I went for long walks together, talking about how we didn't fit in. Once, when I was tired beyond sleep, I wandered to her barracks for morning tea. Before I left, she handed me Milan Kundera's novel *The Joke*. It wasn't until nine years later that I found that book again and read it in an emotional fever. Kundera had me hooked with his tale of non-ideological resistance from within the bowels of the Czechoslovak Communist Party. I said a silent thank you to Hannah and devoured Kundera's other novels recklessly and fitfully.

Perhaps my favorite theme from Kundera comes from his novel *Immortality*, in which a single, elegant gesture becomes the vehicle of both plot and identity. Kundera flips the axis on which we build our self perceptions, the notion that we are unique individuals doing unique and unprecedented things. Instead, Kundera argues, we are the medium through which gestures—of which there are only a limited number, and which are therefore more unique than the billions of people who use them—travel. This idea resonates in me, in my experience of the Army, my role as ideological agent of Neoliberalism—In my own mind I was fighting those damned backwards Arabs for their own rational best interest!—and then later in my time working for peace after leaving the Army. Additionally, we must be clear that the military is both full of various gestures and, as a career, is itself a kind of gesture: anachronistic, maybe even futile, like joining a monastery or burning an expensive art collection.

The Salute

I was never fond of saluting. While the various incarnations of that particular bodily motion can range on the emotional scale from the tragic (a teary war widow standing next to a Marine Honor Guard with arm raised at a precise forty degree angle) to the awkwardly ridiculous (goofy fat bikers with greasy paws held askew at the high school football game), the cultural valuation of our consumerist society does not hold the salute in an especially revered place. Only deluded politicians, grumpy old men, and gung-ho jarheads take the gesture of salute seriously. Generally, I dismiss such antics as empty, like making the sign of the cross before bedtime. But I do admit that there are certain times when seeing a salute can send me over the edge, plummeting into anger or depression, hitting me in the gut like Hannah's antics in front of a company formation.

In the small oil refinery town of Anacortes, Washington, the war came home early. About the time I was joining the Army in 2003, the small weekly vigil for peace that meets on the corner of 12th and Commercial Street for an hour each Sunday afternoon was being invaded. A rag-tag group calling themselves "Go-Patriots" began setting up a massive display of flags kitty-corner to the peace vigil-ers and blaring loud country music from speakers. As if that wasn't enough, their leader—an old man with lung cancer—had been known to grab and rip signs that he disagreed with. All of this, to my mind, is understandable as simple, hyper-dogmatic behavior stemming from a place of deep-seated fear and frustration. When I was first invited to Anacortes in 2007 by a group of veterans for Peace, my friend, Larry, who lost three limbs as a tank driver in Vietnam before choosing to witness against war, warned me about these "patriots." I was intrigued by the contrasting ideological stances and headed out one Sunday morning in my old Army uniform.

When I arrived, I parked in the Safeway lot nearby. The "patriots" had set up early and the peace folks hadn't shown up yet. I walked calmly over to one of the former. I was clean cut and fresh-faced, just out of the Army and not yet even one year back from the war. "Hello, my name is Evan," I enjoined. "What's your name?"

An old man with an American Eagle baseball cap who could've been my granddad squinted at me, then smiled big and broad, figuring me to be thanking him for his patriotism. "Well, how about that. Are you in the military?" he asked. "Recently I was," I answered. He offered his hand and said, "My name is Dan, and thank you for your service!" He clutched my hand and pumped. "Well Dan," I started earnestly. "I am actually here on behalf of Veterans for Peace to ask you to please find another corner to occupy. My friend Byron—you know him, the old Marine Lieutenant who stands with the sign right over there," I gestured—"is bothered by your music and I'm here to ask you to move to another corner, or possibly to come back at another hour."

Dan snatched his hand back in disgust. Suddenly he was acting with absolutely no hesitation at all: "You phony! Get outta here! Get!" he yelled in my face. "Phony sonofabitch!" He spat on the ground. I stood where I was. Dan's face was distorted in anger. "I said get!" he screamed. He shook his fist in the air, "Why I ought'a!" He sounded slightly like Bugs Bunny. I turned and left, waiting for my more peaceable fellow veterans to arrive. Cars drove by on the busy street, with drivers honking and gesticulating in ways I hesitate to interpret. (Because of the close proximity of the opposing political camps, it was difficult to know which honker was supporting which sign.) That didn't stop Dan from taking credit at every honk, however. Hearing each car horn, Dan would hold his wrinkled old hand up to the brim of his Eagle baseball cap in a gesture of salute. He might as well have been hitting me in the gut.

When I left the vigil an hour later, I had to drive past Dan and the war supporters as they stood in the rain opposite the Veterans for Peace. Driving away, I honked at Dan. Without noticing who I was, he saluted me in my car—a stale movement of political remonstration aimed at silencing those "phony" Veterans for Peace on the other corner, my war-wounded comrades. Thank you for your service, unless you're for peace—in which case you should just shut the fuck up.

A Thought About War

The trauma of being a veteran can consume one's identity, or it can spur intellectual development. Nietzsche, Orwell, Proust, Socrates, Aeschylus, Tolstoy, and Gandhi all wore uniforms in the service, no doubt standing next to young guys like Dan and me and saluting one flag or another. When people think of veterans they think of grumpy old bastards marching in parades and drinking in the local VFW post. They don't think of radical teachers under vows of poverty, executed for corrupting the youth. They don't think of prominent philosophers rejecting the world and affirming the principles of justice, truth, beauty, and peace. But to walk barefoot across Russia, to go to jail for making salt, to proclaim the death of God—these things are also veteran things.

I haven't seen or heard from Hannah in about eight years now. I wonder about her, her rebellious spirit and cutting wit. I want to acknowledge her service as someone who appreciates what she was doing, even if it doesn't quite mesh with the gestures of appreciation that are common currency in our culture. I want to tell Hannah, "Thank you for your service!" despite all the contradictions of such a move. Even if it hits her right in the gut. I salute you, Hannah, in the true and timeless spirit of the deep veteran-intellectual tradition. Peace be with you!

In 2011, Ashkan talked about September 11th with the *Tuscaloosa News*: "I was a high school senior when it happened. I think 'surreal' is the best word to describe the day as we went from class to class. I remember sitting in film class, watching the coverage of the attack on TV and feeling like I was watching a movie. Getting Osama bin Laden before the 10th anniversary was the best. The timing of it was great—I'd just lost my home in the tornado and we all needed good news."

Ashkan Bayatpour

I was determined to serve my country. I was still very young and idealistic. I feel like I owe so much to this country.

I was born in 1984, in Mobile, Alabama. I Went to Murphy High School in Mobile. I was supposed to go to college for a year and, long story short, I ended up going in the Navy instead.

My parents are immigrants. They are from Iran and came here in the late '70s, right before the revolution in Iran. So I've lived my whole life basically being told how lucky we are to be Americans and how grateful we should be. On my dad's side, there is a long lineage of people who have served in the military in Iran. This was during the Shah's rule, so my dad had a lot of experience working with U.S. military and he had a lot of contact with them. I think that's ultimately why he decided to move to the United States as opposed to somewhere in Europe or Canada. It was just ingrained in me that joining the military was something I probably needed to do. My parents were a little shocked at first, I think. They were very hesitant, especially since I was joining after 9/11. Ultimately, they ended up signing the paperwork; they had to sign because I joined at seventeen. So I spent my eighteenth birthday in boot camp.

I loved the military from the time I was a kid. I think at thirteen I definitely knew I was going to join the military. When I first told my parents, I was only thirteen. They didn't really think I would remember or figured it was just some kind of a dream that would probably dissipate as I got older. But it stuck with me, and not only was it a dream then, it's still a dream now. I'm considering getting back into the military as a commissioned officer now; it's just a love of mine. I can't pinpoint exactly what it is, but I can tell you it had a lot to do with my parents being immigrants and how grateful we were for being in this country.

Part of me wanted to be a Marine, but I was drawn to the Navy and I really wanted to be a Navy SEAL—probably like many kids who want to join the Navy. That never worked out, because someone decided I could not get security clearance due to my family history. That turned out to not be the case, but I didn't find out in time to actually go through the training. I fell in love with the Navy a long time ago because I felt the Navy has the most diversity as far as where you can go and what you can do. I was really drawn to the tradition of the Navy, too. I believed the United States Navy could fight a war on its own if necessary because it has its own air force—it has its warships and whatever else—but then it also has the Marine Corps, which is part of the Navy. The Navy has its own ground troops too, so it's an all-in-one package—"One team, one fight," as we say. So I felt like if I joined the Navy, I could get a wide range of experiences. I thought maybe one time I could serve in a squadron and the next time I could serve with an infantry unit or something like that. That's essentially what ended up happening and I really love that. Being able to jump from one thing to another and learn about the different parts of the military and how it works was wonderful.

I went to Fallujah in 2005. It was right after it had settled down a bit. It's never really settled down, though. When we got there, Ramadi was the worst part of the Sunni Triangle, because that's the area of operation for the Marine Corps. Once you're on the ground, even though the Navy essentially owns the Marine Corps, the Marines are in charge and the Navy personnel on the ground do what the Marines say because they're the experts. The main body of our unit was in Fallujah. We had an outpost near Syria where we were helping build the Marines and the Iraqi Army. We were scattered all over Iraq.

I ended up becoming our battalion public affairs officer. That was kind of a job I fell into, like most of my jobs in the Navy. I had really good writing and communication skills, so that got me placed in the job and I kind of learned my job on the fly. Being a public affairs officer gave me a lot of autonomy and I could make up an excuse for why I needed to go anywhere. For instance, when I wanted to do something out in Ramadi, all I'd have to say was, "Oh, today I'm going to go out to Ramadi so I can go visit our guys out there." I had to get approval from people, so it's not like I just jumped on a convoy and left, but a lot of times I just basically came up with what I was going to work on and they usually let me do it. For an E-4 in the Navy, that's a pretty great gig, being able to call your own shots.

I had to learn it all. I didn't know anything about anything when I first got up there, so it was a big crash course on photography and journalism. A lot of our audience was the families back home, but I also did my best to get our guys out there in Department of Defense publications or hometown papers. The United States Navy has their own websites and they have their own magazines, so a lot of times I would push for them to be published there. We hosted Chief of Naval Operations Admiral Mike Mullen once, who's now the chairman of the Joint Chiefs. He came and visited our unit so we got to hang out with him. Donald Rumsfeld came out and we got to meet him—there was a lot of that kind of activity. There were a lot of news people that would come and I would be in charge of handling them and pointing them in the right direction when they came to see our unit. So that was some of what I did, which wasn't fulfilling because, again, it wasn't exactly what I wanted to do when I first joined the Navy. I guess for an alpha male type it wasn't the aggressive, combat-driven job I was looking for, but it was a good job all-in-all. I got to go out with the Marines—with some of my convoy teams and things like that—and it gave me at least enough to "snack on," I guess, as far as getting outside the wire.

I think the most commonly heard phrase is, "You just want to show everybody in a positive light." That's the main goal of a public affairs officer. You're not a true journalist; you're not trying to get to the truth, like, "Oh, I exposed the commanding general of the base because he's not doing...." That's not your job. That's up to the *New York Times* and the *Wall Street Journal*. For you, your job is just to put out positive stories about the military and not necessarily lie, but just find the stories so that when people back home open up their magazine or open up their newsletter, they get to read about their own family members doing something great and it makes them feel good—it makes them feel a little better about the fact that their family is deployed.

We had a lot of contact with Iraqis on our base that worked for us; for me, it was kind of a unique experience, because I'm of Persian decent. I'm Persian, not Arab. Persian is different, but close enough, especially in that situation. My unit was trying to convince me to be a translator, but I told them, "No, you still need to rely on real translators because Arabic is not something you pick up in a few weeks." But I did have a pretty good rapport with the Iraqis that I came in contact with. I remember we went to a barbershop and got our hair cut and all the guys in there were Iraqi. One guy looked at my name tag and kind of looked at me, and didn't really say anything. I started chitchatting with them and he asked me where I was from, and I said, "I'm from the United States," and he said, "But what are you?" I said, "I'm Persian," and he said, "Oh, you're Iranian," and he kind of whispered, "Are you Muslim?" I'm not—I have no religious preference at all—but I said yes, just to gain some acceptance. I said yes, and you'd think I'd just told him I loved him and that he was my best friend, because from that moment on they all wanted to talk to me every time they saw me. Some of the workers on base were Iraqi and some of them were from other places who had come over for work, but they were good people, and I had a good time meeting them. Getting to know them, experiencing their culture—you know, making friends with them—was a good experience.

When it came to Iran, I had no problem with what we were doing, except to say that I was more concerned with how we were empowering Iran than anything else. I was not a supporter of the Iraq war—when it happened, before it happened, and even more so after it happened—but that was where my unit was going and I wasn't going to sit it out. But I think because I have a more complete understanding of the region and the people, I could tell certain things were going to happen that most Americans weren't going to be able to understand. I remember saying there is no way that Saddam Hussein is in bed with Osama bin Laden. It's just not possible. I'm still trying to convince people that Iraq had nothing to do with 9/11. People still believe that Saddam had a role, which is insane to me.

I really didn't like Rumsfeld. There isn't a word strong enough for the level of dislike I have for him and his staff, not just because of what they did, but what they didn't do. You know you're going to war but didn't arm us? You didn't armor our convoys, our Humvees? There was just so much that wasn't done, so I have a very big dislike of him.

I think more politics played into it than actual strategic decision making. I've actually spoken with a few generals myself who talked to me candidly about how a lot of people were pushed out; a lot of people who were making noise in opposition were pushed aside. So I think no matter how many experts you had that argued against it, it wasn't going to make a difference and that's the situation. It was a done deal. We were going to war.

I was definitely not a supporter of going into Iraq, but once we were there, it was that Pottery Barn mentality of, "You break it, you bought it," so now it's time to fix it. And I thought that it was more important for me to go over there whether the war was right or wrong—get over there, serve my country, expedite in any way I can the process of fixing Iraq so we can give it back to its people, and get out of there, because we needed to get out of there and we still need to get out of there. It has no strategic value to us, except we now opened up a can of worms. We knew that Iran was involved in the Iraqi resistance. I know for a fact that we captured Iranian officers in Iraq. I knew it was making Iran more powerful regionally. I think that was the worst unintended consequence of the war that's going to affect us long-term, because now we've empowered Iran. We took out their biggest competition.

I think we missed a huge opportunity after 9/11. We got sidetracked. That was something I really struggled with, because I really believed in our mission in Afghanistan. I still do. But the Iraq war was something I had to figure out. What was more important, my oath to my country or my sense of right and wrong? Maybe it was just legitimizing it in my head, or maybe it was a logical perspective that I took, but we had already been in Iraq for about two to two and a half years, so my question of right and wrong was irrelevant at that point. So it wasn't about whether I supported President Bush as an individual citizen or if I supported the war as an individual citizen. This was the mission now.

Once that first step was taken over the Iraqi border, the questions about should we or shouldn't we were over. Now the question was, "What is the best way to fix it and get out?" I think that's how I legitimized it in my head. Our mission at that point was not to invade Iraq. Our mission was to prepare Iraq to stand up on its own so Americans could leave. While the initial invasion may have been wrong, that is a mission I do support. Getting Iraq stable and self sufficient so Americans can leave

Iraq is a mission I think all Americans can get behind, because you can't just leave it, especially with Iran on the border. You cannot just leave that country to its own accord. You have to help it out. So I think that's the way that I, in my mind, made what I was doing make sense.

But as far as U.S. involvement with the Middle East and the rest of the world in general, I think that as a world power we have vested interests all over the world now. A lot of people ask why the United States feels the need to be involved in Iran and China, and all over the world. I think if you look at the last hundred years, the world has been moving towards globalization. Globalization isn't something that happened in the '80s, '90s, or the 2000s. It's something that's been happening progressively for a century. People and nations are more reliant on one another for resources, supplies, and trade, so I think the United States is just at the top of that hierarchy, where it's our responsibility to maintain order and to maintain peace, so that the globalized market can remain stable.

I think a lot of what the United States does is unjustly criticized, but often that is unjust and simply a matter of others wishing they could do what we do. So in the 1950s —I think it was called Operation Ajax—the CIA was called in to restore the Shah in Iran. I think at the time it was the right move, and I think that my family supported that because they were supporters of the Shah. The Shah was probably not the greatest guy if you opposed him. But I think he was also probably one of the best leaders for Iran at the time, because he really brought a lot of modernization to Iran. The Shah made sure the United States was allied with Iran and that Iran played an important role in world affairs. I think Iranians were proud of the country at the time, but there are certain things that he probably did behind closed doors that a lot of people didn't like. He was much better than what happened in 1979. I know for a fact that my dad was a big supporter of him. He served in his military and was a big supporter of the Shah, and a big, big critic of the revolution, mostly because of its religious overtones. One of the important things people have to understand about what happened in Iran is that it did not start as a religious revolution. It started as a political, student-driven, youthful movement and was hijacked by a religious right-wing group who ended up taking over the whole thing. So for me, Iran is not really a place that I feel much connection to.

When I joined, I thought, "this is my chance to do something—I can go join the military, be an intelligence specialist and really help my country with this unique skill that I have"—because really and truly there are very few who speak Farsi in the U.S. military. I mean, it's a handful, so I was really excited about that when I went off to training. One day, they sat us in a room to discuss our clearances. Some guys in civilian clothes rattled off a bunch of things that we needed to talk to the investigators about if they applied to us. I was eighteen, so when I heard, "If your parents are foreign nationals," I didn't know if that applied to me. My parents were citizens. But I wanted to be honest, so I went and explained my situation. Long story short, they told me there was no way I could get a clearance. That was totally not true, but this was less than a year after 9/11. I think that had something to do with what they did next. They told me they'd submit my paperwork, but I found out later they never actually did. They just told me it had been rejected and sent me packing.

I was still determined to serve my country; I was still very young and idealistic. I felt like I owed so much to this country and I think that's something a lot of kids my age that are born here don't feel anymore. They offered to let me out of the Navy. I said no, so they found me a new job that didn't require a clearance. Two years later, when I deployed to Iraq with the CBs, it turned out I needed a clearance to deploy. It took a few months to get it without any headaches whatsoever. So I know that I was lied to when I was in training and it really sidelined the career path I wanted. However, I made lemonade out of lemons and it all worked out nicely.

As far as I'm concerned, once you get back from Iraq or Afghanistan, you have a right to feel and think what you want. You're still a U.S. citizen, especially when you're not wearing your uniform, or once you've gotten out of the military, you have a right to say and do what you please. I can't tell anyone else how to feel and what to think about their experience because everyone is unique. You can have two guys that sat side by side in that Humvee for six or seven months, driving down the streets of Iraq getting shot at, and they'll come out with vastly different perspectives. I think that's just human nature. No two people will think alike or process the information and the experiences that they had alike; some people become angry, some people become depressed. I think a lot of that comes from people wondering things like, "What the hell did we even accomplish over there? What did we get done?" All that sacrifice in blood and treasure, and so far we don't have much to show for it. At least when the guys came home from World War II they could easily see the fruits of their labor.

Because you build a school and the school gets blown up by the insurgency. You build a hospital and the hospital gets a hole blown in the side of it from a mortar attack. It seems like this big, never-ending circle. It just keeps going around and around, where we fix something, they break it; we do something, they destroy it. So I left with an even worse taste in my mouth about the whole war than when I got there. Then I talk to some people who said how much they think the Iraqi people loved us and appreciated us. I think that has a lot to do with how diverse Iraq really is. A lot of people don't know the difference between Sunni and Shia, and of course the Kurdish North. Depending on where you were, if you were closer to Tikrit, you were going to have more Saddam loyalists. If you were in the Sunni Triangle, you were going to have more Saddam loyalists who were violently supporting him and trying to overthrow the U.S.-placed regime. If you were in Baghdad, you were much more likely to be well received because that's where the Shias were.

When someone's come back and they are cheering on the war and they say it's the right thing to do, or that they hate our government for what they did to us over there, I think it's a matter of perspective. I think it's a matter of what they experienced and how they feel about it. For me personally, when I came home in late April or early May 2006 from Iraq, I'd seen enough and experienced enough to be a little bit jumpy and for it to have a little bit of an effect on me. I didn't realize the change at first and wouldn't have admitted it even if I did.

I immediately enrolled in the University of Alabama. By August I was enrolled in school, had bought a house, and was preparing for my first full-time semester of college. I was a 22-year-old war veteran in school with a bunch of eighteen-year-old kids, and that experience was a complete shock to me. I felt like I was back in high school. I felt out of place. I was irritable and angry. I didn't really know what I was doing. While I was in the Navy, I would take a lot of night classes to keep myself occupied and out of trouble. I had a 3.7 GPA from the classes I took through distance learning and things like that. My first semester of "real college" I had a 2.0 GPA.

I didn't know what I was doing there and I felt empty. As much as I said we didn't accomplish anything when we got back, I felt even less accomplished as somebody sitting in a classroom in college, because I'd turn on the news and see people were still going back over there—sometimes people I knew making another deployment—so I felt like somewhat of a coward and somewhat of a let-down to those guys. I was sitting in a school, in a comfortable classroom and going to football games. I was going to parties most nights of the week with my friends and frat "brothers" and my real brothers were over there fighting. It was really depressing.

I joined a fraternity, looking for some of that brotherhood I was missing out on. That was a huge mistake. I can't completely regret it, because I had to do it to realize how big a mistake it was, but it ended up leading me to realize that I'm not the only person who struggles. I quit the fraternity after a while and made friends with a couple other veterans around my campus. Two or three of them dropped out in one semester and one just left town without warning. I realized, "Wow, I'm not the only person who is struggling; I'm not the only person who is having these problems." I decided to do something about it and ended up starting an organization on campus. Initially, it was supposed to be a social organization and veteran support group, but we started lobbying the university to create programs for vets. It's been an uphill battle for almost three years now. From that experience, I learned that everybody processes differently. Some people are angry, some people are alcoholics, and some people immerse themselves in school and do really well. Some people just go home, lie on the couch, and don't move. Some people play video games. I really don't feel the right to tell other people how to think about their experience or what to do.

Now, sometimes you have people like an acquaintance of mine who say, "I hope all those Iraqis die. They're liars, they're manipulative, and they're cheaters." I tell them, "I understand that's probably the interaction that you had with them, but you also have to put yourself in their shoes. You are an Iraqi. One day, all these troops pour into your country and they tell you that they are taking your leader out and they're going to place a good government instead. Maybe you didn't appreciate the old guy, but like one Iraqi local told me, 'I wish Saddam was still in power because when Saddam was here, I knew how to get around without any trouble. You would put your head down, do your job, and you keep your mouth shut so you can go home. Everything was fine. I had water and I had electricity. Now I get two hours of power a day. There are food shortages in the country and I can get killed walking to work because I happen to be in the wrong place when a bomb goes off in a market. This is awful. If this is freedom and democracy, I don't want it. Bring Saddam back.'"

So, I think that just as much as we can't tell a fellow veteran what to feel or what to think, you also have to understand there are different perspectives from those people who live in the places we're fighting, too. Some people cooperated because they saw the bigger picture and they served as translators and things like that for us. They wanted to be part of the government. Some people wanted to fight us because they didn't believe in it. Others took sides to not be standing alone, or because someone paid them to. So really, there's no right or wrong answer to it. It just is what it is.

Here's the way I see the situation with the Iraqis: I live in the South and President Obama isn't really popular down here. I personally like him. I mean, there are a lot of people who do, but what would happen if China flew their jets here and invaded the United States through Florida, made it through Alabama and the Southeast, and said, "It's okay guys. We understand how oppressive Obama is and how terrible he is. We're going to free your country from him and we're going to help you establish a new nation." Every red-blooded American with an anti-Obama sticker would load their shotgun and rifle and start going hunting for Chinese soldiers, because as much as you dislike your leader, you're sovereignty is more important to you. Your nation is more important, even if the leader is not someone you agree with at the time. So I think, again, just as hard as it is for me to judge the veteran, it's hard for me to judge the Iraqis too, because a lot of them just don't trust us.

A lot of them have had bad experiences with Americans. I know one guy that I served with in Iraq who made me really angry, because this little kid came up to him and was trying to sell him gum. Of course, the kid knows that the U.S. troops are paid well. So he came up and tried to sell the gum, but this guy ends up grabbing the kid and shoving him to the ground and yelling at him. We said, "What the hell's wrong with you?" His response was, "Well, I'm sick and tired of this. I'm sick and tired of these kids always coming up to me, trying to sell me something." Again, put yourself in their shoes. I understand his frustrations. I understand the kid's motivation, too. He's trying to help his family and make a living. That kid probably went home, told his dad what happened, and if his dad wasn't angry enough, that kid probably had a negative impression of Americans for the rest of his life now. I told the guy, "You may have just created another insurgent. That kid may not sell gum anymore. Now he may take 100 dollars to carry a duffel bag to the side of the road that's going to blow up on us later." It's based on everyone's personal experiences and you can't really tell people how to feel. You can try to reason with them, but I leave folks to their own devices.

A handshake and a thank you for your service are always wonderful, and it's very nice, but I think that people really have to understand the struggle that some veterans go through, or at least empathize. You probably can't understand the struggle, but try to empathize with what these guys are going through, what they've experienced, and really encourage all levels of government and non-profits to help these men and women. There have been a lot of things that have been done for veterans that are great. For instance, President Obama signed a bill recently for government agencies to try to hire veterans first. That's great, because sometimes people are hesitant to hire veterans for one reason or another. Before you can employ a veteran, though, we have to educate them, we have to rehabilitate them, and we have to help them to readjust and reacclimatize themselves to this life. This is vastly different.

Even if you've never stepped outside the wire in Iraq or Afghanistan, your experience over there is dangerous and stressful. A sailor from a previous unit who never went outside the wire was killed in our camp in Iraq because a mortar landed on him while he was building a wall on base. Camp Knott, in Fallujah, was named for that young sailor who died in the mortar attack. So the threat is real, but obviously, our combat troops see much more danger than the guys who don't venture out much. You have to understand that everyone has experienced something over there and they all need help, even if they don't realize it. Whether it's colleges and universities having services for veterans on every campus across this country, to some of the things that are now being done that may require more funding, like getting job training and things like that, these folks need it and deserve it. A lot of these folks are really hard workers. A lot of them are very organized and strong leaders. They just need to learn how to take those skills they had in the military and apply them to a civilian career.

This could be the next great generation if we take care of them and help them along. I think that most people who are reading this book are going to be interested in helping veterans anyway, but there needs to be some kind of national movement where you really start taking care of your veterans and say, "Whatever the VA needs they will get to help these people." Of course, we want it to be efficient. We don't want to waste money, but whatever they need should be made available. The VA is doing some great work with traumatic brain injuries and things like that, so I think there just needs to be a lot of focus put on taking care of veterans over the next, probably, ten years. If we do that, I think we're going to have a really great generation of war veterans that are going to contribute to our society, our government, and our country's recovery. I think our country can prosper again and these men and women can lead the charge if we invest in them now.

From the *Tuscaloosa News:*

> I was a high school senior when it happened. I went to school like any other day. I worked in the vice principal's office and she walked in and said someone had attacked the World Trade Center. I thought maybe she'd gotten confused and was talking about the anniversary of the 1993 WTC attack. One of the faculty had a small TV she kept on her desk, so we huddled around it, watching the replay of the first building being hit. Thinking logically, I said, "I don't think it's over. If it was a planned attack, wouldn't you fly into both?" We all hoped that wasn't going to happen, but minutes later it did. It still came as a complete shock.
>
> I think "surreal" is the best word to describe the day as we went from class to class. I remember sitting in film class, watching the coverage of the attack on TV and feeling like I was watching a movie. A friend of mine whose parents were from India asked if I was going to be in class the next day. I thought it was a stupid question. I never really did experience overt racism in high school because everyone knew me.
>
> Then I joined the Navy. It had always been my plan to join the Navy after going to college for a year, but after 9/11 that plan got kicked into high gear. It was in the military that I experienced racist backlash for the first time. I lost my security clearance. It wasn't military policy. It was just a couple people who had a bias against me and it was all sorted out in six weeks.
>
> My parents have been U.S. citizens since '91. I was born here, so it's weird to be treated as an outcast. But it didn't affect my feelings about the U.S. I grew up listening to my father talk about how terrible Iran was. Here, we have the opportunity to better ourselves. That's why I felt I needed to give back to my country, because it gave so much to our family.
>
> Getting (Osama) bin Laden before the tenth anniversary was the best. The timing of it was great —I'd just lost my home in the tornado and we all needed good news. There were pains after September 11th. Anti-Muslim sentiment is still around, but because it's become a mainstream issue, it's opened up a dialogue and challenges people's preconceived notions. In the long run, it'll help. It wasn't the most ideal way to start a dialogue, but it's just important that it got people talking.

Sergio Kochergin in Eugene, Oregon, before leaving for India to work with homeless children. He immigrated to the United States from Ukraine at thirteen. Sergio served two tours in Iraq with the Marine Corps. Sergio says, "I want to apologize to all the people in Iraq."

Sergio Kochergin

My family moved to the U.S. from the Ukraine when I was thirteen. I decided to become a Marine after 9/11; I thought it would be a good thank you to the government for providing a home and a job and a normal lifestyle. I joined in 2002, and that's when my journey began.

I went to South Carolina for boot camp. Then I went to the school of infantry. As soon as we got there we started training continuously. Educating us on Iraq and telling us that we have to be ready to fight women, kids, and everybody else. Starting dehumanization to prepare us. We were young, brainwashed, and motivated.

During the first deployment I was in an infantry platoon, patrolling the streets and enforcing the law made by us. We acted like we owned the place and dehumanized people. Treating them badly and being disrespectful. In the beginning, people were giving us cigarettes, they were giving us food, they were offering their daughters for a night. We're not meant to occupy. The longer we stayed, the worse things started getting—IEDS and all that stuff—because they got sick and tired of us. It just kept getting worse and worse and worse.

We were supposed to do humanitarian work. My platoon didn't do it. Other platoons did it for a week or so. We didn't really do anything except harass people and drive around. My second deployment, as soon as we got there, we lost our company commander and one of our NCOs. It just started going to shit. We would go out and look for people to shoot depending on our rules of engagement, which got more lenient, to the point where we had no rules of engagement for a while. It gave us the ability to fight the war the way we thought was the right way. That's pretty fair. Just taking people out.

I got out in 2006 and I lived at home. Then I couldn't take it anymore. Pills weren't helping me. I was drinking and acting like a dumbass. I decided I shouldn't put my parents through this stuff, so I went to live with my friend in Texas. I got there and then it started sinking in, the things that I did. I started realizing what I did was not only for the wrong reasons, but inhumane reasons, I tried to commit suicide by blowing my brains out. Good I didn't do it. I guess I passed out. My roommate started yelling at me, "What the hell are you doing?" It was an epiphany. I realized I needed to start doing something about it.

I don't want anybody else to go through what I'm going through. A friend told me about the IVAW and I joined. As soon as I got a chance to speak I jumped up for it, because I thought they should hear the story. I thought it was just my company, my platoon. But it turned out everything everyone was saying was exactly the same.

I just learned to live with it. It's fine. Alcohol and drugs smooth out the realization of what we were doing. You stay with it and stay with it. Then, when you stop doing everything, it's still there. It's a long process, which for different people happens in different ways. That's how it was for me.

When we came in, we wanted to serve our country. We gave all of our loyalty and all of our everything: our souls, our minds, our bodies. They just used us. We were betrayed. The VA system is just horrible. In Oregon it's great, but in Texas, when I really needed their help, nobody would call me back. Here it's amazing, these guys are awesome, and that's good, but it's not everywhere. That's another betrayal and it's really hard.

I got to finish school right now. I need to concentrate on my VA, mental health, and my knees, my stomach, and stuff, getting fixed up a little bit. There are effects that are always there: anxiety, panic attacks, sleeplessness. You kind of feel depressed; sometimes you just lie quiet. I'm physically there, but mentally and psychologically I'm not at all. I'm able to live in the good world and stuff, but I still get flashbacks. But I kind of got used to it, so I don't react to it the way I used to. I'll take deep breaths, just wait it off.

I learned too much from the war and I don't want to forget about it. Because every time I remember something I learn from it. All I have to do is learn from it and not sit on it. So that's what I do and it kind of works out.

Facebook post from January 2012

So I just had a conversation with the bank about my college loan. I explained my situation and my hardship, being a disabled combat veteran and finding a job and paying back my loan. I asked them if there were any options of getting a deferment or forbearance. They explained to me that they do not offer such privileges to anyone. They told me I have sixteen days to make a payment or my account will be handed over to a collection agency. Then I asked them what would be a way to make sure that my parents don't end up stuck with my debt and they did not have an answer. So I asked them what would happen if I blew my brains out—only then they said that my loan would be forgiven. "So veterans, thank you for your sacrifice and thanks for the bailouts from your tax money, but the only way we can help you is if you blow your brains out!!!!!" I'm proud to be an American where at least I know I'm free, AND I WON'T FORGET THE MEN WHO DIED WHO GAVE THEIR LIFE FOR ME AND I GLADLY STAND UP . . .

Former Marine Garrett Anderson at a monthly poetry reading at Tony's Tavern on West Burnside in Portland, Oregon. He says: "I fell in love with the scene in the back of a Portland dive bar and would write about life through the eyes of a veteran in transition. My future wife would attend 'The Reading,' which captured the perspective of another trip to a VA hospital and the anxiety of living through the famous VA backlog in paperwork, which took nearly three years before my case was resolved, even with two hospitalizations and a clear documentation of my combat experience. During this time, I was warmly received by my adopted poetry family, as I was able to communicate a world most Americans were unaware of, and they were able to talk to me about it and help a member of the community feel accepted. I am honored to call the Tony's poets family who can truly claim to support the troops, even though most did not support the war."

Garrett Anderson

When I was there it was a job, my job. When I returned it became a recycled memory, but all of my fluff won't change your point of view and I understand that each reader will misinterpret my intention. In short, as a human being you should be ashamed of yourself for looking. My war was your television program.

It seems to me that the most interested population in war tend to be middle-aged people who have not served. Many liberals seem to yearn for we veterans to return scarred emotionally so they can say, "I told you so." Many conservatives are too eager for bloodbaths in the name of their savior; they hope we return to stick up for the second amendment. The liberals forget the military is comprised of all walks, and the same with the conservatives. They put us in a box that turns my stomach. War tourists who follow the movement to justify preconceptions of something that can't be defined.

They were happy to send us off, or they were crying in the streets, "No blood for oil!" This was back in 2003, when an anti-war protest made some curmudgeons feel the liberation of a long-gone era. 2004 became a low-key version of 1968: the shitkickers back home versus the peaceniks back home, and once again each missed their mark. I have seen enough to appease both sides' narrow views, and I hate them equally for reading the following and imagining that they could relate or insert a deeper meaning into calculated death and destruction. When I was there it was a job, my job. When I returned, it became a recycled memory, but all of my fluff won't change your point of view, and I understand that each reader will misinterpret my intention. In short, as a human being you should be ashamed of yourself for looking. My war was your television program.

I remember that the top of a young Marine's head had been removed by a bullet. As they managed him across the street, the Lieutenant and I approached. The Lieutenant ordered the Marines to pick up the corpse because the shards of glass in the ground were getting stuck in its legs. He was so heavy, packed inside a combat load, that the Marines were dragging him. This seemed silly to me, since he was already dead and incapable of feeling discomfort. I understood that if he were with us in some ghostly spirit, he might have told the Lieutenant to give the guys a break. One of the dead legs had a posthumous bullet shot into it and was slightly oozing a black circle at the source. I remember telling myself not to look down as we carried him under a drive-port across the street, but I did. His eyes were rolled back, white half-moons lazily open, his face hung agape with an expression I can only describe as stupid. The sun shone into his skull, illuminating the inside of his forehead, casting a glow that reminded me of a jack o' lantern on Halloween. I remembered a few years before watching the street vendors peddling flags the day after 9/11. This macabre scene was the wet dream of patriotism.

The track-suited youth was howling the same thing over and over in repetition, but I did not have to understand his language to know that there was a message being communicated through a death throe. I asked the interpreter what he was saying and the interpreter looked to me grimly and replied in a thick accent, "Where is Islam now?" I laughed. I understood what the "terp" was saying. The poor young-looking jihadi had followed his older mentors into war and they had lied to him. They were dead surrounding him, twisted and mangled in the street. They had told him that God would protect him from the infidels, but it did not take much for a well-trained Marine to sink lead into the fleeing young man's trunk from a couple hundred meters. Islam was his blanket, just as much as Christianity was mine. A medic stood by the wounded fighter and I asked what was wrong. The medic explained that the young jihadi had been hit in each lung and that he was mortally fucked. The young man kept screaming his mantra. Sometimes I summon his chant before I drift off to sleep. I found out nearly a decade later that the young jihadi was only sixteen years old at the time. I was nineteen and hated him for failing a basic math class.

Rick Lawson at his Experience War Project exhibition at Western Washington University. Rick holds Dr. Edward Tick's book about homecoming, *War and the Soul: Healing Our Nation's Veterans from Post-Traumatic Stress Disorder.*[1]

Rick Lawson

We need to look seriously at the true costs of war and acknowledge that the costs are much higher. The human costs of war are much higher than we collectively acknowledge. We must also acknowledge our societal obligation to take care of the people we choose to send into these situations on behalf of our country.

My name is Rick Lawson. I was born in 1982, in Palm Springs, California. I enlisted in the Washington State Army National Guard in January 2002 and went to basic training in March. My military occupational specialty was as a 91K—medical laboratory technician. I went through basic training at Fort Jackson, South Carolina, and Advanced Individual Training (AIT) at Fort Sam Houston, Texas, where I learned my skills as a medical laboratory technician. I then did an internship at the now Joint Base Lewis McChord (JBLM) in Tacoma, Washington. I spent only three months drilling as a National Guardsman before being activated to deploy to Iraq. We trained full time at JBLM before going to the Fort Irwin National Training Center (NTC), where we trained to be in a desert environment. From there we deployed to Kuwait, and then Iraq, where we spent a year.

While in Iraq, I was at a base called Logistical Support Area (LSA) Anaconda, near the city of Balad, Iraq. It is in what is known as the Sunni Triangle. It was a hot spot for insurgent activity at the time. We were in-country from April 2004 to April 2005.

I was medically discharged, honorably, in August 2006.

The War Experience Project started because I was asked in a university class to create an art piece about war in response to the Bayeaux Tapestry. The Bayeaux Tapestry is an embroidered timeline of the Battle of Hastings, which took place in 1066. The Normans beat the Saxons and, basically, the fundamental structure of western government was instilled in the UK at that time. So we learned about that in this class and were instructed to create an art piece. I was the only military veteran in my class. I went home thinking, "What am I going to do? What can I possibly do that would be meaningful?"

When the assignment was presented to me, I took the challenge and thought, "I am going to really do this, and I want to do it really well." So I decided to use cloth because I felt that if I am going to make art, then I want it to be a challenge for me, rather than just drawing something. To use cloth was a little more challenging, so I started looking for cloth around my house that would be useful for this purpose, but the cloth I was finding really didn't inspire me to do anything. I was finding pink polka-dotted fabric, or orange striped fabric, or floral prints, and I just kept thinking that this isn't going to work. But then, as I was digging through the house looking for fabric, I found a black plastic box in the bottom corner of my closet, buried under other boxes. It was my "tough box." We called these black plastic boxes "tough boxes" in the military. It had my uniforms and other memorabilia from my time in the military, my basic training handbook, and all kinds of other manuals and letters that had been sent to me while I was deployed in Iraq. When I opened it there were all these memories that I had been trying to move on from, trying to move forward with my life; when I opened that box, I was overwhelmed with the memories—good memories and bad memories. I actually put the uniform on and reminisced what it was like to be in the military; to put the uniform on and to feel the pride and the commitment that I had while serving my country. It was really intense, because I felt these things while I was serving in the military. So to feel it again years later, it was always a part of me. I had been trying to pretend it wasn't. I was trying to move forward without it somehow. I realized at that point that the uniform was the cloth that I wanted to use to complete the assignment. That cloth was what I knew about that others didn't know about, those who have never worn the uniform.

I cut the back of the uniform off so I could use it as a canvas, nailed it into an old wooden picture frame, and then painted for four hours, first using my fingers to finger paint and using black paint in the direction with the camouflage pattern. As I started doing that, it seemed like smoke emerging. The camouflage seemed to have a natural smoke pattern to it.

I started envisioning an explosion. I took yellow and orange paint and put it on with my fingers, and eventually used a brush. Then I envisioned a Humvee exploding in the midst and so I went online, found a Humvee, and painted that into the scene. The experience was very cathartic for me—I was crying—it was a very intense four hours of painting for me. I took it to my class and showed it to my classmates. When I brought it back home and put it up on my wall, I started talking with my fiancée about what I'd experienced and how this was really more than me. What I had just done was so powerful, and I knew it was bigger than what I had just done. I was trying to figure it out, so I started researching art therapy. I began understanding about the processing of trauma that can occur through the art-making process. This furthered the conversation between my fiancée and I. We talked about what this art could really turn into. At first, I thought I was just going to create my own tapestry. I was going to take more uniforms, cut the backs of them off, and paint scene after scene before and after this Humvee exploding moment, then stitch them all together in the form of a tapestry. Then I thought, "Why?" I thought that idea was really selfish. It was the artist's side of me thinking that this is going to be cool and I'm going to be awesome. After contemplating that for a while, I started thinking about how I have such a small piece of knowledge about this whole experience of war. There are so many other people who have served before, during, and after that all have their own stories to share, their own knowledge about the war experience. So I thought, "What if I ask other veterans to participate?" I came to a realization that it is the uniform that's important! It's the uniform that others don't know about. So I took safety pins that day and I safety pinned the back of my uniform back onto the rest of that uniform, with the sleeves and the rest of the jacket. At that moment, I felt I was taking control of my voice. It was pivotal because, during this same time, I was also being bombarded by questions from people in my community like, "Did you ever kill anyone?" or, "Did you ever see anyone die?" People ask because they're curious; they want to show interest and support, but they don't realize the insensitivity of those questions. For generations, many veterans never shared their stories with non-veterans—even their own families—and not because they weren't asked to.

I think that I was trying to close off my conversation with people by stopping or moving away and not talking because I was getting so fed up with their questions. I really felt that when I safety pinned that uniform back together I could take control of my own conversation again. By starting this project and offering it to other veterans, I started the conversation that I wanted to have with the public about war and its effects on the individual. We were drawing attention back to the humanity of war and to the individual (we have our own individuals in this country, our brothers and sisters that are participating in war), not the concept of war, politics, or the right and wrong of it.

When I presented the artwork to the class people were floored by it—they were speechless. There was a lot of emotional stuff going on. People were crying. I talked about how a childhood friend of mine (we grew up together) had just recently died after being in Iraq for only two weeks. His memory was very fresh and his loss very fresh. For me, this whole process really brought that back up again, so I talked about how that loss was very real to me. This painting was the best that I could do to express the nuances of all of that.

We hold workshops where people can come and paint. Some people paint at home and send their artwork to us to add to the project. When we hold a workshop, we don't stigmatize the participants by calling it an "art therapy" workshop, because it is my opinion that when people are stigmatized, their potential for healing is diminished. When you stigmatize someone, they can't access the depth of their experiences because of the roles the patient-provider relationship creates and people fall into. So we call it a painting workshop because that's what it is—people can come and paint. We are not setting up any kind of expectation of healing. We are not setting up an expectation that we are therapists. We let people know that choosing to participate in this is choosing to engage their experiences at the level they are comfortable with. Ultimately, when one paints with the intention of accessing such memories, it is a very deep process. Most participants move on with their life and we don't hear from them again, which is to be expected. There are a few who have kept in touch who say this process changed their lives. That is a pretty amazing expression of what art has done for them and it would be easy to dismiss it, but I don't. I'm thankful to have introduced, or in some cases reintroduced, art as a positive outlet of self expression to so many.

An active duty captain (CPT) painted in one of our workshops. After that painting experience, the CPT decided to come to an art gallery we had in Tacoma. The CPT continued to come back to our gallery to paint canvasses, then eventually began selling paintings to friends and patrons of our art gallery. This person then decided that having painted on one uniform wasn't enough and wanted to paint another uniform. We said, "OK, who are we to tell you no. Go for it." A second uniform was painted and, looking at the progression between the first and second uniforms, it was really interesting to see how the first uniform was just patches sewn onto the uniform and writings with a permanent ink marker. The second uniform was painted using acrylic paints, has a face with a magnifying glass over one of the eye, and the figure is holding the magnifying glass. It says, "I'm a veteran not an animal." What was interesting for all of us is that we saw a lot of introspection beginning and emerging through the canvas. The CPT kept painting more and more canvasses and then decided to paint a third uniform jacket, and we said, "Wow, ok . . . two, ok, but three . . . we can't stop you!" This time, when the CPT painted, it was using only acrylic paints and was intense. The painting depicts a skull up in flames and says, "Post Stress Demon Disorder (PSDD)." It's so intense that there is someone who now, through this process of painting, is really starting to access some deep stuff and getting it out, and it was all done at the individual's own pace.

This soldier is currently an active duty mental health professional; someone who can't go for help because it would be seen as not being able to fulfill the mission of the job. The stigma presented in the military around mental health is one of its downsides.

So, basically, the CPT said the art-making was life changing. Today, the soldier has an art room in a garage for painting and continues to sell paintings. This is extraordinary stuff; we can't ask for anything more than that.

One day at our art gallery in Tacoma, at around ten in the morning, a guy walks by, looking at our window display. He comes in and asks, "What is all this?" We explained our project to him and I asked if he was a veteran. He said he was, so I asked if he'd like to stay and talk, or maybe even paint. He ended up staying in our gallery for about four hours that day, which is interesting, because four hours is the length of our painting workshops. It was the time it took me to paint my uniform initially. It's a good amount of time for a complete process to unfold. He had been on his way home from a night of drinking with his buddies after his thirtieth birthday, or something like that, and he was emotional in our gallery, saying he had never really talked to anyone about his experiences. He said his friends didn't understand when he would become emotional about things, presumably after being triggered. He said these so-called friends would call him derogatory, insulting names. He painted onto a uniform, inscribing words like, "We are shouldering the burden so you don't have to." In this case, our gallery was a space for veterans to find camaraderie when it couldn't be found elsewhere. I have been privileged to witness the process for every single person that has participated in the project so far. It's an immense journey that we have all taken together.

We've held twenty-five workshops and have eighty-five veteran-painted uniforms. We have shown the exhibit fifteen times, including London and at the Department of the Army's force health protection conference, two exhibitions we're particularly proud of. It's a very challenging exhibit. When people come in to view the exhibit they have varied reactions. Sometimes a person can only get through eight or ten uniforms before leaving. Others have viewed the entire exhibit and stayed to talk for hours. Many of those were veterans or family members of veterans.

In addition to creating The War Experience Project, I am also a survivor of military sexual violence. I spoke at the White House with senior presidential advisers about the topic as one of only three veterans invited. It was a huge honor for me to be able to be a part of that. I also gave an interview to the *New York Times* on the topic around the same time.

For me, what my military unit called "hazing" began during my first National Guard drill and continued during training at Fort Lewis before deploying to Iraq. The culture of the military and the type of behavior that is bred allows for perverse joking and other perverse behavior that ends up leading to sexual harassment and violence.

At the White House, our discussion was about the health and national security implications of sexual violence in the military. The basics are that it has personal health effects on people, and I attested to that from my personal experience. The larger picture is the national security implications created through a degradation of morale of the victims, bystanders, and eventually others, who lose trust in their peers. If our soldiers cannot trust those they serve with, they cannot serve to their full capacity. The hostile environment created is not good for the readiness of our military. Some recommendations were to look at the possibilities of taking the judicial authority away from these commanders so that there can be some type of neutral third party oversight. The military commanders hate that because they don't want to have anything outside of their control; it has become a very exclusive environment with no oversight. Our commanders aren't doing what needs to be done and that's been proven. Even though they like to implement programs and say, "Look, we are doing something about it," their placating measures don't really work at the end of the day.

We need to look seriously at the true costs of war and acknowledge that the costs are much higher. The human costs of war are much higher than we collectively acknowledge. We must also acknowledge our societal obligation to take care of the people we choose to send into these situations on behalf of our country.

It's amazing that only about one percent of our country is serving in the military at any given time. As a whole, about thirteen percent of our country can call themselves veterans. That's pretty amazing to me. That's a small percentage of our country—and yet a large number of people. It is very difficult to get into the military. There are so many people who say, "I was going to join the military, but . . ." but they never did. Their draft number was low, they couldn't pass the physical tests, or they failed to make it through training. That isn't to say anything bad about people who haven't joined for whatever reason, but rather, to make the point that serving in the military is very demanding and a job few in our country take up. It took a lot of drive for me to get into the military. It took a lot for me to get through the physical and mental training that went on during basic training. I guess I'm proud of the part of me that is idealistic that wanted to serve my country and that I want to make America a great place. That's what I'm proud about. I survived my experience and I'm thankful to be alive today. Not everyone has been so lucky, like my friends that I grew up with. So to come through that and come back, I can wear my hat that says "Iraq War Veteran" and be proud, because I know that I lived through it—not that I'm necessarily proud that I was a part of any of it. But I am proud that I survived it and went through something that no one else in our country—that very few people in our country—know anything about first hand. What I am proud about is the wisdom that has come from that. If people would just be willing to listen to that, rather than just talk about politics, they might learn something. Most people want to know if you are for the war or against it, but the truth is that for myself, and I think many other veterans, going through such an intense experience and getting to see world dynamics from a different perspective, we can gain some pretty deep insight into the way our government functions and the way the world functions. Whether it is right or wrong, our country depends on our foreign policy the way it is currently. Our privilege as Americans is dependent on our foreign policy today. It may not always be that way, but I think that if it changes then we, as Americans, will have to make sacrifices in terms of our quality of life. I'm proud of my service that way, but I am not proud that civilians die because of the war.

You can't tell a nineteen or twenty-year-old anything, right? I mean, at the end of the day, when I was eighteen or nineteen and I wanted to join the military, no one could have told me shit. I was either going to do it or I wasn't going to do it. I know that the American Friends Service Committee groups have pamphlets about the risk factors about going into the military, and they are legitimate, but you really can't say enough about any of it to really make a difference.

I applied to public health programs at Yale, University of Washington, and The George Washington University. I was accepted into all three programs and ultimately decided on Yale. It will be a Master in Public Health with a focus on Health Policy. Turning my negatives into positives has really set me up to be where I am today. I'm thankful for the people around me who help keep me going every day.

"Another Gold Star Day" by Rick Lawson, 2008, depicts a Humvee exploding from an Improvised Explosive Device (IED) with a small pickup truck driving away in the distance.

Ian LaVallee at the Burning Man Festival in the Black Rock Desert in Northern Nevada in 2013. Ian's Playa name is "Mammoth." There are three sets of antlers—six antlers from white tail deer: a pair that his grandfather killed, a pair that his father killed, and a pair that he killed. The coyote and possum skins were his uncle's. The boar's tooth necklace is from a pig that Ian hunted with dogs and a knife. Ian says: "Hunting is something that connects me as a participant in the cycles of nature—we are a part of it, not separate or above. It is a base that has helped me to come home from war, and where I find my most connection to source."

Ian LaVallee

One of the most profound lessons I learned from my experience in the military and Iraq was seeing myself change and seeing other soldiers change. I did things I never imagined I would do. I also saw the same in others. All people have the capability of doing the greatest "good" or the greatest "evil," and it is a matter of our circumstances and choices in life.

I was born in 1984 in Orem, Utah. My mother, my uncle, my grandfather, and my great uncle had been in the military. My great uncle was in France and Germany, and my grandfather was a submariner in the Atlantic, both during the Second World War. I remember when I was a child my grandfather talking about how the war had affected his brother afterwards. He wouldn't talk about his experience.

Since childhood, I've been influenced by what our culture deems the most honorable thing to do as a young man: we would play war and we would kill each other. You go from GI Joe to video games, films, etc.

I joined the Army on 19 March 2005—two weeks before my twenty-first birthday. I was in Iraq the first days of September the same year. I got out at the end of 2006. I was an airborne infantryman in Bravo Company, 2nd Battalion, 325th Airborne Infantry Regiment—part of the 2nd Brigade Combat Team of the 82nd Airborne. I was in Iraq from early September until the end of December 2005. I was in Tal Afar, which is in northwestern Iraq, about equidistant from the Syrian and Turkish borders in Nineveh Province.

I really wanted to believe in the good that we could do with our military. That was something I had always believed in since I was a child, and that's what we were taught. I always felt very strongly about that. But is it really "supporting and defending our constitution against all enemies foreign and domestic" (as our oath of enlistment stated) to send military troops to over 100 countries across the globe to have military bases everywhere? Is that really what it's about? We are just promoting our own shortsighted economic and political interests. It's about hegemony—dominance.

When we were in Iraq, we were occupying buildings to live in. I started seeing a lot of extremely upsetting things that made me question the validity of us being there, and feeling that we weren't doing what the government and media said we were doing. We were just making more enemies for ourselves, for America; we weren't making America safer. If people were doing in our communities the things that I saw and did, every "red-blooded American" would pick up their grandpa's rifle, AR-15, .22 shotgun, or whatever, and fight them too, just as the Iraqis were doing. We were really the terrorists. Nobody wants a military occupation or war in their home on somebody else's terms. People should have self-determination. We weren't bringing "freedom" or "democracy."

I saw a commonality between what we talk about: the "freedom fighters" of the American Revolution and the people who were trying to fight us off. The vast majority weren't "hardened terrorists" from Al Qaeda; they were just people who lived there that didn't want a foreign military occupying their homes and killing their families, whether it on purpose or accidentally. No one would want that. That's what I want people to know. Sometimes we did do good things: we were helping people by giving them blankets, mattresses, and vitamin-fortified milk for their malnourished kids. But at the same time, we would turn around and do things that far overweighed—in a horrible and negative sense—the positive things we were doing.

The way we treated ourselves—as soldiers and each other—didn't assist our own health in many ways.

We destabilized the region by our haphazard invasion and occupation; we essentially shifted the center of power to Iran. Our government disbanded the military and put hundreds of thousands of men out of work who knew where all the weapons were and who knew how to use them. Generals were surrendering with whole units and asking how they could be of help to us. The Iraqis then started seeing what was happening to their country under the Americans. They thought the Americans were going to come and do the right thing. They told us to go home. We could have done so much more to help them, but we didn't, because our government didn't know what they were doing.

President Maliki of Iraq was in exile in Iran while Saddam was in power. He's a Shia. If you look now, the Shia dominate a lot of the military, and that's about sixty per cent of the population of Iraq, whereas Saddam was Sunni. Since the invasion we have divided and conquered. Before the invasion, the Iraqi people were less sectarian, with Christians, Shia, and Sunni living together.

There are so many things that linger from our war against Iraq, one huge one being all the effects of the white phosphorus and depleted uranium (DU) munitions. There are extremely high rates of birth defects, cancers, and other diseases linked to DU. This is also affecting our soldiers who served there. This is our war's Agent Orange.

For me it's really about, "Do unto others as you would have done unto you."

Sometimes we'd give children candy, other times we'd put explosives on their door at two in the morning. We'd blow the door in and then wake them up with a gun barrel and flashlight in their face, yelling at them in a language they didn't understand; separating the women and children to one room, teenage and older men in another place; then zip tie them and take all the men and teenage boys away. They didn't know where they were being taken; the women and children don't know where they were going. I've pointed my weapon more times than I can even count at children because they weren't doing what we wanted them to do. What would we do if that happened here?

Sometimes we'd give them candy, a water bottle, or an MRE. Sometimes we would throw water bottles at them from the trucks and try to hit them.

I initially signed up for four years and nineteen weeks. Nineteen weeks included the training. When I returned from Iraq, after about four months I began developing symptoms of PTSD. I was having a lot of panic attacks, anxiety, and night terrors. I reached a point where I thought my best course of action would be to end my life. I attempted to kill myself at a bus station bathroom by stabbing and cutting myself in the arm with my knife. I was taken to the VA hospital. My platoon leader came and picked me up that week. At Fort Bragg, the military doctors recommended I be separated from the service with an honorable discharge. This led to about nine months of what I call purgatory. During that time, there was a large command change from the Brigade level down. My new command structure told me they thought I was faking it to get out. This astounded me, as I had been supported by my previous command and encouraged to reach out if I was having any more problems during the process out. Through their misconduct, the process of six to eight weeks became nine months. I was barely receiving care or help navigating the system. I felt a huge sense of betrayal from many of the so-called brothers and leaders I would have killed and died for. The behavior on their part was just the norm. I was not a special case in this, as I witnessed other soldiers while still in and those I've met after getting out. This was as radicalizing as my time in Iraq.

I still feel guilt that I didn't go on the later fifteen-month deployment. This happened after I was discharged. I knew people who were killed, wounded, and saw a lot of combat on that deployment, and I know I am lucky. I still feel guilty because I didn't fucking kill somebody over there, but I know that's just the training and the expectation, and that's still with me. I see now what many of my friends who did experience some of those things have to deal with now in their everyday lives. I didn't kill anybody in those situations, protecting my buddies. It's what you train for every day, and it not happening is like one not accomplishing the mission. It is still imbued in me, even though I know I am lucky and glad to not have killed. This is what people refer to as "brain washing"; it's just training and habituation of thoughts and actions.

One of the most profound lessons I learned from my experience in the military and Iraq was seeing myself change, and seeing other soldiers change. I did things that I never imagined I would do. I also saw the same in others. All people have the capability of doing the greatest "good" or the greatest "evil," and it is a matter of our circumstances and choices in life.

I have quite a few veteran friends that I would consider to be my most reliable and closest friends. Most of those I didn't serve with, but I have met them afterwards through activism.

Seth Manzel and his daughter near their home in Lakewood, Washington, preparing for a Fourth of July BBQ party at his house. Manzel spent two tours in Iraq with the Army infantry. He is the founder of Coffee Strong, the veterans' coffeehouse near Fort Lewis, Washington.

Seth Manzel

There were four men on top of the prisoner: one was smothering the man with a blanket; one was pummeling the poor man's kidneys with his fists; another was striking him with a cleaning rod from an AK-47; and the last was trying to push a water bottle into the prisoner's rectum. Television always portrayed torture as a rather well-ordered affair that involved sodium pentothal and dental picks. In reality, it looked like a frat house gang rape.

I joined the Army Infantry in 2002, after losing my job at a gun store. I was stationed at Fort Lewis, in Washington State. In the four years I served, I was very fortunate to have only been deployed to Iraq once. Many of the people I had gone through basic training with had two or three tours under their belts by the time I went to Iraq in 2004. I was also lucky to be deployed for a year, instead of the fifteen months that later units had to endure. While I was deployed, I served as a Stryker driver, machine gunner, and a vehicle commander.

The first half of my deployment was spent in Talafar. While we were in Talafar, we were tasked to guard the castle—a literal castle from the Crusades that overlooked the city and contained the last vestiges of civil government. This is where I met Ali. Ali had been an Iraqi Special Forces soldier in Saddam's army when they fought the Iranians. After the war, he returned to Talafar, the largest city in Northern Iraq, and became a police officer. He had the distant stare of a man who had an intimate relationship with war. He was a Turkman with black hair, a weathered face, and a mustache that curled down around the sides of his mouth.

"This is Ali. You see that I am giving him my own personal pistol; this is how much I trust this man," said the gray-haired police interpreter. Ali took the Glock 19 from him and stuffed it into his waistband. "These are not like most of the men you capture. They have money and some are related to police officers. You cannot trust the police, but Ali will go with you, he will show you the house and point out the men." The police interpreter had just lost his three-year-old son to an insurgent bomb that was placed in front of his house and was the first Iraqi to help us actually target insurgents.

Most of the police would feed us information on their own political or tribal enemies. For months we had been fed bad information. Our missions were a series of disappointing dry holes. This man was motivated to help us. The police interpreter took my hand and spoke to me in hushed tones as we walked along the ancient walls of the castle. Ali walked a few steps behind us. "When you take them, be careful. The police may try to set them free. These men bring in money and weapons from Syria. You must arrest them."

I convinced my platoon leader and platoon Sergeant that this man was genuine and that these men were high-ranking members of the insurgency. They allocated two Strykers and two squads to secure and search the house and capture the insurgents. I rode in the air guard hatch with Ali. He pointed in the direction we needed to go and I relayed that information to the vehicle commander. As we drove, Ali adjusted his Kafia to cover his face. Being seen on this mission could have put him in danger.

After snaking through the ancient streets, Ali began pointing at a building ahead. The dismounts secured the building and Ali and I entered a few minutes later. The courtyard was cool and shady. Rabbits hopped around a pomegranate tree that grew in the middle. There were women in the corner weeping as the men of the house were brought into the courtyard and put on their knees, with their hands behind their heads. Ali wouldn't speak for fear of having his voice recognized. It wouldn't have done any good, as he spoke Turkish, not Arabic. Ali walked behind the men and tapped four of them on the shoulder. As he did, soldiers put bags over their heads and zip-tied their hands. They were stood up and marched out of the courtyard.

When we returned to the station, the police gawked at the prisoners as they were lead out of the vehicles and into the courtyard. While we waited for one of the police officials to open the door to a holding room, a crowd formed around us. They whispered to each other and stared. I unsnapped my thigh holster and rested my right hand on my sidearm. The Police Colonel came out of his office and protested. They were good men, men of standing in the community. This was unthinkable. The police interpreter approached us and, as he did, the policemen in the yard accosted him, yelling at him in Turkish and grabbing his arm. He shook them off and went into the room with us. He said nothing, but examined each of their faces and left. I followed him out the door, through the courtyard, and into the street. I pulled him into one of the Strykers and we spoke to the platoon leader. Inside, he detailed each name and their role in the insurgency. We relayed the information to our squadron command. All four names came up on our blacklist of wanted insurgents. When we returned to the forward operating base, the squadron commander chided our platoon leader for running our own operations to capture blacklist individuals.

In the weeks that followed, I dealt a lot with Ali and the police translator. Ali would often bring liquor from Cinjar, the Kurdish town to the north, and we were happy to buy it from him. His friend, the police interpreter, would often come as well, giving me pictures of insurgents or lists of names.

After assisting with the interrogation of one of our prisoners in the police Colonel's office, I stayed as Ali and another police officer brought in a prisoner. Things soon got out of hand. There were four men on top of the prisoner: one was smothering the man with a blanket; one was pummeling the poor man's kidneys with his fists; another was striking him with a cleaning rod from an AK-47; and the last was trying to push a water bottle into the prisoner's rectum. Television always portrayed torture as a rather well-ordered affair that involved sodium pentothal and dental picks. In reality, it looked like a frat house gang rape. I had left the room a few minutes earlier to get a translator. Before I left, I had told Ali not to hook electrical wires to the prisoner's feet. Ali told me through pigeon Arabic and sign language that if he touched one of the wires to each of the prisoner's feet, he would feel it in his genitals. I told him no and went to find the Army interpreter to help interrogate the man. Ali must have interpreted my leaving as an insult to his interrogation skills.

When we entered the office, we saw that more people had joined the interrogation. The prisoner's hands were bound and he was lying on his stomach. His eyes were blindfolded and his flannel shirt had been torn open. I could hear him trying to scream through his gag. His face was a mask of pain. "No," I said, "You can't torture him." The man with the bottle got up, the punching stopped, and the man with the cleaning rod struck him once more for good measure and sat him up facing me. He had cried through his blindfold, and when they removed the gag he drooled bloody saliva onto his white clothing. "What has this man done?" I asked. The Army translator repeated my question in Arabic. One of the police officers then translated that into Turkish. After much discussion, the translator returned with the answer, "He is bad." "In what way is he bad?" I asked. After more discussion it became clear that the man was Sunni and was found in a Shiite part of town. "You can't torture him," I said. The police responded that he was their prisoner and they would do with him as they pleased. "He is my prisoner now, and I want him released in the morning." The next day I found him in the holding cell. I instructed the police to let him go and walked him to the outer gate of the castle.

One day, while we were guarding the castle, our platoon leader was called away to the hospital to capture an insurgent who had been brought in for emergency medical treatment. His cohorts had burst into the hospital with AK-47s and forced a medical team to stitch him up. When the platoon leader found them, they were trying to leave the parking lot in a station wagon with the gunshot victim in the back, IV bags hanging from the hanger hooks. The Leader went into the hospital to take statements from witnesses. "Alpha 26 this is Alpha 24 Delta," I called to the platoon leader over the radio from the castle. "Alpha 24 Delta this is Alpha 26 Mike," replied the platoon leader's radio telephone operator. "Alpha 26 this is Alpha 24 Delta. Tell 26 Actual that I have to kill Ali." "Alpha 24 Delta, this is Alpha 26 Mike. Did you say you were going to kill Ali?" "Yeah, he is fucking shooting random people. He is drunk and out of his mind." "Alpha 24 Delta, this is Alpha 26"—the platoon leader must have grabbed the mic from his hands. "Do not kill Ali. Just try to restrain him."

Soon thereafter, the wounded started arriving at the hospital. Earlier, Ali had shown up at the castle, drunk and screaming. I asked what was wrong and one of the police told me that his brother had been shot and killed by insurgents. Ali went to the roof and I followed him. The roof overlooked a large wadi. On the other side was the al Serai district, which was known to harbor many insurgents. Ali oscillated between crying and rage. He turned and spoke to me in broken Arabic. He renounced Allah and said he wanted to be an American. Then he shouldered his AK-47 and fired into al Serai. It was common for the police to randomly fire into that part of the city, but there was something different about this. He turned slightly and fired again. This time, I saw a dark figure in an alley drop to the ground. "What the fuck are you doing?" I screamed. He turned 45 degrees, leveled his rifle at a small red silhouette on a rooftop, and fired. I grabbed his arm and he turned to me, holding his AK and staring at me with hollow eyes. I retreated to the nearest Stryker. That is when I called the platoon leader. By the time I returned with flex cuffs, the other cops had subdued him.

At the hospital, the platoon leader saw a bleeding young girl being brought in by her mother. He watched as she convulsed and then went limp. He said that he had never heard something so horrible as that mother's scream. Ali was taken into U.S. custody two days later on the insistence of my Platoon Leader. He was held in our detention center. I wrote out a sworn statement explaining that Ali had aided in the capture of blacklist insurgents. I dropped it off with our Human Intelligence. He was released a short while later. My Platoon Leader has always resented the fact that I wrote that. I have always resented the fact that he ordered me not to kill Ali.

Seth Manzel testifying at a Winter Soldier Event in Seattle, Washington, in 2008.

"Michael William Michaels" at the Rotture Lounge in Portland. Michael is AWOL and lives in the Pacific Northwest. He is an artist and an activist. Michael wears a button that reads, "Daddy's Little Hero."

"Michael William Michaels"

It's not death you fear, but the infinite bliss on the other side. Come close, feel the vibrations of the universe.

As for now, I've taken up the maddening task of reminding my (a)pathetic civilian peers that there are wars going on . . .

a sonnet for potential deserters

made miserable 'gainst each broken will,
made to shout with shouting, made to fire
reflexively, like a machine without
conscience, made to unquestioningly kill

the residents of occupied nations
which are defending their own liberty,
made to believe that there is nothing which
they, the malcontents crowding formations,

can do to resist what they have been made
to do by the warmongering rich,
those bloated subverters of liberty.
You can put an end to this quagmire.
You can throw down your machine gun and shout
against a government which has betrayed.

I was wondering where my tax return had gone. "As authorized by Federal law, we applied all or part of your Federal payment to a debt you owe. The government agency (or agencies) collecting your debt is listed below." Oh desertion, you are expensive.

Erhen Tool creating cups at his residency at The Museum of Contemporary Craft in Portland, Oregon, in 2011.

Ehren Tool

My wife calls my work "World Awareness Art," because I really don't care if you're for or against the war, but ignorance of the wars is inexcusable to me.

My name is Ehren Tool. I was born May 16, 1970. I live in Berkeley now, but I was raised in sunny south central Los Angeles. I was in the Marine Corps from 1989 to 1994. Gulf War One was in 1991. I was a Lance Corporal during the war.

I joined because I wanted to be a man. My dad was in the Army in Vietnam and my granddad was in the Marine Corps in WWII, and they were men. I respected them and I wanted to be like them. My father was a Lieutenant in Vietnam. When I told my granddad I was going to join the Marines, he laughed and said, "They're going to take your soul." I think it's kind of true. It's like that Humpty Dumpty thing: I'm pretty much like who I am, but I'm definitely someone different than I was before—I'm a little sadder.

I was in Saudi Arabia and then Kuwait for almost seven months; I was in Desert Shield and Desert Storm. I used to joke. I used to tell people that they just put us on a plane and flew us around for twelve hours, and that we were really some place in the desert of California, that they had actors in there. I was in MP Company, Headquarters Battalion 1st Marine Division. We did "battlefield circulation and control," convoy escorts, and enemy prisoner of war handling.

During the '91 oil fires, there was cloud covering and the smoke couldn't dissipate. We had to use flashlights to read during the day, everybody's uniforms were all stained, and the vehicles were all stained. I have an entry in my medical record that I was exposed to dangerous levels of chloral floral carbons. Not seeing the sun in the desert, the Bible bangers were always talking about Revelations and saying, "This is the end!" I'd say, "Yeah, yeah, whatever." But then the sun was blocked out and I was like, "Oh, shit, this is it! I'm never going to see my family again." I really thought that if I died there and then, that would be it. There wouldn't be an escape from evil or whatever it was that, even in death, would follow.

I'm a ceramist. I've been making cups and giving them away since 2001. The idea here [at The Museum of Contemporary Craft in Portland, Oregon] is "occupation." I want to build a bunker out of clay in a space or in a community. Ideally, it would be on the street some place—an empty lot or something—but I would build the bunker out of clay and then make cups. I would fire the cups and then give the cups away and make some kind of abstract community.

My wife calls my work "World Awareness Art," because I really don't care if you're for or against the war, but ignorance of the wars is inexcusable to me. I think as an artist or mediocre potter, you have the opportunity to focus light or whatever on whatever you want, right? The work is kind of like a conversation that you are having with yourself or through the work. My father used to think I should be making happy sunshine things, but I just can't avoid issues of war and violence. And part of that is because it's still going on. At best, the cups become a place for veterans and people that care about them to have a conversation about unspeakable things. I thought I was a big man in '91. I was going to do something important, make the world a better place, a safer place. To have guys in the same piece of sand doing the same thing so many years later is really crushingly disappointing to me. I just make cups. As far as trying to change the world or make any kind of grand statement, I feel it's pretty weak and impotent, and I don't have much hope for art's ability to change things. They talk about *Guernica* and what a strong anti-war statement that was, but Auschwitz, Hiroshima, Vietnam, and other wars happened after that. So fat chance cups are going to do anything. I'm just trying to make work that's honest and mine, and navigate the art world with some integrity. I don't think that anything I do is going to change the world, but nothing in the world releases me from my obligation to try.

I have a few images that are like self portraits: one of them is the scene from *A Clockwork Orange*. The guy has his eyeballs peeled open and they are making him watch all this horrible stuff. It's kind of the same with the cups. Sometimes it's stuff that is hard for me not to cry when I am looking at, but I think that's the thing: we try so hard to remove ourselves that images of war and violence become entertainment, whether in video games or movies. I'm trying to bring war home and into your life another way. There are some cups that are just completely blank for guys who have seen stuff. They don't need to see it burned into their freakin' retinas, they don't need an image of that. But for the rest of us, I think we should share some of that burden of knowledge. Some cups have insignias. I only use them if someone rates the insignia. Someone who rates the insignia gets a cup. So the Purple Heart I have is from a guy who was in the Battle of the Bulge—he got a cup. His grandson was in my class. That's important to me, the hand-to-hand aspect of it. It's not just going to the swap meet and buying medals and decorating cups with them, but somebody who really rates the thing has the thing. It's funny; I think using ceramics and talking about war is strange, but these objects will last 500,000 years. What is Islamofascism going to mean in another hundred thousand years?

I think all artists think they are freaking geniuses and the world needs their work, but most of us are nuts. When someone picks up the cup and something resonates with them, that's when it's alive. So when giving the cups away, I know it's not going to help me get a commercial gallery, but it feels right. And it's more interesting to me knowing the cups are going through the world hand-to-hand instead of just sitting safely in a white box.

I think I've done over 14,400 cups, which is kind of cool, but 20,000 or 40,000, that'll be really cool. I got a grant to go to Vietnam, and my wife and kid and I went and made cups near where my father fought. It was crazy to think that forty years before we thought we had to kill these people or western civilization would collapse.

I have a few images that are like self portraits: one of them is the scene from A Clockwork Orange. *The guy has his eyeballs peeled open and they are making him watch all this horrible stuff.*

Tamika Faye Moore at a rib joint in Memphis, Tennessee. Tamika posted this on her Facebook page on April 19, 2011: "Raise your hand if you have laced up combat boots, killed, and faced death in Iraq for the United States and currently live with Post Traumatic Stress Disorder? I'll raise my hand."

Tamika Faye Moore

You got a lot of people around here with PTSD who are being labeled crazy . . . well, guess what? These crazy people were taking care of y'all so you could sleep at night.

When I saw the first plane hit, I was getting ready for school. I was in college, going to school for veterinary medicine. I had my radio on; my radio went silent and I'm like, "What happened to my music? I need my music!" And basically the people on the radio flipped out and told everyone to turn on CNN. I saw the first plane hit and I was like, "Oh my gosh, what's going on?" I didn't even know what the World Trade Towers were, that's how I was about politics. And then the second plane hit while they were talking live, and then it turned into "America is being attacked." I was like, "Oh my gosh." And I guess the part of my generation, my grandfathers being in World War II and Vietnam, I guess that kicked in and I said, "I gotta tip my two cents in." I said, "I've got to do something." I officially signed up on the delayed entry program on September 16, 2001.

I was the first woman in combat at Davis–Monthan Air Force Base. I'm not going to confirm or deny any killings, but we were at war and I had a machine gun. I was told to protect the U.S. military from anything, so with that said, I felt like I was handpicked. I loved that machine gun. I could tell you in my sleep how to take it apart, the names of the parts and everything. I was good at what I did. People don't know that there are women in combat. I'm living proof of that. Yes, I have seen combat. I have been through combat. As a black woman, I felt honored and privileged to be a woman of combat. Being black, I have to work three times harder. And then being a woman on top of that, five times harder.

The U.S. military in general is predominately controlled by the Caucasian male, and it was designed for Caucasian males as far as promotion. My senior Staff Sergeant was racist: he thought we were thugs and he would tell us we were thugs. I've heard it's modern-day slavery; I've heard that from the black community in the military, yet when we are in the military there's a camaraderie. We don't see color. The higher-ups or the brass, they do.

I got out on medical retirement December 14, 2004. Basically, my homecoming has been an insult. I was in a parade one time and I had this sign that said, "I'm an Iraq war veteran and I'm against the war in Iraq." I got booed. This is my welcome home, and people turned their backs because they didn't want to see. I got maybe two or three, "Hey, I'm proud of what you did." I passed out *Obama Keep Your Promise* ribbons to people. That stood out. I laughed it off because none of them were ever in my boots.

It's one thing when I talk to my mom and dad and try to tell them what's going on, but sometimes they just don't want to hear about it. No one ever wants to hear about it because it gets so technical and political. Just listen and take the time to get to know a veteran. Stop the labeling of PTSD and crazy together. The mental illness has a huge stigma. I talk to people and I tell people, "Yes I have a mental illness." If that person walks away from me, then they walk away from me. If that person wants to stay in my life or hang around me then hey, that's great.

I just keep doing it because that's my passion: to help other veterans. And whatever I had to go through, and am going through, I'm sure the world wouldn't want the next veteran to go through. So I try to make their path easier. I'm excited and ecstatic that Obama passed that bill so PTSD claims can be a whole lot faster and easier. It took me three and a half years to get Social Security to get to my PTSD. I was already retired from the military at seventy percent and it took me like a year after two denials. That's how fast I was writing them back, and I mean I would put "Help Me" in big bold letters with a marker on the back of my form, like seriously, I need help. "Someone please help me."

"John Doe"[1]

I was sleeping. It was about 11:30 at night when my wife ran in and said, "John, the Sheriffs are here to arrest you." I woke up in a panic, didn't really know what to do, so I just kissed her for like five seconds. Then I walked out into the garage with my hands up and he said, "John, come out. We have a warrant for your arrest for desertion of the U.S. Army."

I was sleeping. It was about 11:30 at night and my wife runs in and says, "John, the Sheriffs are here to arrest you." They knocked on the door, then my wife's mother went up to the door and they asked if they could come in and she said "No," but they barged through anyhow and pushed her with force . . . no badge number, no card or anything—and then they took me away; no respect for anybody in the house at all.

The entire "Doe" side of the family is affiliated with the Assemblies of God Church: my grandfather is the former General Superintendent of the Assemblies of God, and my dad was the black sheep. I've been getting guidance from all my family. We do our daily prayers and all that, but we really just try to stay on the same path that they were on.

I joined the Army because I needed some guidance. I dropped out of high school my senior year. I had no idea what to do. I was working at UPS, but for me to get further I needed a GED. I knew the Army would help me with that. I was in the delayed entry program for two months and then I went to basic. I had no idea where to start.

I started off with "Name" Company and we made our own patrol base out of West Baghdad in an old train station. It was all Combat Engineers, and I was the only Infantryman there, so really it was just fall-in as a Combat Engineer, building fences, doing patrols, and making sure all the tribes in the area were secure. They got food, random inspections, and house searches—just the basic routine.

I was in a Humvee when we were called to a Bradley getting hit by an IED, which blew the tracks off. We got out to secure the area and we started receiving gunfire, which started shattering metal and different things. I got stuff in my knee, but it wasn't important enough to pull out or anything. It still hurts all the time.

In West Bagdad, at an Iraqi police station, a truck rolled in with a bunch of explosives in the back and blew. It was just such a loud noise; it just banged out my ears and I couldn't hear much after that. I got my hearing tested and they say, "Yeah, well, you lost seventy percent, you can't hear high-pitch." Then I got it done again and they say, "Oh you are at sixty percent, you can't hear low-pitch." It's just different every single time. I've heard two medical doctors saying you are legally deaf in your left ear, but I've never left with paperwork.

Coming back, my struggles were just keeping my cool: temper, anxiety, and major stress. Everybody deals with driving in the middle of the road; I still do it with my wife when we are driving around. "IED! IED!" It's having anxiety and stress all the time. It clicks in your head and you just start to panic and say, "Oh God! Wait, I'm not there anymore."

Pretty much most of the people in my squad were suffering pretty bad from just "freakin' out," not wanting to go back. A lot of the guys there just started a family, panicking. I know a couple people that just baled, but everybody, almost everybody, had one reason they shouldn't be going. But it's "military needs you," so they say.

Now I have severe pain in my back. I can't move around. I can't sit in a car for more than an hour; I've got to stand up and stretch. I toss and turn all night long and sleep with a heating pad. I was doing cortisone shots once a week and narcotics all the time. I've probably seen a dozen doctors, none of them helpful until the last two doctors, who actually want to pursue some surgery.

Because of my medical reasons, I didn't find myself fit to go back and survive in Iraq. I do have a lot in religious beliefs, and my great-grandmother—an amazing woman—said, "If you go back you may die."

---

[1] This person's attorney requested that their real name not be used due to their pending case.

Conscientious objector SPC Nicole Mitchell, U.S. Army, at Coffee Strong, near Fort Lewis, Washington, before she was sentenced to thirty days in jail in a Summary Court-Martial proceeding at Joint Base Lewis-McChord for the offense of AWOL.

Nicole Mitchell

I told him it was because I didn't want to shoot the target. It represented a person, and I didn't feel right shooting somebody. He replied something like, "oh . . . " and went to get somebody else.

The day of the range came, and at first I chickened out. I fired two iterations and failed miserably, not wanting to hit the target and all. Between each iteration a Sergeant pulled me aside to go over the fundamentals again and try to correct whatever was making me fail. The second time, the Sergeant asked me why I thought I was missing the target, and I told him it was because I didn't want to shoot the target. It represented a person, and I didn't feel right shooting somebody. He replied something like, "oh . . . " and went to get somebody else. My Lieutenant came to talk to me and told me regardless, I would have to shoot. She said to go eat an MRE and collect myself, and come back to fire again.

To kill or not to kill? I am going to admit something here that I have not openly admitted before in regard to a question that I have been asked numerous times. Why did I wait to apply for CO status? Why did I wait until I was in Iraq? The answer is simple. I was afraid that I was going to be in trouble for it, so I thought I could change my mentality simply because I thought I had no choice. That lack of choice was not because of my own moral standards, but because I had signed a contract with the military, and if I did not do what they said, I would be unacceptable in the military. I found that I was unable to deceive myself once the reality of the situation was no longer in training. Then I waited some more. I went out on missions, and thank goodness nothing ever happened where I might have had to kill anybody, because I was waiting for justification that might have seemed more acceptable to my command and to my peers. I was going to wait until I did have to kill somebody that one time and then use my guilt to justify never doing it again, but in truth, I was already guilty, and one night I realized how ugly it was that I was waiting for such a thing, so I stopped waiting.

For those who don't know much about military law, a Summary Court-Martial is the lowest level of Court-Martial with the least severe maximum penalties, and also does not result in a criminal record. My bargain kept me from being tried under Special Court-Marital, which is the next step up and could have led to a federal conviction, and up to a year in jail. That would have been terribly inconvenient.

I gathered a number of character references in order to show that I was a decent soldier, and that my unauthorized absence was not the result of irresponsible tendencies, but a last resort to taking care of my needs. My friends and family came through with some very well-articulated and positive things to say. The convening authority (the "judge") reviewed the record and read the character references in private before announcing my sentence. She started by talking about how I have some very loyal friends that clearly think very highly of me, that she appreciated my candor throughout the proceedings, and so on . . . however, "the person in these documents is not the same as the person in this case." "There are two kinds of failure: failure of the brain and failure of the heart. I believe your case to be a failure of the heart . . . "

I was given the maximum penalty under a Summary Court-Martial: reduction in grade to E-1, forfeiture of two-thirds pay for one month, and thirty days confinement. Hooah! Can I get out of the Army now?

Twenty-five days in a Naval brig—it wasn't very exciting. I read a lot, and I returned to my unit. That was not quite a week ago. Now, I'm just adding the final touches to a packet for Chapter 14, which is an administrative separation for misconduct. I'm hoping to be out of the Army in just a couple weeks.

Corey Moore at Benjamin L. Hooks Central Library in Memphis. Engraved on the column is an excerpt from Homer's epic poem about war hero Odysseus's ten-year long journey from the Battle of Troy to his homeland and wife Penelope in Ithaca. Engraved: "Man of misery, whose land have I lit on now? What are they here—violent, savage, lawless? or friendly to strangers, god-fearing men? Where can I take this heap of treasure now and where in the world do I wander off myself?"

Corey Moore

I think the American people appreciate what we've done. When I tell them I am a veteran and I serve, I see that they appreciate that. They show it and their response is enough for me.

I was born in 1980, here in Memphis, Tennessee. I graduated from high school in June of '99 and enlisted in the Army in May. I went to basic August of '99, and I spent eight years in the Army. I procrastinated throughout high school and I didn't have my college stuff taken care of. I didn't want to stay at home and I'd do anything, so I joined the military. First, I was a truck driver in Germany. Then, in September 2003, I did my first six-month deployment in Iraq. My second deployment began December 2004, for just under eleven months. I left my kids with my mom both times.

There was a big difference in the two deployments: the first time I was in Anaconda, and the second time I was in Taji, just about thirty minutes from Baghdad. The first time was living hard because we didn't have a lot. We basically had to build everything up from the ground. The second time was a little bit better; we actually had trailers, we had stores and cafeterias, and it was a bit better.

We didn't have armored trucks and we didn't have the updated Kevlars or flack vests. It happened so quickly that we didn't have time to order the stuff that we needed. I was basically in harm's way because, with my job as a truck driver, we had to deliver supplies. We were in harm's way every day, and also on base because of RPG and mortar attacks. We were under fire with RPGs and had to evacuate to the bunkers often.

I was a truck driver and I saw a lot. Being in Iraq made me appreciate our life here in the U.S. The first time over there was an eye-opener. Not having a lot of things that we have here, like running water and electricity, makes you appreciate being home. Don't take the United States or living here for granted.

I saw a lot. I saw car roadblocks, bombings, and IEDs. One particular day, we were on a convoy and were stopped because they had the road blocked because of an IED. A man—an Iraqi citizen—came up, carrying his child. The child had drowned and there was nothing that we could do. That was hard, that was really hard, that was very . . . that didn't happen as a result of the war, but . . . yeah.

A lot of Iraqis worked on the base during my second time. We got along great. They provided basic services, haircuts, and sold DVDs and things of that nature.

Coming back has been good. I don't have any complaints. Being over there, you get used to doing things in a certain way. Coming back home, you have those moments where you go back and you think you are there, but the last couple of years have been great for me. It was hard at first, but now it's a little easier.

I've only been in touch with a few of my fellow soldiers on Facebook. Some are doing well. As a matter of fact, I have a battle buddy; he's in Afghanistan. He got out of the military but he's still serving. He's a contractor and working with a contractor, so they're doing pretty well. They're coping and that's about it. I've been out of the military for four years. I'm a law enforcement officer now; I have been for about three years. I got out April 2006 and applied as soon as I got out. I got hired and have been doing it ever since. I think the American people appreciate what we've done. When I tell them that I am a veteran and I served, I see that they appreciate that. They show it and their response is enough for me.

1SG Phillip (Vinnie) V. Jacques training troops at Camp Rilea before deploying to Iraq.

First Sgt. Phillip (Vinnie) V. Jacques

I never really told them this—but after going out with the wire and getting into it a few times with them, I said I would always watch out for them. And then you lose a few of your guys and you're like, "I've got to make it right. I've got to make it right." The ones that come back home are going to have a shot and I will kick in doors to do it. Stay out of the way. You can get on the train or you're going to get run over.

We were some of the first guys that came back. There was a big difference between wounded and injured, you know: injured—I tore my thumb off playing volleyball; wounded—I was shooting at the enemy and I got shot or blown up.

We decided we've got to do something for our buddies. Our number one priority was getting people back on their feet. We knew our buddies were coming back, and they were going to need jobs, they'd need help getting back in college, and we kind of prioritized things. It was just amazing how it rolled.

We were interviewed by CNN about what we were doing and we got inundated with calls. My wife was very good about this; she said: "You know, Vinnie, you can't do everything. You're going to have to focus." And I said, "You know what? I'm going to focus, I'm going to focus on *all* three things: careers, education, and health—be that mental or physical—health, and welfare." And I kind of broke it down to where the concept of the team was to become the ultimate NCO program. I've kicked soldiers' asses in training and I've done what they expect you to do as a Ranger; that is just a portion of what a non-commissioned officer does. A non-commissioned officer is also there to make sure their troops have every opportunity for a great education. If they don't take advantage of it, shame on them if they don't step out of the military with a degree.

I had two roles in the reintegration team. The first role was pretty much the establishment of the team between myself and three other veterans. After meeting with congressman Joe Wilson and General Coldwell, we went back up to Albany and were just like, "Hey, we've gotta do something for our guys." We had a number of our other buddies sent home wounded. There were some of them at Fort Lewis, and I personally don't believe they were receiving the best care they could. They needed to be home with their families. And then the one that really drove me nuts was my machine gunner—he was wounded, had extensive hand and arm damage. We found a doctor that would accept TriCare and was one of the best hand specialists that we could find. Fort Lewis still wasn't releasing, so we had to stay up there. And at that time (2004), Fort Lewis wasn't a place to be. They weren't ready for all of us coming back. No fault of their own. They fixed it, but at that time it was horrific.

Our mission was to make sure no one fell through the cracks. One of our warrior ethos: I'll never leave a fallen comrade. We knew our buddies were coming back. Some of them were broke down range, some of them were ready to continue with their lives. And I remember just making an oath to them—I never really told them this—but after going out with the wire and getting into it a few times with them, I said I would always watch out for them. And then you lose a few of your guys and you're like, "I've got to make it right. I've got to make it right." The ones that come back home are going to have a shot and I will kick in doors to do it. Stay out of the way. You can get on the train or you're going to get run over.

We reached out to all branches of the military. During my first meeting with the Marine Corps I met with First Sergeant Owens, and at the end of the meeting he was just like, "I can't believe you're coming down here to hire one of my Marines for the team." I said, "This is how we take care of each other. You guys were on the same boat." And he goes, "I have loaded up just as many Army personnel on helicopters and evac'd out as I have my Marines. I know where you're coming from, and there's a few of us that think alike." He said, "God bless you and I will get you a fine Marine."

We started seeing success almost right off the bat. With some of the guys that were sent home early that were wounded, we were able to get them access they needed right away. Samaritan Hospital, Roseburg, VA, was absolutely amazing. Absolutely amazing. Greg down there did a tremendous job with the invasion PTSD clinic in the start. Some of the great things I saw too were that we didn't just help out our generation. We helped a lot of Vietnam veterans, Korean War veterans, even World War II veterans. We were out there getting the communities involved. They wanted to do something and we were an asset for them. A bunch of other people in the community asked, "What can we do when they get home?" So we started lining up in that general area. If they wanted to go back to school, housing, if they were looking for jobs—we kind of had our feet to the ground for jobs. So we were trying to make a seamless transition for our guys, but it was getting bigger and bigger at that point. We were able to help them get the paperwork they needed.

Vets have been hired. My last year on the team we got 328 people hired. They're not receiving unemployment benefits anymore. I'm still trying to work in college graduates. You know, they make roughly a million dollars more throughout their life than somebody who is not, so let's get them in school.

In our first year I believe there were 128 suicide interventions. Some of those were multiple, some had times where there were a few individuals working it, so if you break it down, that's how many man hours were put into it. Each one of these suicide interventions takes a huge toll on the team. That's a dark place to go. And it's a tremendous amount of time to get them the help they need. If you just go "they're good," no, they're not good. You need to make sure they are okay. They need following up, and following up is huge.

I thought it was very helpful when Sergeant Major Comely said, "You're not authorized to kill yourself." Some people have a biff with that, but when Joes see a leader come out and say, "You are not allowed to do that," they go, "Oh, I'm not allowed to do that." It's something funny that clicks and it just makes sense. That's not part of our warrior ethos going down the line, but it did help.

The people that went down that dark road, they had no goals when coming home. They spent their money and then they were like, "What the heck do I do now?" And they go through this depression; maybe they start drinking or whatever. That's probably the worst thing you could do at that point. Having a goal when you come home is probably the single most important thing I've seen out of anyone; that's the difference between success or the dark road...that simple.

"This is how we take care of each other. You guys were on the same boat." And he goes, "I have loaded up just as many Army personnel on helicopters and evac'd out as I have my Marines. I know where you're coming from, and there's a few of us that think alike." He said, "God bless you and I will get you a fine Marine."

Mariya Cables and her partner find shelter near Fort Lewis, Washington. Mariya has been homeless and struggling with injuries from basic training. She says, "It's just heartbreaking because I didn't even get to go over."

Mariya Cables

Today we don't have anywhere to go. We will be on the streets, and I don't feel like I deserve that. I don't feel like anyone deserves it. I have a whole new outlook on a lot of things, based on this experience and the past two years.

I was born in 1985, in Oak Harbor, Washington. I joined the National Guard in 2003. I was sixteen when 9/11 happened and, like all young impressionable teenagers, I felt a very strong sense of duty to my country. I figured I'd try to do my part to help the situation. I dropped out of school. I didn't have my diploma yet. My recruiter was very nice—paid for me to get my GED and everything—but completely mislead me about boot camp and AIT [Advanced Individual Training] and all of that. My signing bonus was about $25,000 less than everyone else was getting at the time, but it was okay. I grew up in a lower middle class family with a single parent, so I went in thinking everything was okay.

I don't believe in war, but I do believe in security, and that's why I chose the National Guard. They had never gone to war before, so I thought I'd be at home doing my national duty, and all of a sudden I'm going to boot camp; they're sending National Guard over and I'm like, "crap."

I finished boot camp. That was my MOS [Military Occupational Specialty] training school. I was in a program that puts your basic training and your MOS training all together. During that time, we were still doing some basic training exercise just to keep us on top; we were repelling down a building and my buddy didn't catch me until the very last second, when I hit the ground. I ended up breaking both of my heels and kneeing myself in the face so hard I had a four-inch bruise from the bottom of my chin to the cheek. I hit my face so hard it knocked me out. I had orders from the doctors to go on convalescence leave, but my drill sergeants and my first sergeant wouldn't approve it, so they kept me in training for the next month. I had broken heels and still ran my miles.

When I finally left for convalescence leave, they just gave me a pair of crutches and said keep going. Now one of my feet is deformed. It's basically readjusted my hips. So now my hips are off balance and it messed up my back. I have TMJ from that incident, from smashing my face. They finally let me go on convalescence leave and then I got back and, magically, they were going to discharge me for being gay. I requested attorney after attorney after attorney without any assistance. I filled out about forty pages about my sexuality. I stayed true to myself. The whole "don't ask, don't tell" policy failed.

I filled out my forms and they were going to discharge me, and I actually thought they had discharged me. For that reason I was okay with that, because they gave me two years to come back and say being gay was a "phase" so I could get back into the military. That was my intention. I thought, "Okay, that's what I have to do, wait my two years."

So I left and I went to South Carolina, and after about two years a warrant pops up for my arrest for being AWOL. I didn't go AWOL. They didn't have any records of my medical history in my personnel file at all. They didn't have any records of the Chapter 14, which is the discharge for being gay. There was no record of that. Nothing. So for the last four years now I've been just trying to get by, and my condition has deteriorated.

I'm homeless now. I'm trying to get a job, but it's hard to get a job when you haven't worked for years because of a medical condition. I'm becoming unemployable; there was a time I could get a job any day of the week, and now that there is this break in time, I can't get a job. For the past few months I've been homeless, hopping from place to place trying to get on my feet, but it's very, very difficult.

There's definitely a place I'd rather be, but I can't go anywhere. I can barely get enough food every day to eat. My fiancée and I share a sandwich every day. We eat what we can and go to the food banks as often as possible.

For a while we were panhandling to stay in a motel, but we weren't able to keep doing that. That's $200 a week. It's just real difficult now. Today, we don't have anywhere to go. We will be on the streets, and I don't feel like I deserve that. I don't feel like anyone deserves that. I have a whole new outlook on a lot of things, based on this experience and the past two years.

AWOL with honorable discharge, right? I still have the option to get in . . .

Former Marine Lamarris Williams in his apartment in Starkville, Mississippi. Lamarris says about his faith: "Reading the Bible has been a big thing in my life, even as a child. I think when I joined the military I kind of pushed it aside. I've basically reconnected with God. I feel like He blessed me, and I didn't give Him the appreciation that He deserved."

Lamarris Williams

I sat quietly and watched, because we always heard and talked about those who were dying around us. But it didn't hit that close to home until I saw those around me who were affected by it, and I was like, "Wow." What little problems I was having, it helped me to value life being over there.

I went to Natchez High with dreams of grandeur. I thought I was going to college, but never really knew that you had to sign up for college. We were never really taught that. I signed up for the Bill Gates scholarship. I didn't get it. I think it's because I didn't sign up for college. So I went off to the Marine Corps. I told my parents about it and they weren't too happy. The war was going on. It was after 9/11.

I went off to the Marine Corps—Parris Island and boot camp training. Then we were sent to Afghanistan. It wasn't even six months before they shipped us off. I kind of cut off communication with my family; I didn't talk to them. I didn't want to make them worry. My mom and dad were already worried about what was going on. My mom and dad watched the news so much that when we did get a chance to talk, it was always about body counts, dead, and casualties. It was depressing my parents. Eventually they cut the cable off because of that.

We were on a base called Bagram. It's in the mountain area somewhere. I had a situation that actually taught me about the value of life and the necessities of life. I was on security detail most of the time. I would always talk to the kids. They talk pretty good English. It kind of made me laugh; the kids would always talk like, "Oh what's up man?" I met this kid. He was trying to sell me porn and I didn't want it. He had the whole bling-bling slang term thing going. I gave him a water bottle and went about my business. He got a bottle of water but, in the end, he was killed at our main gate. I'll be honest with you; I was hysterical. I don't think it was about the bottle of water. I don't know. That's what bothers me. That's what's been bothering me for the longest time . . . I prayed about it and I feel that God always shows me things in his own way: the good, the bad, and the ugly.

Lamarris posted these words on his Facebook page:

"Oh you're in the military? That's cool. I wanted to do that when I was a kid. What do you make?" (I always loved this question.) What do I make? I make holding your child's hand possible everyday. I make five minutes seem like a lifetime when I go. I make going to war for your freedom a duty that I will die for. I can make your children have a future before terrorists attack us. I can help you by spending a year away while you complain about your job. I make myself get out of bed at 3 a.m. to risk my life to preserve your freedom. Today I might make the ultimate sacrifice to save your life. I make a difference. Now, what do you make?

It's sad that military service is frowned upon as much as it is. We have about 1.5 percent of our population protecting the other 308 million. It doesn't bother me that people don't want to serve, but it does bother me when you give a false perception about something you are too scared to experience. Freedom is not free. I have scars to prove it, mentally and physically.

Happy Birthday, Marines. We are 235 years old, baby, and steadily pushing forward. I'm proud of our tradition, our ethos, and the service that we have done for our country. No one can understand the Brotherhood, the Camaraderie, or the blood, sweat, and tears that we have all shared. I am proud to call myself a United States Marine.

OOORAH, SEMPER FI TIL I DIE.

Allen Huck a few yards from Coffee Strong, a GI resistance coffee shop located across the tracks from Fort Lewis in Washington State. Allen is a one hundred percent disabled Marine. He has back injuries and epilepsy from TBI. He is protesting the illegal detention of conscientious objectors Travis Bishop and Leo Church at Fort Lewis, across the tracks from Coffee Strong.

Allen Huck

I'm not saying that immediate attention would have solved everything, but they kicked me out because they fucked me up.

We were driving on a night convoy where we were in blackout in a hostile area. We hadn't actually been trained in driving with night vision. We took hostile fire from the port side and then my vehicle left the road. We hit a berm and jumped way up. I hit my head, compressed my back, and that was that.

Now I have epilepsy. They say that there is a two-year period between head injuries and the introduction of seizure disorders. Two years later, in August 2005, it started happening.

I asked to talk to the chaplain for counseling. I talked about some self-destructive things that had been happening. He immediately left and brought back the JAG attorney, who walked me down to Medical. Medical filled out paperwork and said that I wasn't allowed on base, or anywhere near the unit, and I had to get medical attention within seven days at no cost to the government. I'm not saying that immediate attention would have solved everything, but they kicked me out because they fucked me up.

I was living off base, but after the discharge happened I lost my means. For a little while I was able to stay in my apartment, but then, after the lease was up, I had to live in my car for a period of weeks. Then I pulled the guts up to go back to my mom.

Essentially, I was banned from the Marines for requesting help. Perhaps this is the reason that Post-Traumatic Stress Disorder is so rampant. Had we been given the help we so sorely needed, perhaps the homeless rates, drug use, domestic violence, and completely shattered lives would not be so rampant. We're not hearing about people who have come back and were denied health care at the Veterans Administration and so they've shot themselves. That's the real tragedy. It's a shame when someone dies at war, but it's more of a shame when they die here at home.

We drove through a lot of villages. There were lots of kids, and we were told we had to maintain forty miles an hour in the convoys. We were told that the kids would try and slow us down because the insurgents would tell them we were distributing candy. I never heard one report of actual ambush, but I did, um . . . I did hit a child who was riding a bike. She crossed in front of me and just, Humvees can't stop very fast. That was one that . . . I . . . don't think that I reported and . . . that one . . . just, it never got reported, just . . like it never happened.

On our return to Kuwait, we were handed forms to fill out. We were given strict instructions on how we were to fill out these forms. Awful things. Ridiculous questions. Especially since we were never really informed of what exactly war crimes were. Did you see a dead body? The guided answer was no. Did you kill anyone? The answer was also no. Do you feel you need immediate help and/or counseling? Absolutely not. The questions went on. And of course, the answers were almost always "no."

Maybe I did.

Those thoughts continue to haunt my daily life and my dreams.

Vincent Emanuele, former U.S. Marine Corps rifleman in Iraq, testifies before Congress in May 2008. Iraq vets spoke about their experiences in Iraq. Among the topics they addressed were hardships experienced by military personnel in Iraq and Afghanistan, equipment and combat conditions, and the quality of mental health issues.

Vincent Emanuele

During the last four months of my second deployment in Al Qaim, my best friend was killed less than thirty yards from me during an ambush and failed patrol. Our platoon morale hit an all time low and I obtained my first official "kill." The moment I shot that Iraqi man in the back of the head, I knew my life was forever altered.

United States Marine Corps, 1st Battalion, 7th Marines Alpha Co., 3rd Plt. I was in Kuwait March '03 to May '03 and Al Qaim, Iraq, August '04 to April '05. I was an infantryman and machine gunner.

I was born in 1984. I'm a rust belt kid. The country I come from is called the Midwest. I grew up on the south side of Chicago. My family were all union members, labor activists, steel workers, railroad workers, pipe fitters, and iron workers.

I joined the military at seventeen, even though my father had warned me not to join, particularly after 9/11. The atmosphere was very scary, a lot of jingoism and racism. The general attitude towards those from the Middle East and Muslims was very toxic. To some degree, I did feel like I wanted to be a part of what was happening at that time, and in an ignorant way.

I'd grown up around weapons. I had become militarized at a very young age and I figured, "Hell yeah, the Marine Corps, this is for me." I wanted to be in the infantry. They didn't have a tough time finding me. I went right away. I walked in, walked straight to the Marine Corps office, and told them I wanted to be in the infantry. It was like a recruiter's gift from heaven.

I didn't join for any kind of patriotic reasons. For me, it was straight up: it was going to be a job, it was going to be exciting, and I was going to get to travel, see the world, and meet different people from different cultures.

My grandpa was in WWII. He got two Purple Hearts and landed in Anzio. He went through all kinds of stuff, and when he came back, he never talked about WWII. He told my dad not to join the military, but my dad joined the military. And when I was going to join the military, my dad told me, "You're an idiot. Don't join the military." He said, "This is going to be just like Vietnam. This is bullshit and you're going to hate it." And of course he was right about everything. You know, I was seventeen years old, and that's the short of how I got into it.

You're born into a violent, masculine culture that, to be defined as a man, you have to be a badass motherfucker. You grow up with plastic guns. You grow up with real guns in America. Everybody in my family had guns: my uncles, my dad. I was shooting pistols, rifles, and shotguns by the time I was twelve years old, and shooting assault rifles by the time I was fifteen. I watched Arnold Schwarzenegger films. We grew up on that shit. There was an entire generation of kids who grew up in the 1980s and the early 1990s who grew up with Bruce Willis, Sylvester Stallone, Arnold Schwarzenegger, Steven Seagal, Jean-Claude Van Damme, Chuck Norris, Bruce Lee . . . you can go down the list.

One of the biggest parts of the military was the de-humanization of the Iraqis. They were calling them sand niggers every time we trained for four years. They were referred to as camel jockies, sand niggers, hajis. There were even some black guys who were saying that shit.

You are trained to be a killer. People forget this. I joined because I thought it was a job or some bullshit. You are trained to kill people, then you kill people, and then you come home. I don't know who the fuck expects anyone to come home having done this without having catastrophic results? That's why veterans are coming home acting violently, shooting places up, killing themselves, acting crazy, and getting addicted to drugs and alcohol at a disproportionate rate. I mean it's crazy. Besides the military, there's nowhere else where they expect people to go kill people on a regular basis and then come home and say, "Oh, I have a nine to five job. Punch in, punch out, come home, watch some baseball and just go to sleep." It's crazy.

During our deployment, we were constantly in convoys patrolling the streets, looking for snipers, IEDs, land mines, "insurgents," or anyone else that wanted to engage us. This, along with shooting at innocent civilians, destroying their property, beating up prisoners, and the occasional guard time made up the majority of what I saw and did during my eight-month deployment to the "Sand Box." Soon I became aware of what I was doing. We spent most of our time doing house raids and prisoner detention. Many Iraqis told us they didn't want us in Iraq. The U.S. forces were conducting some very brutal actions. Most of the prisoners we took were tortured. There were a lot of shootings and massacres of civilians—things that were not on the daily news in America.

During the last four months of my second deployment in Al Qaim, my best friend was killed less than thirty yards from me during an ambush and failed patrol. Our platoon morale hit an all time low and I obtained my first official "kill." The moment I shot that Iraqi man in the back of the head, I knew my life was forever altered. Looking back on it now, it seems like a dream. I'm sure a lot of veterans say the same thing. For me, it's been cathartic talking about it. Unfortunately, that wasn't the last time I shot someone during that deployment.

I began to see exactly what the Iraq War was all about and what I was participating in: an illegal, immoral, unjustified, and unneeded occupation of a sovereign country. It was apparent that we weren't spreading "Democracy and Peace" and winning "Hearts and Minds."

Because of these things, I decided I could no longer support the war effort. They told me they were going to send me on a third deployment to Iraq, and I refused to go. At that point I was discharged from the Marine Corps.

I remember in the barracks in 29 Palms, people talking about Smedley Butler, that he was a badass Marine, that he had killed all these people, and he was somebody we should look up to. He wrote a book called *War Is A Racket*.[1]

When I got out of the Marine Corps, I eventually took college courses and got into Marx, Weber, Kurt Vonnegut, Howard Zinn, Chomsky, and Cornel West. You start to understand why it is we go to war and who profits from war. You realize how drastically things have changed in this country from when a Republican President, Dwight B. Eisenhower, could make a speech about the military industrial complex seventy years ago.

There has been a long history of veterans protesting. 50,000 veterans occupied DC after WWI. You can go back to the 1780s, to the Pennsylvania Line Mutiny. You could go back to Civil War militias all across the South and the North by several different factions of both armies, who were looking for pay and benefits for their service. You could go back to the Vietnam Veterans Against the War, who had maybe 40,000 members at their peak. So I think on one level it's very disingenuous for Americans to say about veterans protesting, "Oh, this is so crazy. I've never heard anything like this . . . "

I've been traveling and speaking around the country for the last eight years, and the world for three years. I have to explain this to white men, usually in the South or the Midwest. I don't have to explain this to the black community. I don't have to explain this to the Latin-American community. I don't have to explain this largely to the Jewish community. I definitely don't have to explain it to the Arabic and Muslim communities. You don't have to explain this to women, either. I've never stood in front of a crowd that is primarily African-American and someone has stood up and said, "My goodness, I can't believe you say this about the United States of America." The only people I have to explain this to are white men over the age of thirty-five.

I've learned through work with Disabled Americans, trying to get people into the VA hospital for benefits and treatment. You ask a vet, "How ya doing?" And they say, "Man, I'm doing fine." Even if they're honest and say, "Hey, I'm struggling a little bit" or "I'm struggling a lot," the people you really need to ask are the relatives—their loved ones—because these people will tell you, "Look, this person is a totally different person than when he or she left for the Marine Corps."

I can honestly say, after having some very candid conversations with my parents, cousins, friends, and close relatives, that yeah, I used to be happy-go-lucky. I used to play sports. I used to be able to laugh and smile and hang out. You know man, I mean, now you're lucky if you can get to sleep. You're lucky if you can wake up without the urge to blow someone's brains out, or wanting first to blow your own brains out, or thinking to yourself, "Oh, damn, it would be nice to have a kid someday, but I don't even know if I can fucking take care of myself." Or, "I don't even know if I'll feel like waking up next week because it's going to be the anniversary of another guy's death." I've got three buddies who have died since I got out, all under the age of thirty, all stage-four lung cancer. Come on, now you're telling me that this depleted uranium and all this shit isn't affecting people? I've got Post-Traumatic Stress Disorder and I've got a traumatic brain injury because my head's been rocked around. They have a CAT scan of whatever the fuck is bruised in my brain. I've got hearing loss and tinnitus, so my fucking ear is ringing all the time, and I've got migraine headaches. I'm twenty-five years old and I go to the doctor more than my dad, and he's sixty-eight. I mean, what the fuck?

Right now, the VA estimates there are about 15-20,000 Afghanistan and Iraq veterans who are sleeping on the street any given night, and the suicide rate—what are they saying now—is from eighteen to twenty-two per day. The unemployment rate is twice that of the national average.

If I had one wish, it would be that progressives in America would start calling America what it is; it's an empire. We need to recognize that we have a thousand military bases around the world, that we're in well over a hundred countries, that we're overthrowing democratically elected governments and torturing and killing and droning, that we're assassinating innocent people all over the globe, and that we can choose to spend close to a trillion dollars on the empire every year. We could choose to spend a trillion dollars taking care of our people at home every year. We're not going be able to change a damn thing. I don't care how much you raise taxes, I don't care how many progressive reforms domestically you think you can accomplish, you will not be able to do anything positive in this country until we rectify the the fact that we are an empire around the globe. I think that, finally, some conservatives are getting this. That's why you see splits in the conservative party. I think that some progressives are getting this. This is why you're seeing splits in the progressive parties. People are starting to wake up.

Former Marine Nick Benas reads the Vietnam War timeline at the Oregon Vietnam Memorial: "On land, at sea, and in the air, the U.S. greatly increased its offensive against North Vietnam. U.S. troops numbered nearly a half a million, using two thousand tactical aircraft and dropping two million tons of bombs. This massive offensive prevented the fall of South Vietnam, but did not defeat the North Vietnamese, who withstood the bombing and increased their infiltration of South Vietnam. The cost to the U.S. was high: an average of a thousand and more Americans killed each month. This lead to increased opposition to the war at home; in the Congress Senator Wayne Morse of Oregon, in the streets of the nation's capital the 200,000 who marched for peace." Nick expressed his dismay at the one thousand casualties per month in that war.

Nick Benas

"Chaos often breeds life, while order breeds habit"
—Henry Adams, American Historian

Serving in Iraq was an amazing life experience that I wouldn't trade for the world.

Serving in Iraq was an amazing life experience that I wouldn't trade for the world. As a young kid, I always fantasized about being a war hero. A Washington, DC field trip in the 8th grade to the Vietnam and Iwo Jima Memorials was a life-changing event. My father and uncle both served during the Vietnam era. My mother is the toughest woman I know. For me to match her courage, I would have to do something bold. I always tried picturing myself soldiering as a tunnel rat in Nam because of my smaller size. Until the age of twenty-five, I was able to successfully achieve most of the goals I set for myself. Age six, I wanted to become a martial artist: check. Then it was on to earn different belt colors, get the whole rainbow: check. Age fifteen, I test and become a 1st Dan Black Belt in TAE KWON-DO: check! I spend my remaining high school summers training with the U.S. Olympic TAE KWON-DO Team. My senior year of high school I test and become a 2nd Dan Black Belt. Graduate high school, off to Parris Island to become a recruit, and I survive boot camp and become a U.S. Marine. I'm still small, but now I feel like I can fuck people up. From 1998 to 2002, days are spent training my ass off as a Military Police Officer and Marine Corps Martial Arts Instructor with the 1st Marine Division, 1st Tank Battalion, at 29 Palms, in the Mojave Desert. Time flies. These happen to be some of the best days of my life.

Sliding into my spring semester of Southern Connecticut State University, the year was 2003, and the invasion of Iraq kicked off. This was hard for me to stomach now that I was a civilian and student on the sidelines. Checking up on the casualty list, I find a friend's name from my former unit who was killed. It turns out his tank dumps off a bridge into the Euphrates River and the whole crew drowns. Couple weeks later, a few NCOs and a Staff NCO I greatly admired were seriously injured by an RPG attack. Watching this in the news and hearing the stories being relayed back was weighing on me. On a positive note, a few friends made the national spotlight for their heroic actions.

I had spent so much of my time and energy training to become a Marine and I wasn't even serving my country. I did four years, received my honorable discharge, and that was it? I felt like a draft dodger. Another year went by and I carried this feeling with me. Then, one day in May 2004, I received a phone call from the Marine Corps to check in and update my height and weight standards for the inactive ready reserve. I asked the Sergeant on the other end if they were calling me back in. He replied, "No, but would you like to?" I said to him, "Can you get me orders to Iraq?" He said, "I will call you back in ten minutes." Sure enough, he called back and said he had a unit that was leaving in a month or so out of Pittsburgh. "Sign me up!" Next thing I knew, I was working out and wrapping up all the loose ends with school, work, family, and friends. A week later, I'm back in uniform and happy to be back fulfilling my childhood fantasy.

As soon as I arrived in Iraq, I was in paradise. The country, the people, and the culture were amazing things to take in—we are talking about the Cradle of Civilization. Palm trees, amazing food, and hard working women, children, and men who appeared to be relaxed and unmotivated (by my standards). My time in-country was fragmented, spending time with different platoons in my unit. I spent time training the Iraqi Police in Al Asad, watching several of them get wacked by a vehicle-borne improvised explosive device; patrolling the streets of Fallujah and Al Qaim while only firing a few shots of my weapon to warn an approaching vehicle; getting hit with the compression of an improvised explosive device that we had cordoned off; and tying a naked dead guy to the hood of our Humvee for transport, all flanked by a lot of down time. The down time is what I enjoyed most. I was able to barter for things I desired, like the new Iraqi Dinar currency and booze from civilian contractors. The Marine Corps prepared me well for this opportunity. Sgt. Bilko was an amateur compared to some of the things I pulled off in-country. I got to play the whole time I was there. This was an opportunity to vacation with my brothers and two sisters who were in-country. We were fortunate to return with no losses in our unit. I see the many struggles veterans are having and feel for their pain. I owe my resilience to my great friends, family, beautiful wife, and amazing career. I'm honored to be a U.S. Marine, always.

Warmest Regards,
SGT. Benas, Nick U.S.M.C
Served 1998 to 2002, 2004 to 2005

Homeless vet Clinton Carroll at Union Station, Washington, DC. Clinton asks travelers for change. Everything that he owns is in his bag.

Clinton Carroll

Even though I'm homeless, I'm out here on the street, I'm cold, I'm hungry and I'm this, that, and the other, I wouldn't even give it a second thought. You know, if they needed me to go somewhere and defend the freedom, I wouldn't think about it twice, man.

I'm from Washington, DC. I joined the United States Army and I was in the 82nd Airborne. Initially, we were deployed to Beirut, then I was deployed to Afghanistan. I was a communications specialist amongst other things, but that's my primary MOS [Military Occupation Specialties].

That in itself is putting yourself in harm's way, but anywhere they drop us off in somebody's LZ [Landing Zone] in conflict, you are in harm's way. I would do it all again for my country. Even though I'm homeless, I'm out here on the street, I'm cold, I'm hungry, and I'm this, that, and the other, I wouldn't even give it a second thought. You know, if they needed me to go somewhere and defend the freedom, I wouldn't think about it twice, man.

Actually, the military prepares you for homelessness (laughs). You can survive. Yeah, it's almost like basic training, and I laugh, because it's kind of funny, but some of the things I learned in the service I actually use out here. You know, how to stay warm, how to make water drinkable, stuff like that. Defense techniques, shelter—ya know, I can make shelter out of almost anything. I've been homeless for about six years—about six years of actual homelessness.

The VA is trying to help; they're trying to get me into a—what do you call it—a VASH [HUD - Veterans Affairs Supportive Housing]. They have been trying to get me into VASH for a while, and I have this excellent counselor/nurse, Martha. She's awesome, but it's not them; it's the paperwork or whatever it is after them. Because, ya know, the people at the VA are so anxious to help. I mean, they will stay on the phone for hours calling places and trying to do stuff. Like all these clothes that I have on—donated to me by the VA—these tennis shoes were brand new—kind of messed up now—but they're brand new. I actually got this sweat suit from them, but they got it from CCDC [College of the University of the District of Columbia]. So I'm wearing it.

My future? That's just hard to say, man. I need a job, man. I need to be able to work or, ya know, really, I just need to work or to get a check from somewhere. You know, right now I get two hundred dollars of food stamps. It feels hard, man, I don't know; I have no idea where I see myself in five years, but I know one thing: I don't want to be homeless. I mean, I have adapted to it, but I can't, I can't, I don't want to do this. I'm 48 years old now . . .

There is no way for anyone to contact me; I don't have a phone. I'm moving around. This is part of my house [Union Station] right here. My bag, yeah, so . . .

Philip Nannery in Iraq in June 2009. While the Advisory Team (of which he was a member of the Personal Security Detail) inspects Iraqi units in bases around Baghdad, Philip, then a Private 1st Class, poses in front of a weapons cache uncovered by the Iraqi Army's 6th Division that morning. *Photo provided by Philip Nannery*

Philip Nannery

Going to war was the easiest thing a kid in his early twenties like me could've asked for. Coming home from war is Hell.

I used to make life and death decisions and signed, or at least was responsible for, hundreds of thousands of dollars' worth of equipment. Now I'm just another civilian, getting by, and since I recently graduated from college, I'm being told by other civilians who don't know I'm a combat vet what to expect in the "real world." I volunteered to go to Iraq right after Basic in 2008. I was going to community college and my National Guard unit had just gotten back from a nine-month deployment to Iraq. I didn't want such a defining historical event to pass through my fingertips and felt the need to deploy so badly. I joined the Army after going broke backpacking Europe and wanted a new adventure. It's not exactly the stereotypical Hollywood conditions people expect of guys who join the Army.

I went to Iraq in 2009, where I spent nine months on a personal security detail for a bunch of high-ranking officers, driving them all around Baghdad. It sucked, of course, and by the end I was burnt out, fatigued, and heartbroken, but most of all frustrated that I never got shot at. I was ashamed, and my family would ask, with eyes as wide as saucer-pans, about a photo of me that somehow made it into the newspapers and TV. It was a picture of me grim faced, dour, and stoic (although secretly scared shitless), pulling security in front of a blown up school bus from a massive VBIED (car bomb in the civilian tongue) that had just gone off in the city at a spot where we had been one week before. Despite being in such a desensitizing environment, surrounded by violence and the far off sounds of insurgents committing war crimes in the distance as I tried to sleep, I never got hit by an IED or into a firefight in Iraq. When I got home, I didn't know how to reconcile the violence I had witnessed with the frustration of not having felt like I had done my job as an infantryman. As burnt out as I was, I swore to never volunteer for another thing in the remaining four years of my contract and to ride my time out quietly. About six months later I volunteered to deploy to Afghanistan.

It's no mystery to me why I enlisted, or why I picked the Infantry, or why I volunteered to go to Iraq. I was a broke, clueless dreamer in search of meaning in life and a sense of belonging—both of which I now have, though at what price I don't know. But I still wonder why I volunteered to deploy a second time and why I still miss Afghanistan, where I did take part in the kinetic combat operations that had eluded me in Iraq. Despite all that, though, I am still working to get sworn statements needed for my Combat Infantryman's Badge (CIB) two years after the fact. I am still sending them "up to Brigade," despite being a civilian. Some in my unit thought I was a glory hound or a medal whore. Fuck them. Even without the recognition, and all the bitterness and resentment towards my unit and my chain of command and the Army that motivated me to get out last year and still burns in my heart, I know what I've done. I know I've done much less than many, much more than most, but never enough to not feel I should've done more. I did enough to justify volunteering to go back, but not enough to not want to go back again, if I could.

People ask me, "Have you ever seen a dead body?" or, "Have you ever killed anybody?" or, the more subtle version of that: "Did you ever see any combat?" Fellow veterans ask me what my MOS was, which province of Afghanistan I was in, whether I had an M16 or an M4, etc. Civilians ask me personal things that make me cringe, shudder, and regret ever having fought for them. And the questions don't bother me the most. It's the need that every American seems to have to tell you the tale of how they "almost joined" themselves, as if expecting some form of kinship or respect to form between us, or to tell me the war stories of their cousin or friend. "Oh," they will say, "You were in the Army? That's cool, my cousin Steve is a Marine sniper" or, "Yeah, you were infantry? That's cool, I almost joined, I would've gone Special Forces." Fuck you and fuck your cousin, I want to say. I want to tell them all, sarcastically, "Well, I was only in the Infantry and all we do is get blown up and kill people, sorry I wasn't a Navy Seal like in the movies you watch or the books you read." Instead, I swallow the pit in my throat and try to politely change the subject.

They tell me things like, "Well, I can relate to that sense of fatigue, you know, working as a (fill in the blank)." No you can't. So I keep the stories to myself these days. My family, my friends, the whole outside world sees me graduate college, they see me applying to jobs, and that's all they see. They tell me they understand. All I've ever wanted since coming home from war is for someone who has never been to war to sit down and frankly tell me that they will never understand what I've been through. But instead, they all pretend that they do and hold me to the expectations they hold of a man who has never been to war. They don't understand, and I get that. But it pains me that none of them—my friends, my family, none of them—would ever acknowledge that and just tell me, "Phil, you've been to war and I haven't, I will never understand what you're going through or what that's like."

I once made a girl cry when I told her I would go back to Afghanistan tomorrow if I could, so now I don't tell people as much. Or worse than getting upset, they'll nod and say, "Oh, you must miss the camaraderie," as if they get it. But our camaraderie is born not from any positive experience, but from the shared negative experience of this endless alienation. It is born from the alienation we feel around those who never went. When I went to war, I made the best friends I have ever had. Every decision in my life was made for me. All I had to do was show up when and where I was supposed to and do what I was told. My only concern was getting blown up. Going to war was the easiest thing a kid in his early twenties, like me, could've asked for. Coming home from war is Hell.

Penny is an active supporter of the Doug Fir Veterans Farm project. Their mission is to facilitate a holistic transition for service members to post military life and to support active duty military, veterans, and their families, regardless of politics. Doug Fir Veterans Farm project's slogan is "From the War on Terror to the War on Terra."

"Penny Dex"

Don't let your children grow up to be dead soldiers.

Dear Citizens,

Stop telling your sons and daughters the best thing they can be when they grow up is a dead soldier. Until you can show me how killing children in foreign nations helps ensure our freedom, stop telling them that fighting for it is a good idea. When you can explain to me how becoming government property makes you better suited for life, then you can tell them enlisting makes you a better person.

While I was a pharmacy tech, it was my job to make sure people got better and able to go back to work. We were the people that fixed the cogs so that they could go back to the machine. That was our job. We knew you were hurting . . . take some Motrin. Can't sleep at night? Take some Zolpidem—be careful with that, don't drink and drive.

I was always asking, "What do you need to make yourself better?" I never asked, "Why are you hurting in the first place?" "Why aren't you sleeping at night?"

My real epiphany was when I was on staff duty one night. One guy had his room bolted. He was in the Wounded Warrior Transition (when people get hurt they go into Wounded Warrior Transition). As per orders, I walked in; if the door is open, you have to walk in to make sure the room is all right. The soldier was naked, on the bed with a bottle of Zolpidem (generic Ambien) in one hand and a plastic bottle of vodka in the other hand. On his arm he had written in sharpie, "THIS IS YOUR FAULT."

Of course, that was the arm that had the bottle that had my signature at the bottom; I had given him these meds at some point. He wasn't breathing. He was gone and there was nothing I could have done. I went and got the Sergeant on duty. I was freaking the fuck out. I called the ER, then all of a sudden the Sergeant came out and said, "I got this, don't worry about this, just go to bed, we'll take care of it." Later, when I saw people going up the stairs, one of them had a bottle of rubbing alcohol and cotton swabs. Why else would they need that except to take the writing off his arm? When I saw that, I thought it wasn't right.

My parents told me of the "honor" that came with serving, not the guilt of having to wonder if you were ever a real soldier because you didn't kill anybody. You have to kill people who kill people because killing is wrong, right? They told me about how eager companies would be to hire me when I got out, not about the misogyny and patriarchy the military is drenched in that would keep me feeling subhuman for years to come. They told me I would see the world and meet new people, not that I would become owned by Uncle Sam and would have to put my hopes and dreams on hold during what were supposed to be the best years of my life. They didn't know any better. They were operating under the same mythology as many.

Do I blame my parents for me joining the military? Four years in and an honorable discharge later, no, not by a long shot. I raised my right hand and took that oath; I signed that dotted line, no one else. At the time, I was young and dumb and looking for the quickest way out of my one stop sign town. It was an experience I wouldn't trade for the world and wouldn't wish on my worst enemy.

But I have trouble to this day—five years after leaving the U.S. Army—looking my parents in the eye. If they had challenged the mythos of military service, if they had cared to know what path their daughter was getting lost on while on her way to college, they would have known the facts.

They would have known that one in three women who serve in the military will be raped. They would have known that the trauma experienced by women during military service often makes the transition to civilian life more difficult for them and contributes to an increased risk of homelessness.

They would have known that a servicewoman was nearly one hundred eighty times more likely to become a victim of military sexual trauma in 2013 than to have died while deployed during the last eleven years of combat in Iraq and Afghanistan.

Is every woman who serves raped? No, but I was. Twice. By people who called themselves my brothers. By people, I was told, who were the only ones I could depend on when shit hit the fan. In March 2013, I was finally diagnosed with PTSD from my military sexual trauma. My parents still think I'm making up my mental "disorder" to claim my "entitlements" from the government. I wish they could handle the truth.

That's the social contract. I signed on the dotted line. I do not regret it. Others like me served our country and, in return, the veteran should be taken care of. We kept our end of the bargain. We need to stop having such a shortsighted view. If we are going to go to war, we need to know these are the repercussions of war. Children will die. Our children will die and suffer.

Don't lie to yourselves or your children when it comes to military service. Don't let them grow up to be dead soldiers.

Sincerely yours,

"Penny Dex"

Joe Callan with his daughters at his home on Thanksgiving, at Kirtland Base in Albuquerque, New Mexico. Joe says, "I have a really good support system with my family. But I see a lot of other veterans that don't have that."

Joe Callan

I like the George Orwell quote: "People sleep soundly in their beds at night because rash men are prepared to do violence on their behalf." You know? And I was like, "Wow, that's me. That's cool, you know, I'm down with that." So I stuck around for a while.

I was born in 1978. I joined the Marine Corps in December 1996. I didn't really want to go to college and never really put the effort into applications and stuff. Then, a recruiter came in and told me stories about Australia and beautiful blonde women and beer, and I said, "That sounds super! Sign me up!" I come from a family that everybody has been in the military; it's just kind of like one of those things that you do. And I guess that's kind of part of it; I was like, "Well, I'll just go do that." That's what all my uncles and my dad did. My great-grandfather was a Code Talker.

Around here in Albuquerque—because there's such a high Native American and Chicano population—the recruiters prey on that shit all the time: "Your people are warriors, you come from a warrior culture," blah blah blah. They're totally twisting and distorting the definition of what a warrior is. It's incorrect. And they're taking advantage of children. I definitely fell for that "adventure." I was ready to go and I was ready to get out of Albuquerque. I graduated from high school on the reservation. I was ready to get going, and I didn't understand or know of any other opportunities. So the military seemed like a super idea: get out, get paid, come back, and they'll pay for me to go to college. There's so much of that around here. It's unbelievable . . . the promise of adventure. They tricked me with stories. I never got to go to Australia.

There's a lot of family history and tradition, so I joined the Marine Corps and I did eleven years. For more than a few years, I kind of really believed in it. I considered myself a warrior, like I'm protecting my family, my people, and my country. My uncle had been through most of the eighties and nineties in places like Somalia and liberating Kuwait, and the way he talked, he was out there helping people out. And I was like, okay, cool. I liked that idea of helping people out. I liked the George Orwell quote: "People sleep soundly in their beds at night because rash men are prepared to do violence on their behalf." You know? And I was like, "Wow, that's me. That's cool, you know, I'm down with that." So I stuck around for a while.

First, I went to Okinawa, and then all of my deployments were in Iraq. I did three deployments to Iraq. I was there for the initial invasion from Kuwait to Iraq, and then I was there for the first election and the takedown of Fallujah. I've always been right up in the mix, right up there. I was in the infantry. I was in a light armor reconnaissance battalion, so I was at the tip of the spear [chuckles].

When I was in Japan, I fell in love with the idea of the samurai. My job was just to train for battle, be glorious, and die. Like that's awesome, I'm so down. The problem I have is allowing somebody else to tell me who my enemy should be. That's the disconnect. What did any Iraqis ever do to me? Nothing. You know? Even the ones that shot at me or tried to blow me up, they weren't doing that to me, they weren't doing that to Joe Callan. They were fighting this machine, this huge force of occupiers.

After 9/11 I thought, "Let's go to Afghanistan, these guys did this, let's go get it done." And then we were going to deploy in Iraq? I never understood that. I remember a huge amount of guys in my unit were all like, "Why are we deploying to Iraq?" None of them knew why. They were all fired up to go because it's the big game; it's the

Super Bowl, that's why we were ready to go. Honestly, the only ones who were like "We were attacked" were the really redneck stupid ones who were like, "They're all the same, hajis this and hajis that. We were attacked and we have to get 'em." Everybody else was like, "That's stupid. That's a retarded argument. That country didn't have anything to do with it." But nonetheless, "It's the big game. Let's mix it up." To me, it just showed the depth of thinking of the individuals in the units.

Then I deployed to Iraq, and at first we did whatever and survived. And that's cool. But it never made any sense to me. I never felt like we were really the good guys. I kept doing more and more deployments. I never was for the war—I've never been—but I was in the Marine Corps.

I've come so far from believing in that stuff anymore. If somebody wanted to invade our country and put down martial law like what we are doing in Iraq, it just wouldn't happen. One, it's too big. Our country is ginormous, and we're so geographically isolated it's not going to happen. If it were some foreign army, it would be game on. It just wouldn't happen; it'd just be ridiculous.

Now I'm a field organizer for Iraq Veterans Against the War. I helped start the chapter here in Albuquerque and right now I'm the treasurer—and a lot more—with the national organization. I'm basically responsible for the western region of IVAW. I'm still kind of doing what I'm supposed to do. I'm still fighting for everybody: for my family, for all the folks here. I don't see it as much different. The other thing is, I think a lot of guys returning don't necessarily have a family to identify with. I think one of the things that I define myself by is my family.

I'm doing pretty well. I get fifty percent disability or sixty percent disability: fifty percent for PTSD and ten percent for my ears. I get random weird ringing and muffled stuff. I got blown up a couple times (laughs). I got hit by three IEDs [improvised explosive devices] on my vehicle at different times—shew, pshew, pshew—amongst numerous other crap. Now, I actually work for IVAW as a field organizer. IVAW is my full-time job. I've only been working for IVAW now for like two months. When I first got out, there were definitely more than a few lean times.

I know a lot of guys who couldn't get jobs with the police department. The police department wouldn't take them because they have combat experience in the Marine Corps. These are not the kind of guys the police want handling stuff, 'cause they handle things differently.

That's a reality. There's so much violence committed by returning veterans it's unbelievable. Just because you've gotten some extra training and are wearing a badge and have a spiffy uniform, it doesn't take away from the fact that you are an inherently violent person. It's not going to change any of that. It'll just allow you to be more justified in what you're doing. Over the last two years, Colorado Springs has had like eleven people murdered by guys from that unit. Here in New Mexico, in Albuquerque, we had (let's see, yeah, two years ago, too) a Marine that had gotten out. Someone was breaking into his car and he grabbed a shotgun (this was on the other side of town) and he chased 'em down. He chased 'em down for two or three miles and then killed them both. He got off. He was a combat veteran from Iraq. That's not normal. Normal people don't do that. Once you've chased them off, a normal person would have stopped and called the police. That's what you do. There was another veteran in another town, in Las Lunas (he wasn't an Iraq veteran, but he was a Marine veteran from a few years back), who ended up killing two guys down there over a traffic altercation or something.

I definitely believe in non-violence. Non-violence is the way to go to get things accomplished that you want to be accomplished and respected for. I'm not a pacifist. I reserve the right to punch a motherfucker in the nose. Like, phfft. Overall, violence as a means isn't productive. It's just going to end you up in the same spot that you were.

We are living on a military base and have a peace sign in our window. Nobody's said anything, really. I've had a few gate guards say, "Hey! Right on!" I've tried to talk to some of the airmen around here, but the Air Force is a different animal than what I'm used to. I'd imagine it might be a little tougher someplace like Camp Lejeune, where I was with a bunch of infantry Marines. There would be a bit different reactions about some stuff. Around here nobody's reacted aversely; everybody kind of really just accepts it.

I'm trying to educate young folks about joining the military. Going into the military isn't what they say it is. There's a reason that recruiters have such big budgets, because they have to sell something that nobody wants (laughs). The war is wrong. We need to stop both of these occupations. You can't win an occupation.

I get sick of those magnets on cars. You see them; they start to get faded and they're just faded stickers on somebody's bumper. There's the other thing of, "Thank you for your service," and this slap on the back. But brothers and sisters need jobs; brothers and sisters need understanding and acceptance. It's not so much understanding and acceptance that, "Oh you were a soldier, a sailor, a Marine, whatever, and now you're back. Okay great. C'mon, go to work." That is important but, at the same time, accepting them as a person and not as this machine, I think that's really a big thing. I have a really good support system with my family. But I see a lot of other veterans that don't have that: they're not accepted as people, they're just "that veteran guy."

My definition of a warrior now is someone that's making a positive change for the betterment of their community. That, to me, is a warrior. Whether it's picking up trash, manning the after school programs, volunteering at a food bank—whatever it is to you—as long as you're making that positive impact on your community, even if it's just having a job and taking care of your personal family and that sort of stuff, that's fine. You're in the struggle.

Daniel is currently an MFA candidate at Montana State University. He says: "I was invited to the LH residency in the foothills of the Wallowa Mountains in Oregon through a random series of events, being in the right places at the right times. Jakob Haßlacher, founder of the LH project, is a wonderful supporter of the arts and troops. Working at the residency was the first time I ever actually tried to make work about my experience in the Army. I'm sure that, subconsciously, a lot of that sort of darker dialogue, and the violence that I was exposed to, leaked out in different sort of ways, but I never before liked to relate myself to the Army directly, openly."

Daniel Donovan

When she found out, she told me that I should regret having ever signing up, and that she didn't want to go out with me again if I didn't admit to regretting that I signed up for the Army and went to Iraq. I told her, "Even if you didn't go to Iraq, just living here in this country you are guilty by association for everything. Everyone here is complicit. And just because you didn't hold a gun doesn't mean that your taxes didn't pay for that gun and pay for that person to be over there." That's what I told her. We never went out again.

My name is Daniel Donovan. I was born January 9, 1983. I grew up mostly in Kent, Washington, pretty close to Seattle. I joined in 2001. I was eighteen, right out of high school.

My older brother was the first of my immediate family to join the military. He joined the 82nd right out of high school. There was a point when he came home on leave. If you recruit while you are home, you get additional days of R&R. It was required that you bring people in—if only to talk—for you to earn the leave. I was talked into going down to the office so he could get the points. He said, "Just go in there and just say 'hey.' I mean, don't sign up, but just go in there and talk."

I ended signing up anyway. Like I said, it seemed like fun. We've had a member of our family in every war since the Revolution. I had a cousin that joined the Marines just recently and ended up going to Afghanistan, so the tradition is still being maintained. It was before 9/11, and it seemed like an adventure and a little college money. I left not long after signing up. Then, during basic training, 9/11 happened.

I didn't go to Iraq until 2003. Most of the Army's transportation lay in the reserves—the branch that I had joined. I was leaving for what was a dangerous and hectic period of the war with a unit that had next to no up-to-date gear and, outside of our first Sergeant, a suspiciously misguided commander. I will say that there were a suspiciously large number of rumors of how our Major had volunteered our transportation unit for some dearly needed promotion points. It was not long after that the mission was dubbed OSL, or Operation Silver Leaf. That moniker was spray-painted on a lot of jersey barriers and concrete walls, and written on hats and bandanas.

The mission had an interesting beginning. Fourteen hours on a plane put us in Kuwait, then three months driving container trucks from Camp Doha to Camp Arifjan. That was the easy part: nice weather, civilians on weekends, and the Marble Palace. I don't really know what the Marble Palace used to be, but it became a recreation center for troops. The place had everything: pool, sauna, billiards, video games, a driving range, and an old Kuwaiti man that would sell chicken shawarma.

Three months in we got our mission. We hauled 8,000-gallon fuel tankers from the south at Camp Cedar II through to the north, into Baghdad, as well as LSA Anaconda, or Camp Anaconda. Cedar was not so far from the Iraq-Kuwait border. It was a long drive north with fuel. Our company would haul those tankers hundreds of miles up to Anaconda and Baghdad. The drives were made longer and infinitely more dangerous because we didn't receive armor for any of the vehicles. None of our tankers had armor of any form. Even better, they were 1980-1990 civilian over-cab tankers leased from a Kuwaiti Sheik. I always enjoyed getting a firsthand opportunity to see where all those billions of dollars were being funneled—directly into Halliburton and to Kuwait.

I remember my first contact was on the Fourth of July. A tracer round snapped in front of my face, inches from the windshield of the over-cab style tractor trailer. All the training pays off: the radio blew up, my copilot had my weapon in my arms, and I was shooting, being shot at, and driving close to seventy mph. Exhilarating, to say the least. We would try and drape our chest armor over the doors for some minimal protection, but were always threatened with Article 15. Chalk up another reason I dislike the Army—just a tool of men like Bush to make money for a select few. A lot of lives could have been saved if we had the supplies and armor we needed.

Being there came to a head when the embedded journalist who was with us came out with an article about how our commander was pushing us to exhaustion for nothing more than numbers on paper, trying to make himself look good for pride and promotion points. It is sad when someone like Commander Bendtner will sacrifice the safety and welfare of his troops for personal gain and pride. They wrote an article for our home cities' papers all about how we were driving 48-72-hour missions with no sleep, living on Rippled Fuel and Red Bull. After the article came out, the journalists were excised from the unit by the commander and sent packing; they got a little too close to the truth for his liking. The 48-hour mission was the cherry on top, or the straw. We had driven fully-loaded from Cedar II through Scania to BIAP—a long day of driving. The long day was made longer by flat tires, assaults, and most notably, a foolish Platoon Sergeant that got the convoy separated in Baghdad and drove us down a dead end alley. Good job, 737th 1st Platoon Sergeant—we had to back our 8,000 gallon tankers out of the alley one at a time. He could have got us all killed. It was then that we were told we would not be allowed to stop for sleep. We would download fuel and drive back at night so that another mission could go out in the morning. This was close to 24 hours in; we drove back and one of the drivers crashed his truck out of sheer exhaustion. Many accidents were a product of sleep deprivation as much as enemy fire. I would buy a flat of twenty-four Red Bull before every drive and split them with my copilot. We would drink all of them and eat ephedrine pills. Sometimes I drank twenty-four to myself—twelve there, twelve back—and then puked blood. When we got back from this mission at three in the morning—close to forty-eight hours later with no sleep—we were awakened for PT (physical training) at 6 a.m. A soldier filed a complaint with the post commander; we were ordered to eight hours of sleep and our commander was reprimanded (we were told and hoped), but things never changed. It is my understanding that Commander Bendtner, of the 737th transportation company, received his silver leaf not long after we returned—good for you buddy, hope it was worth it. Upon our mission concluding, the post commander addressed us: we had spent the longest of any transportation unit in the combat zone, we had completed the most missions and hauled more gallons of fuel, and we were to be commended. Hazza.

There never seemed to be a plan while we were there, and there was never a real reason for going over there. We went over there under what seems like false pretenses—9/11, and then Saddam was killed, which, turns out, was the whole point, or not the point—who knows. We could have done some good, but you have to think about it before you go over there. There wasn't a real plan for helping anyone specific. We tried to put a new leader in charge, but we think about it through the lens of being Americans. We wanted to Westernize them; we wanted to change the country to suit ourselves, regardless of their views.

It is my opinion that the majority of the public is ill informed outside of a simple partisan perspective. It takes an effort to really know what is going on. No one really cares that Iraq developed as a patriarchal society; that they trust leaders with larger families and more influence, not some shmuck that is voted into office by someone with a lot of money. There are dozens of cultural differences between our two people. Our ignorance of them has created, and continues to create, a growing resentment of Americans. I think (hope) that with the next generation this is changing, and that youth are better informed and less closed minded than previous generations.

The Iraqi people were amazing while we were there; the ones we met in towns and villages while driving were truly incredible. Confused as I was about why we were in Iraq, and what it was that we were actually doing, they were so happy to see us. We did get opportunities to make small differences, tossing out water or food. We would drive through a town and there would be kids trying to sell or trade for American food. They would try and grab onto the truck if we were driving slow enough, pointing at things in the cab that they wanted.

I left Iraq in early 2005. The homecoming was good and bad. We got to the airport and there were a whole bunch of people there, and this little old lady came right up to me and gave me a huge kiss on the cheek. They were super excited to see us back, and it was exhilarating to be home and to have people actually be happy.

But then there'd be instances when I got home, like when I went out on a date with a girl who didn't know I was in the Army. When she found out, she told me that I should regret having ever signed up, and that she didn't want to go out with me again if I didn't admit to regretting that I signed up for the Army and went to Iraq. I told her, "Even if you didn't go to Iraq, just living here in this country you are guilty by association for everything. Everyone here is complicit. And just because you didn't hold a gun doesn't mean that your taxes didn't pay for that gun and pay for that person to be over there. And if you really want to separate yourself from that, you're not allowed to live here. You're not allowed to participate in the society that we built and that the military supports. If you don't want to support what's going on, then you need to either try and make some serious change happen and be in vocal opposition to it—or leave."

That's what I told her. We never went out again.

I went back to school toward the end of my military career and I focused on art philosophy. I got a bachelor of fine arts degree, but also a minor in science in philosophy, primarily in ethics and existentialism. I am currently an MFA candidate at Montana State University.

People have been shocked to find out that I was in the military, and I guess a lot of times I distance myself from it. This current body of work is the first time I've actually openly referenced the military in art, but even in doing so, I still try and distance myself. A lot of times you'll see, if I do use imagery of soldiers, it'll be a World War II soldier or a Vietnam soldier, because I guess I'm now impossibly associated with the Army forever, but I don't identify with it.

When I think back, I would still sign up for the Army, because I see life as an opportunity. I am always open. That's why I went into that recruiter's office and I signed up then and there. I said, "You know what? This is a great opportunity to go experience an adventure and see the world through the eyes of a soldier." Similarly, through the eyes of an artist, or through the eyes of a student, or carpenter, or any of these smaller lives I have led.

More than just experience, though, it is gaining perspective, and will help you empathize more with other humans and gain some real perspective. Most days, it leaves me with an overwhelming guilt. I hope to continue to learn and share through making art and teaching. I also hope to be able to help where I have failed to help, but there is only so much time. I might be slightly angry with the Army, but I treasure the time I spent in Iraq; it was something I would never trade for the world. Many of those crazy missions going haywire are the only reason I still remember much of what happened there. I was young and dumb and got in trouble a lot, but it was an amazing adventure, and a chance to help support what so many in my family have fought to support in the past.

Scott Dawson in his daughter's bedroom in their apartment in The Tri-Cities in Washington State. Earlier that day, Scott and I spoke at a Veterans Day event where Scott talked about finding WMDs in Iraq. Later that night at his home, I asked him about this claim, because WMDs were the premise for the Iraq War and the Bush administration would have been eager to know that American troops had found WMDs. Scott said: "I'm not a bomb guy but, in my opinion, a bomb with a kill radius of a mile or two miles, and which can kill from 100 to a 1,000 or more people, is a WMD."

Scott Dawson

As it turned out, joining the Marines would be one of the singularly, most intelligent decisions that I would ever make.

I was born in 1982, in Richland, WA, and graduated from Richland High School in June 2001.

Before I graduated from high school, I got a job at McDonald's, and then moved on to be a sales rep at an up and coming air filtration/vacuum company, or so I thought—turned out to be a go-nowhere job. After the vacuum company job, I just got on with being a nineteen-year-old: drinking, having fun, partying—basically being a punk—and going nowhere and fast.

I wanted more for my life. I wanted to make a difference, but I just needed to get motivated. 9/11 motivated me. I joined because terrorists attacked us and I wanted to return the favor. I wanted to return the favor—that's exactly why I joined. There was also the added perk of the GI Bill to help with a college education.

So I met with recruiters from the Navy, Army, and Marines. I had always thought about serving, but was not sure which branch would be best. I was very nervous. I took the test for the Navy and then the Army. I failed both. I don't know why, but I decided to try one more time. This time, I took the exact same test for the Marine Corps and passed the test. I took that as a sign. Even though others advised me not to join the Marine Corps, I said, "The hell with it, I think I will." I really thought that at that point in my life I had no direction or self discipline. I was becoming a mouthy little punk. As it turned out, joining the Marines would be one of the singularly most intelligent decisions that I would ever make.

I officially signed up for the Marines in November 2001, but I didn't actually ship off to boot camp until December 11, 2001. Marine Corps boot camp was tough, one of the toughest things I have ever done. I started out after boot camp and MOS training with most of my energy directed at wanting to go fight. I wanted to be able to stand next to my dad—who served in the Air Force in Vietnam—man to man, as an equal. Every generation of my family has served. My grandfather served in the Army during WWII, and my great grandfather served in the Army—after becoming a U.S. Citizen—during WWI. It was important for me to be in that line-up.

In the Marines, my MOS was heavy equipment operation: building berms, filling Hesco barriers, moving concrete dividers (aka Jersey barriers), digging trenches, and expanding bases. While not fitting my original idea of being a Marine, it turned out to be a job I really liked and I was good at it.

Our battalion left for Iraq in February 2004. We spent a week in Kuwait and then convoyed from Kuwait through Iraq to our first deployment base near Fallujah, in the Sunni Triangle. We convoyed on highway 12, which was, as I was told, the second most attacked highway in Iraq. We were attacked. That was scary and thrilling all at the same time. I was glad we were not fighting on American soil. If the Iraqis wanted to kill American soldiers, I thought I would rather be killed over there.

There was a lot of controversy regarding weapons of mass destruction (WMD). At the time I was in Iraq, I did not know what the official definition/description was for WMD. Of course I had an opinion, which may or may not have coincided with the average American citizen's. My idea of WMD could be completely off; I'm not a bomb guy. But, in my opinion, a bomb with a kill radius of a mile or two miles that can kill from 100 to a 1,000 or more people is a WMD. And a biological bomb is just as much of a WMD as a nuclear bomb. I've seen videos of what biological weapons and bombs can do.

I was trained to handle machine guns, handguns, and rifles, not bombs. Yet, as a heavy equipment operator, I had actually been part of an excavation of bombs from a mountainside. We weren't just digging based on a hunch or suspicion that bombs were buried in the mountainside; we knew the bombs were there because of the pictures we had seen. I wondered why something hadn't been done about these bombs before. What we excavated were crates of bombs—big bombs—with bio stickers affixed. I saw these with my own two eyes. Then all excavation was shut down. We were issued gas masks and were told not to inspect or go near the bombs. So the bombs were left right where we found them; in the dirt, with soldiers and civilians driving nearby. Maybe I misunderstood what I think I saw, but with the stickers I had seen on the surface of the bombs that said "biological," it then seemed clear to me that these were WMDs.

Rules of Engagement. Historically, the military has always observed "Rules of Engagement." The military does not allow soldiers and Marines to indiscriminately start shooting people, but I think the rules have changed. The bad guys don't observe any rules; you cannot always recognize the bad guy. Yet, some politician who doesn't know shit about the military, or what being in combat is all about, sits in a cushy office and writes rules of engagement to appease the bleeding heart liberals and the news media. The reality is that the rules of engagement we [soldiers, Marines, etc.] have to follow and still be able to defend ourselves only get military people killed; not the insurgents, not the bad guys. I talked to a couple guys attached to the light armored vehicle (LAV) and amphibious assault vehicle (AAV) crews. They said they were losing guys because of the rules of engagement: cannot fire until fired upon; need to be under sustained fire before returning fire; and cannot fire upon a hospital, a school, or a mosque (yet that is precisely where the insurgents were hiding, waiting to ambush).

The insurgents knew our rules of engagement and used the rules against us. They would hide amongst their own civilian population, all dressing like civilians. We couldn't go up and check out every single person because we might just find that one child or woman who was willing, or unwilling as the case may be, to blow us up.

Being in Iraq was confusing and nerve wracking. While we were told to build a positive rapport with the Iraqi people and socialize and befriend them (not all Iraqis wanted to do the Americans harm), you never could quite trust them. In fact, I met plenty of Iraqi people that were just ecstatic we were there. But our rules of engagement and eagerness to befriend them allowed the insurgents to get dangerously close to us and betray our positions to their bombers later.

In my opinion, the current rules of engagement are crap and should be thrown out, or at least rewritten. My dad told me before I went over, "I would rather be tried by twelve than carried by six any day of the week, any time."

During my deployment, one of our commanders said: "Our rules of engagement are gone and this is how it's going to happen. It's basically shoot first and ask questions later. We are losing too many people because of the rules of engagement. If there is a rule that says it is okay to be fired upon but you must be under sustained fire, the hell with that. If there's fire coming, know where the fire is coming from and return fire." Sometimes you are fired upon by a sniper whose location you do not know; you just know you are being fired upon and it's "duck and cover."

While I was with my fellow Marines and Navy guys everything was fine. I didn't think about the dangers so much while deployed. I was excited about what I was doing. My experiences were awesome. However, after one particular firefight, after the adrenaline wore off, I just started crying. I think it was a natural reaction. I wasn't scared. There were guys screaming and laughing and crying. It takes a firefight to get the heart pumping so hard. That's why I think they say war is one of the most addictive drugs. There is nothing else that will give you that kind of a rush again. Go skydiving, whatever, it won't be the same. I think a lot of Marines drink and drive too fast, trying to recapture that feeling of danger. I heard a statistic that said more Marines die out of combat then in combat, looking for the thrill. It's a feeling you want back, that adrenaline rush.

I was in the service for another year after I got back from Iraq.

At the beginning of my enlistment, I felt great about the war and was gung-ho for it. And now I almost feel like it's another Vietnam. When I came home, it almost seemed like nobody cared. But it wasn't ordinary civilians I felt this from—it was from our own government. The U.S. government was not there for us.

The Marines had the best training for dealing with blood and guts and dealing with wounds while you are in service, but not for life when you get out. The Marines did send us to classes, such as "how to separate," the kind of places to get a job, various things we could do, unemployment benefits, and all that stuff. When leaving the Marines, I was sent through medical and psychological checkups. The doctors would ask, "How are you coping with it, son?" But I don't think they really cared to know. Anyway, the Marines can only train somebody just so much to deal with going back to your previous way of life. For me, Post-Traumatic Stress Disorder (PTSD) didn't set in while I was in Iraq, or in the year following Iraq before I got out, but it sure did after I came home.

One of the first times I felt the affects of what might be PTSD was after attending my sister's wedding. After the wedding, I went outside and broke down—I just lost it. I wouldn't be able to tell you why, but I just felt overwhelmed.

There were some tough and scary times for about a year and a half after I got home. I became more violent. My mom and my girlfriend at the time can bear witness to some of my outbursts. I was drinking heavily, always angry, and extremely paranoid. Still am paranoid to a certain degree. Even now. There are some Iranians at WSU, and I would get into my car and think, "What if one of those guys put a bomb in my car?" I tell myself that it is just me being paranoid. Even going into a bank or a post office, or anywhere, I see trash on the road and my heart starts pounding. I'd be driving, zone out, and think I was back in Iraq. Sometimes I could swear that I could see people in my room who really were not there. I would wake up in my bed with my girlfriend next to me, in a panic looking for my rifle, feeling like I'm getting attacked. When I was home on leave for New Year's (2004/2005), while celebrating at a bar balloons started popping, corks were going off, and I just freaked. I had to get the hell out of there. The next morning, we went to a Seahawks game. The Seahawks lost the game and I went into a rage, yelling, "Get the hell away from me. You don't care, none of you care. You are all liars and doing it for own your benefit." That was a rough time. Thank God, I knew deep inside this was not the way I wanted to live. I knew that I needed to go to school.

I still have bad dreams, but the bad dreams and waking up looking for my rifle and all that stuff does not happen so much anymore. But for that first year and half out of the service, it seemed like the bad feelings would never end. I wanted to cry. I thought, "What the hell is wrong with me?" People I would talk to about my thoughts and feelings would say, "There is nothing wrong with you. This is just what happens. If you didn't feel anything, then that might mean there is something wrong with you."

I saw a doctor at the Veterans Administration (VA) clinic in Richland. I told him about the drinking, the dreams, the violent outbursts, and he tells me, "There is nothing wrong with you," and sends me away. And I almost wanted to say to him, "You know what man, if I do something terrible it will be on your hands. Thanks for not helping me, you scumbag." I worked at the same VA office, too, as a work study. I had to deal with him every day. He was just a long-haired hippie. I won't name him—he's retired now anyway—but there were lot of people who didn't like him for the same reason. This guy was a real prick.

For those military people who do not support the war now, I think maybe they should keep that information to themselves in certain situations. It doesn't help morale when former soldiers who served in Iraq now say they don't agree with the war there. I mean, I believe that people should be able to voice their opinions, but maybe not at certain times or places, such as morale-building for the troops, welcome homes, and sending sons or daughters off to combat type occasions. It sends the wrong message.

I have seen pictures of troops from Vietnam with signs that say "Veterans Against the War" and "Veterans for Peace." That's fine if those troops have really been there, in combat situations I mean. They have earned the right to voice that opinion over others who have not "been there, done that."

The support for the troops is much better now than it was for the Vietnam veterans, from what I have seen and experienced, even if the people are kind of fed up with the Iraq war. But there are these military guys crying about Iraq, saying how it was pointless.

There are entertainers who want to support the troops, and that's great. I appreciate that they want to support us. However, there are some entertainers who want just as much to burn us: Sean Penn, Danny Glover, and Alec Baldwin. I think they just need to keep their mouths shut. They don't have a clue.

Up to that last year or two, I felt good about the war. My belief at the start of the Iraq war was that America went to Iraq to dethrone a dictator, a tyrant, and to stop the tyranny against the Iraqi people. I thought we were protecting innocent people. I thought our mission in Iraq was good, and when their government was in good shape and functioning as a democracy then we could leave. It would then be up to the Iraqi people to hold onto that democracy. The Iraqis who I talked to did not want Saddam there. They wanted freedom. They wanted to be able to go to work and know they could come home. We, the American military, fight for people to be able to say what they want, and even for those who want to say they disagree with us. I think some people who are free take freedom for granted and don't want to face the reality of sacrifice in helping those who do not have that freedom. They live in a shell and don't want to face reality. People need to be exposed because they can't handle the truth.

We cannot be the rescuers of the world. The U.S. has come to the rescue so many times, but would any other country come to rescue the United States, if needed?

As time goes on, I am becoming more opinionated and political about the war. Some people think the U.S. was in Iraq because of oil and George Bush, and not to help the Iraqi people achieve democracy. I don't think oil was the reason. Oil may have been part of it, but not all of it. What did George Bush have to gain by fighting for oil? Bush's family was already rich in oil thirty-plus years before this war kicked off. His family was hanging with Saudi Arabians long before the U.S. decided to go to war. It was not all George Bush's fault. As the President he had a say in it, of course, but so did Dick Cheney. Even George's daddy was pulling some strings. I kind of think George Bush's decision to go to Iraq was based on making up for Bush senior's prior failure. It didn't matter what people had to say—whether you were Democratic or Republican—it was off to war we went.

Is it better to use another country's resources? I suppose, if you believe that your own country should horde its own resources for an eventual end of the world or something . . . At any rate, there was a positive outcome: Saddam Hussein was eliminated.

Josh Simpson sits at G.I. coffee house Coffee Strong during a fundraiser and rally for conscientious objector Travis Bishop. Sergeant Bishop refused to serve in Afghanistan, based on his Baptist upbringing and current convictions that Jesus practiced a strict pacifism. His convictions earned him the title Prisoner of Conscience from Amnesty International.

Joshua Simpson

Another thing I need to state is that we need to stop worshiping veterans (and I'm saying this as a veteran); that using language like, "fought for America" or "defended freedom" is not what anyone's done.

My name is Joshua Simpson. I'm twenty-seven years old [Interview 2009]. I joined the Army in July 2001. I was in Iraq from 2004 to 2005.

At the time, there were definitely lots of reasons why I joined. I think I joined for the classic reasons—patriotism, adventure, college money—but it was a little bit different for me; I definitely didn't have a stable home life. I was really interested in history, grew up hearing about the military, and always wanted to see what it was like. When I applied, they said, "Do you want to be a counter-intelligence agent in the Army?" I thought, "That sounds really cool!" So I jumped at the chance.

I was deployed from September 2004 to September 2005. I was a member of a THT team, which stands for Tactical Human Intelligence Team. When I was in Iraq, we were involved in all the different processes of collecting intelligence based on human sources. A lot of times we would collect information by doing interrogations of detainees. Other times, we would talk to informants who would give us information about what local insurgent leaders were doing. Many of these informants basically had bones to pick with members of their community. They would tell us that they were insurgents so we would arrest them and send them to jail. Sometimes, we would talk to informants who were solely motivated by money, who just wanted a paycheck. I don't think they gave a fuck who they sent to jail. That was actually how we collected most of our intelligence. I spent most of my time there doing interrogations. Generally, you gather more information by working with informants than you do through interrogations. But in Iraq, there's a view that interrogation is the most important process of gaining information. If you think about it, it's much easier to get information from people who want to give it to you than to try to pry information from people who don't want to give it to you. One of the things about interrogation that I noticed was that most of the people I interrogated had nothing to do with the insurgency. So even if they wanted to tell me information, they had nothing to tell me. Our chain of command was unwilling to believe that the everyday Iraqi didn't have some sort of affiliation with the insurgency. The truth of the matter about Iraq is that there's nothing wrong with Iraqis being involved with the insurgency. It's totally justifiable because they're under occupation. Iraqis are a very resilient people. They live in a poor country (mostly due to years of U.S. sanctions) and they have a strong will to survive. Obviously, the occupation and the fact that they don't have running water or electricity has a huge effect on them. But most Iraqis are just trying to get by day to day, looking after their families.

When I first got there, I was already pretty much against the war, but in a real liberal way, which is that basically, I'm against the war, but now that we're there, we should finish up and attempt to bring stability to the country. I think the longer I was there, the more I tended to see what was actually going on and got more and more disillusioned. It was a slow process. I didn't quite realize what I was doing, until after I got home and had more time to reflect on what was happening and what I was doing while overseas. Plus, I learned more about the history of U.S. imperialism while attending college. While there, I realized that a lot of things we were doing were really ineffective; whether they were right or wrong was not even important. I remember one time making an argument with a member of my chain of command about how I was opposed to torture. We would send off Iraqis to get tortured by the Iraqi police, the Iraqi National Guard, or even Kurdish militia groups. It was well known that we would hand over these people and they would be tortured. During that process, they would come back to us as horribly mutilated individuals with long lists of confessions; they'd confessed to everything, right? Command would always want me to re-interrogate them because they figured, "Well, the Iraqis tortured them, but they don't really know how to interrogate, so you should actually ask and clear the information they got." I would ask, "Okay, what about this? You said you were involved in this bombing," and they would say, "Actually, I wasn't involved in that bombing, I was tortured, so I just admitted to it." The thing about it is, I don't really know if that individual was involved in a bombing. He could have very well been, but he also could have been tortured to the point where he just admitted to it. What I would say to people is that torture is inhumane and ineffective.

My military experience definitely radicalized me. I became more radical while in the military, but also while going to school. It's kind of like this: another soldier can go to Iraq, see the exact same things I saw, and come out with a completely different view than I have. It's all about the lens you view it through. If you don't have any kind of critical consciousness that's been developed, you'll see a torture and think, "Hey, this guy was a murderer, it's okay if he was tortured." That's what you've been told and that's how you're choosing to view it.

I work at Coffee Strong. Coffee Strong is a veteran-operated service member and veterans' rights center located next to Joint Base Lewis-McChord in Washington State. I worked here all day today, and soldiers came and we talked about stuff. Today we talked a lot about the recent Fort Hood shootings [November 5, 2009] and how people feel about that. It's been a big news item. Should I talk about the Fort Hood shootings? Basically, my view on the Fort Hood shootings is similar to what Malcolm X said about the JFK assassination, it's "The chickens coming home to roost." You know, the United States is the greatest purveyor of violence in the world, and then people are shocked when violence comes back to the United States. They're also shocked by the idea that maybe a brown person doesn't want to go overseas to help rich white people kill more brown people, just so they can make more money. It makes perfect sense to me. I don't support the individual gunning down of random soldiers, but I'm not necessarily against it, if you want to frag officers in Iraq and Afghanistan that are committing war crimes and trying to get you and your comrades killed. I'm totally for that, but at the same time, I'm not for the killing of seemingly random soldiers by disgruntled troops. It needs to be somewhat thought out and rational.

When you think about it, this guy was talking to people with PTSD that had horrible experiences in the war. When this guy—whose job is to treat soldiers—goes crazy by talking to soldiers, it's a definite guilty verdict on the war. It says that what's going on is so fucked up that the people who are supposed to be treating returning troops are messed up as well.

While I was in Iraq, we locked up people; we incarcerated people for printing anti-American propaganda. That's the freedom we brought to Iraq? That's not a freedom, that's us being terrorists. We need to understand that the U.S. government is the biggest source of terrorism in the entire world and it has been for a long time; I would easily say since Vietnam—probably before then—back to Mossadegh in Iran.

Another thing I need to state is that we need to stop worshiping veterans (and I'm saying this as a veteran), that using language like "fought for America" or "defended freedom" is not what anyone's done. Every war in my lifetime, and in my father's lifetime, has been an imperialist war. People do join for honorable reasons, but the fact that anyone in the military has fought for an honorable cause is a complete fallacy. It hasn't happened in a long fucking time. People need to support the troops who refuse to fight. The troops that are fighting are already getting supported by every right-wing nutcase in the world. We should reach out to them, but we shouldn't necessarily support them for being "good Germans." For example, IVAW Fort Lewis is not going to be campaigning for body armor for troops tomorrow, unless we're giving body armor to the Iraqis, too.

I don't want U.S. imperialism to succeed—I want it to fail. I want the U.S. to lose in Iraq. I want the U.S. to lose in Afghanistan, as well. Do I want soldiers to get killed? No. I want them to refuse to go and, instead, fight the terrorists that rule us here. I want them all brought home immediately. If bringing about radical change in the U.S. and the world means the U.S. has to lose in its imperialist adventures overseas, then that is what it takes.

Heather Wakehouse at St. Patrick's Catholic Church. Heather said she was drawn to the Catholic faith as a child. She says, "I asked to go to Catholic school because I felt like it would offer a good faith-based education. I am drawn to the Church for the tradition, ritual, and community."

Heather Wakehouse

Recovery here could cost him his life over there. I've accepted that. When he comes home, when he is out, that is when the real healing will begin. Until then, we find ways to be get through.

I had a child in my early twenties. I have cousins that have been in the military, grandfathers, and an uncle. But I didn't grow up with much understanding about the military or anything specific to military.

I never really thought about it.

I had never been married and didn't have much relationship experience when I met someone that was in the Army. Right away he drew hard lines about the nature of our relationship and the behaviors within that relationship. I assumed this was in part due to his military training and the rest was kind of how people did things in relationships. I actually appreciated the lines. I felt like I could rely on things and know what I should or should not do when everything was so well defined—there is right and wrong and everything is black and white. I really thought this was just how people do it. And when things weren't going well, I convinced myself I was the problem.

He had come back from his third Mideast deployment about two years prior to my meeting him. Though he was still in the Guard, he was no longer in an Infantry unit. He was teaching military science at the university. He had just bought a house. He had custody of his two young kids and I had custody of my son. And he did the whole dating part perfectly, right out of a storybook. He took me to nice places, he did all of those things that you do when you want things to work. We talked about marriage, our kids, and our plans for the future. I really didn't want to live with him before we were married, but it became clear he needed help with his kids and that we all needed time for the transition, so we decided to get started by moving in together.

Looking back, I feel like as soon as I was there and he could count on that, he completely changed. I am not sure if he was just doing a really good job of holding himself together before this or if it was a subconscious thing. He was rarely home. When he was, it was apparent he didn't want to be there. It felt like he didn't even like us. My best description of him during this time would be emotionally violent. He has never laid a hand on me physically, but his emotional outbursts were disturbing.

Just sitting and watching TV, he would react so intensely to things and it made no sense to me. They were real things on the TV that would be disturbing, but his reaction was not like the rest of us would have. If there was violence against a woman he would completely lose it. The veins in his head would throb and he would growl like an animal.

There were a lot of things that set him off. Going out in public was never easy and never enjoyable. Crowds were not a good idea. And worse than crowds was going anywhere that had people that were native to the Middle East. He has friends that are Muslim; he even has family that are Muslim, and he's always been fine with people that we know. But seeing strangers that were clearly from over there, he didn't take it very well. He never physically did or said anything to these people, but he would just be fisted up and you could tell something wasn't right. You could feel his fear. My best guess is that it took him back to combat and he saw them as potential threats. He really thought people here to be a threat.

I learned to spot all of his potential triggers quicker than he did and distract him or change course. When we talked about things—his time over there—it was easy to see why he felt the way he did—the places he's been, the experiences that he's had—those are the reasons. It isn't that I agree with him. But I do understand he has reasons for the way he feels.

I always stay calm—maybe grab his hand, not do something stupid like pat him on the back or startle him from behind. I was a wreck on the inside, but outside I never reacted. I actually started to become a target of his because I failed to react. To him, it meant I was dead inside and didn't care. And I was really just, you know, trying to figure out what was going on and keep things together.

He was a sleep talker for a long time and a sleep reactor. He could be in a deep sleep in the middle of the night and, with the slightest noise, in a flash he would be at the door, armed with a Katana, ready to defend and attack. The look on his face when things like this would happen is one of the worst things I have ever seen. It's a mixture of the deepest fear and a readiness and willingness to kill. A few of the times that I saw this face I knew I was going to die. I'm sure I was scared, but all I could think was, what is he going to do when he realizes that he f***ing killed me?

If I were to stupidly startle him in his sleep—even if it was just a midday nap—before I could even think about the mistake I had just made, I would be flat on my back with hands around my neck. He didn't hurt me. It was just eerie. He didn't know where he was or who I was. And it was very strange in those moments, because though he seemed to be awake and I would lock eyes with him the whole time, I could see the flash where his consciousness came to and he realized what he was doing. He really had a hard time with this. He did not like knowing he could do that to me and that he had no control over it. He began to spite me for it.

I don't take it personally. I think that is one big step. He is doing these things to me. This is happening to him, too. The next step is making sure I can connect with him soon after in a way that makes me feel comfortable and safe again. I just need to make sure he is still there; the person beneath all that crap, the person that I know. I let him know how I feel. I let him know it is OK. And I make sure that I recognize him again so I can move on from what just happened.

PTSD is an illness. So why would I just walk out on him while he's struggling? I had to ask myself, if his illness were physical would I leave? And then I thought about the kids. My son wouldn't want to leave. And his kids—when all of these things were happening, more times than not, at least one of the three kids was there and I had to shield them from things and talk to them afterward. It was *so* hard. But at the same time, in between the episodes, I was always happy to be around him. I was also completely mentally and emotionally exhausted from always having to be "on."

I've also had to be sensitive to the fact that he is still in the military. So recovery or therapy and getting him to a good place is not necessarily the best idea for now, because those things could make him unable to do his job. Recovery here could cost him his life over there. I've accepted that. When he comes home, when he is out, that is when the real healing will begin. Until then, we find ways to be get through.

At the time I didn't have anywhere to go or the tools to help me work through things. I was still trying to figure out if I was the problem. I wasn't going home. My war was here. The person I'm supposed to trust most in the world was treating me like an enemy and reminding me that I might really be the enemy. The difference is that when they go to war, they have each other.

I know this isn't Baghdad. But my home felt like a combat zone. I didn't feel safe or trusted in my own home. How could I heal from a war that I'm *still* fighting? I don't think it is worse than combat. It is just different. And it should absolutely be acknowledged.

I still love him. I don't pity him at all. And I don't hold grudges for stuff that has happened. Those things haven't disrupted loving him. He is still there, beneath all of his war scars. That is the man I know.

I am a completely different person than I was before. I think a lot differently. I've picked up little things, like scanning for danger or, more accurately, scanning for things that will be disruptive to him. I am always so aware. If we go into a restaurant and sit down, I know it is not going to be a pleasant meal if he is seated in the wrong spot. I've learned to be one step ahead regarding those things. Even if I am not out with him, I still avoid the things that would bother him. It's not even conscious anymore. It's just there.

I don't think anyone should feel sorry for me. My hope is that people in situations like mine can be understood and respected. I wouldn't change the past; I am alive in the present and I believe the future will be better.

From *The Telling*, 2014

Joe Dunn in front of the United State Customs House in Portland, Oregon.

Joe Dunn

It's sort of ironic, because here I was feeling like I was being shit on by the Tea Party. And it's certainly not the first time these fuck'n hypocrites have insulted me while I'm wearing my uniform. I wonder if they see the irony?

I joined active duty right out of high school in 2003. I signed my papers before the Iraq War started, but after September 11, 2001.

My whole family has been in the military. My mom and dad met each other in the military; both were in the Army. My grandfathers from both sides were in the military. My grandfather from my mom's side was in the Air Force for thirty years. My dad was an Army officer for ten years. My dad was a positive influence in my life and, seeing him in his uniform pretty often, I knew that was what I wanted to do. I knew I wanted to be a soldier since I was eight and playing with GI Joes.

I served from 2003-2005 in active duty USAF, deploying to Al Udeid (Qatar) in 2004 and 2005. I additionally served from 2005-2007 in the USAF Reserves, completing four years of service in total.

Following is a journal entry from October 20, 2010. At the time, I was an organizer for the local chapter of Veterans for Peace and also an active organizer for Iraq Veterans Against the War. I had recently had dinner with the national board of directors of Veterans For Peace. A board member out of Florida came up with the slogan "How is the War Economy Working for You?" I thought this was dandy and made a large banner from a king-sized bed sheet for Obama's visit.

A lot has changed since then. Today, I no longer believe in the utility of standing on street corners with banners or passing out books on the street. If I have anything in my life that resembles activism, it is to encourage self improvement, civil disobedience, and questioning of authority.

This entry was selected because it provides insight into the duality of pro-war and anti-war veterans, and also Vietnam veterans and veterans of my war.

October 20, 2010

Last night the President was in town. I created a giant banner with the words, "How is the War Economy Working for You?" I didn't do any chanting, any marching, or make a scene. I stood silently, with a huge banner in front of about 5,000 people waiting to see the President. Several people took photos while waiting in line. A couple crazies came up and chatted with me, "Did you know that oil is basically rocks, and we have no shortage of rocks, so we can't have a shortage of oil?" And a few tea party folks walked by and gave me a thumbs-up. A couple independent news reporters came up and interviewed me. I spoke about Iraq, Afghanistan, Pakistan, Blackwater, war profiteering, and why Veterans for Peace is out here.

At around 5:30, everyone waiting to see the President was inside. Just the peace activists and the Tea Party folks were outside. Things got weird; there was some more yelling. I had about thirty copies of *War is a Racket* by Major General Smedley Butler on me and decided to pass them out. I read this book when nearly out of the military and it immediately changed my life. Read it—it's a short read. It so profoundly affected me that I personally paid for, published, assembled, and distributed 2,500 copies of this book as an activist.

One guy told me, "You should be ashamed of yourself." I should be ashamed because I joined the military and am now handing out *War Is A Racket*? He said it was "peace activist propaganda!" Oh well, I think the dude was stereotyping me. Maybe if I'd had a different hair cut this wouldn't have been a problem. (Sometimes I get my hair cut very short to be within military regulations. Other times, my hair gets long and I look like a hippie. I notice I am treated very differently by military/veterans depending upon the length of my hair.)

My favorite lines from this guy were, "You know what happened the last time peace activists got on to the military? Don't you have any shame? We lost Vietnam!" That made me smile. "We were this close," he shows me his hand with his index finger and thumb an inch apart, "this close to beating the North Vietnamese! To winning the damn war, and you people stopped us."

Then he said, "You know what you need to do? You need to get smarter . . . ." I stopped him, "I need an education?" "Yes, you need to read books. You need to find this book, *A Better War*." I told him okay, and then said, "Well here, have a copy of my book. It would be hypocritical of you to suggest to me to read another book if you will refuse to accept and read this one." He took a copy, folded it, and put it in his back pocket. Clearly he was not interested in even looking at my book, much less reading it. So I attempted to make a compromise. "Tell you what, man, just read the first page of this book, just to find out who Smedley Butler was, the guy was a Marine Corps general and a war hero." A small crowd of Tea Party folks assembled around me and another man asked me for a copy. Then someone asked me to read the first page, so I agreed to read one of my favorite Butler quotes: "I spent thirty three years and four months in active military service, and during that period I spent most of my time as a high class muscle man for Big Business, for Wall Street and the bankers. In short, I was a racketeer, a gangster for capitalism. I helped make Mexico and especially, Tampico, safe." Some shouted, "Gangster for Capitalism?!? What does that mean? What is this commie crap!"

I really tried my hardest to be polite and answer their questions, even though one dude was absolutely adamant that I was betraying my country by advocating for the end of the war. He told me the peace activists of the 1960s were funded by the KBG, and that the kids killed at Kent State were being manipulated by the KGB. If he truly believes that, then I guess I'm funded by Osama.

I never really made any political comments, nor did I really express many of my own views, but this guy kept saying, "If you think . . ." and, "If you say . . ." and, "People like you," putting words in my mouth and making assumptions about my intentions. Scapegoating is the tool of the angry and ignorant who do not wish to be corrected.

It's sort of ironic, because here I was feeling like I was being shit on by the Tea Party. And it's certainly not the first time these fuck'n hypocrites have insulted me while I'm wearing my uniform. I wonder if they see the irony? A few of them engaged me like I was human. Some of them outright insulted me. While I'm wearing my uniform, they're mocking the "peace movement" of the 1960s.

My work is very discouraging. It's like being a performer and having everyone boo at the end of your show. Some people assume I'm stupid or crazy for standing around with a banner. I'm not trying to spark a revolution; I'm trying to provide an avenue for dissent. We can't work for a more prosperous country if the entire middle class is wrapped up in hatred or adamant love for the contemporary President. I meet many people who are not even critical of the government anymore, and that's simply not okay. If there's a better way to move the country forward, I'm all ears. This bullshit I'm doing is just the best solution we've got going and I fucking hate it. It's driving me fucking insane.

When I came back, I definitely had the mentality that if somebody fucked with me—if a civilian fucked with me—I was going to kill 'em. I've been a gun owner all my life. I was pretty much convinced that if somebody fucked with me, they were going to die.

Lucia Enriquez in her apartment in the Tri-Cities, Washington State.

Lucia Enriquez

I think people in this area are very vet-centered, very welcoming to the vets, support the troops and stuff, so I've had a good feeling. When we got home there was a big crowd of people in the airport.

I was born in Mexico in 1987. We left Mexico when I was less than a year old. I joined the military when I was seventeen, in 2005. All of my brothers and sisters went straight into college and I just wanted to do something different. The military was kind of there. A recruiter was at the high school and I just looked into it one day and enlisted. Now I'm a biology major and I'll look at pre-med in a couple years. I'm hoping to be a doctor. But one school at a time.

We were stationed in Camp Taji, which is about thirty miles north of Baghdad. We did logistics operations, which means we transported anything that was needed from base to base. I did operations control. Anything that moved I controlled, and I made sure that everything went where it was supposed to. I did all the reports and was in charge of everything that was transported.

I got to see a lot of foreign nationals on base. They were in charge of cooking, laundry, and any type of maintenance that needed to be done in our facility. The Iraqis were really welcoming. We'd go to their side and they would give us their bread—it's kind of a thin flatbread. They showed us how they make their flatbread. They were really welcoming; they had these little shops and they'd always want to give us gifts. Like, "gifts, gifts," you know. I didn't run into many female Iraqis, but I did run into a lot of male Iraqis. I also came in contact with a lot of Iraqi military people as well. I didn't get to train them, but from the things that some of the soldiers did with them, they seemed like they were really eager to learn; they got to learn how to shoot our weapons. It was interesting, one of the banquets I went to was an Air Force banquet that the Iraqi Air Force and the U.S. Air Force hosted. They had this huge party and the Iraqis had their food, and they talked about how they had been trained by the U.S., and it was a good thing.

Now that I'm back in school, I'm doing pretty well, though I know there are times when loud noises kind of startle me. Even though I didn't leave base that often, our base got hit quite frequently. The buildings that you are living in aren't exactly bomb shelters, so when you feel a mortar coming in, your whole building shakes. I didn't experience what combat soldiers experienced, but I stay alert. I think my fiancé and I are both very particular about what's going on in our lives, and one thing we both do is we always have to be facing the crowd. It's really hard for us to have our backs to the crowd because of that.

You can see a shift in some people. My fiancé has PTSD and there are times when he isn't himself. It doesn't keep him from functioning, but it's just something you have to work through. There are times when he says he just feels empty. He was a foot soldier, so he experienced and saw a lot of stuff. When he feels that way I just have to be there, and if he wants to talk, we talk. I think a lot of combat soldiers get an adrenaline rush—it's a high. So when they get back and they're living as a regular person, they don't feel that adrenaline rush. I'm not a psychologist by any means, but I think it has some association with not having that adrenaline high.

Soldiers need the help and families have to really support and understand. I think families and close friends also should know the signs. I think that would be the next step for families—to recognize signs.

I actually think that most of us did pretty well as a whole when we got back. When we were in our demobilization training there was a lot of PTSD talk, and what we can do to get in school and what resources are available. There are a lot of resources out there for soldiers, but the thing is that some soldiers just don't take it. It's more on the soldiers, because there are so many resources like scholarships and VA clinics after you get back from deployment. You have a five-year medical, but some soldiers don't take advantage of it. I really don't think civilians can do more, because I feel like they already do a lot for us.

I think people in this area (Tri-cities, Washington) are very vet-centered, very welcoming to the vets—support the troops and stuff—so I've had a good feeling. When we got home there was a big crowd of people in the airport. Some of them were the American Legion and some of them were just friends of friends that came and welcomed us at the airport, so I think this area is really good at supporting troops.

Jonathan Sanford at U.S. Senator Ron Wyden's offices. Jonathan says: "War is only half of the challenge; the second part of the job rests squarely with the people who go out of their way to meet, work, and think about veterans' needs. There is hope, and it rests with all of us."

Jonathan Sanford

When my boss, U.S. Senator Ron Wyden, asked me, "What can we do for Vets?" I answered, "Stop making them."

I was born in Portland, Oregon, in 1982. I'm a disabled veteran and the Veterans and Defense Advocate for United States Senator Ron Wyden from Oregon. I have made a personal mission to help veterans throughout Oregon.

I joined the Oregon National Guard in March 2000. I joined because I thought it was the right thing to do, plus for economic reasons, to get money for college. I wanted to be part of the military. I wanted to live honorably, and to possibly die honorably. There was part of me that expected to go into the military and die for my country and be happy with that. When that didn't happen, I had to change my plans. I was in Iraq from February 2005 to March 2006. I was in Camp Caldwell, about seventy miles east of Baghdad, and then Ramadi, in Anbar Province.

When I got home in 2006, there were many challenges regarding freshly returning veterans that society and the government weren't ready for. Because the military couldn't get enough service members for the wars in Iraq and Afghanistan, they had to pull the reserve forces. Not since the Civil War had we seen such a dramatic change in the military structure in such a short time. Regular Army soldiers, Marines, seamen, airmen, and Coast Guard members were fighting right along with their reserve component equals. I read somewhere that around fifty percent of the fighting forces in the last decade were from the reserves, meaning they were from our hometowns, from Salem, Medford, Bend LaGrande, and from all over Oregon.

But the military wasn't ready. The reserve members were put in sub-standard jobs, looked down on, and treated as second class. This thinking permeated into our laws and even to the GI Bill, tuition programs, veterans' health care, and reintegration programs. All were ill equipped to handle the thousands that participated in our current conflicts.

So I became involved with congressional offices, wrote legislation, and lobbied in DC and in Salem. In fact, I vividly remember shaving my head on the capitol steps in front of the speaker of the house and the governor. I later became student body president at my university and was a special envoy that hosted Secretary Shinseki, both in 2008 and 2013. Eventually, I migrated to U.S. Senator Ron Wyden's office, where I currently serve. This work has allowed me access to most every political and social event for Veterans in Oregon and the nation in the last seven years . . . and I am truly proud to be at the Oregon Military Support Network.

After over a decade of war, America is tired of hearing about Iraq and Afghanistan, weapons of mass destruction, drone strikes, suicide bombers, and angry veterans. This shouldn't surprise any of us; we all know these wars have asked so terribly much from so terribly few that even the statistics are numbing. Just one percent of our society were directly involved in the wars in the last decade. To put this in perspective, it is estimated that the World War II generation had about fifty percent of the population directly affected by that war. You could not walk down the street and find someone who wasn't affected in one way or another. It's even important to point out it is estimated that about half the enrollees for college in Oregon were using the GI Bill post-WWII.

Today, a veteran or someone affected directly by these two wars is an anomaly. Knowing that few were directly affected by these wars, and that popular opinion is not largely swayed by America's actions overseas, we expect some effects to the veteran community. We can expect limited funding for any group that isn't sharing the veterans' public spotlight, regardless of the work they are doing. For example, the Josephine County Veteran Service Office was defunded this year.

There is a lack of public support of other programs that directly influence veteran's lives, like funding for veteran service officers, mental health programs, and suicide awareness training and outreach. Also there is, and will be, an ever-increasing demand for veteran services. We know that when veterans come home their needs increase over time, not the minute after they get home.

Does anyone know how to prove a veteran was exposed to a toxic, life-threatening chemical like Agent Orange? And when did the large percentage of Vietnam-era veterans get granted service-connected status for Agent Orange related illnesses in the last few years? The reason is that statistically, veterans from that era were coming down with severe health conditions that were outside of the norm, and the only correlating factor was their service in Vietnam.

But the government knew these chemicals were toxic when they poured it over our troops in the '60s and '70s. It seems the answer to how the government is willing to support a veteran who is exposed to toxic, life threatening chemicals is to examine postmortem, or by examining the escalating amounts of cancers that their fellow veterans are facing, but it took over forty years to do so. How many of our friends, loved ones, and relatives have we lost in that time due to Agent Orange?

What I am pointing at are some direct problems for us. Oregon is made up of seventy-three percent Vietnam-era or older veterans. As they age, they will need more and more help. I am telling you this because the message we all need to hear is that funding is going away.

Popular support and funding slacks after every war, right when veterans need it most. We know this. This is what happened after World War I with the Bonus Marchers of 1932, who stormed the White House and Congress, demanding their bonus checks. This happened after World War II, when a generation fought PTSD, depression, anxiety, and other challenges, often turning to alcohol. This happened after Korea, Vietnam (with the added bonus of getting spit on when they came home), after the Gulf War (with the government drawdowns and limited government funds), and all the conflicts between, like Granada, Columbia, Somalia, Bosnia, etc. And we know it is coming after today's wars . . .

America has a great push to get its sons and daughters, fathers and mothers into war, but when they come home support is lacking.

War is only half of the challenge; the second part of the job rests squarely with the people who go out of their way to meet, work, and think about veterans' needs. There is hope, and it rests with all of us.

We need to get information out to veterans and their communities as soon as possible, in every way we can, to ensure they don't become another lost generation. We also need to create lasting conversations that can provide the reference material for the next generation that is affected by war. By creating an organization that listens, we are filling a vital role that the American government does very little of. Our goal is to not only archive these conversations, but use them as material to fight misinformation and provide a greater understanding.

I founded the Veterans Media Project last year while working on a documentary called *Project Tahsoon*, which provided a space to interview people affected by the Iraq War. Veterans are coming back home in the thousands from Iraq and Afghanistan, and VMP incorporates the basic elements that they need to get across: the stories of their experiences, what their main challenges are, and how they are finding success. VMP is created by veterans, for veterans, and for the public. We are using all media sources to get our message across.

When I went to Portland State University, I became President of the PSU Student Veterans Association and then PSU Student Body President. I studied Cultural Anthropology in the Middle East. One of the things I want to do is go back to Iraq and listen to people. I'm working on a project to listen to Iraq veterans and Iraqis and ask them the same set of questions.

One of my life goals is to go back to Baqubah—where I was at—to work to provide economic assistance in the ways they deem fit—not ways any outsider Western American deems fit—if they need water, schools, whatever. When I came home, I set my four goals for Iraq: first, a direct apology from America; second, to provide reparations for the people of Iraq; third, to provide economic support for schools, transportation, and infrastructure; and fourth, an apology and promise that we will never bring the U.S. military back to Iraq. The reason is not totally altruistic. It's pretty simple: I know what I would do if somebody kicked in my back door and killed my friends and neighbors. I know what my job would be for the rest of my life. I'd go to their country and kill every one of them, especially if they killed one of my family. I personally feel guilty about being in Iraq. It was a waste of life, money, and time. We killed around a million people because of our presence. For what? The thing that just smacks me in the face is that nobody gives a shit about why we were there. We wasted a trillion dollars and a million lives, and I don't see the political or social will to dig deep to find out why we went to Iraq. Who benefitted from this war? Part of being a veteran is feeling bad about being in Iraq. I studied to be a pastor. I tried to cleanse myself any way I could. As an American citizen or a Unitarian, I don't feel like I'll really rest until I can *ameliorate* or cleanse my experience there. I didn't kill anyone; I was ordered to, but didn't. But I was part of a group that did. One million people died. We don't seem to understand the true costs of these wars. If the American people would listen, I'd say just look at the experiences that we've had going to these wars. We all need to pay more attention. The drums of war are beating again.

When my boss, U.S. Senator Ron Wyden, asked me, "What can we do for vets?" I answered, "Stop making them."

Ryan Endicott speaking at Lafayette Park—in front of the White House—on the eighth anniversary of the Iraq invasion.

Ryan Endicott

As the months pass and more active duty troops die as a result of suicide rather than in combat, it is now time for the veterans of this country to take a stand.

To my fellow Marines,

In March 2005 I deployed to Ramadi, Iraq, as an infantryman. I remember being more excited than anything else. I was excited because I believed I was serving my country, protecting my family, and helping an oppressed people fight for their liberation. However, after taking part in combat and witnessing the war first hand, I came home a different person.

Nearly 5,000 Marines, sailors, soldiers, and Air Force members gave their lives in Iraq, including sixteen Marines from my battalion in Ramadi. And today, we recognize that these troops were sent to kill, and be killed, for the profits of a tiny few. Today, as more evidence surfaces as to the oil interests, defense contracts, and war profiteering taking place in Iraq, we see that our government will stop at nothing to expand its power.

There is no longer any doubt that the war in Iraq was waged for corporate profits. We see that the government has no qualms about sending brave men and women in uniform from Main Street to their deaths for the interest of Wall Street. We see that the government has no qualms about terrorizing and killing innocent people around the world for the interests of the super-rich. And lastly, we see that this government has no qualms about what happens to those veterans who do return home and suffer the highest unemployment rates and the highest homelessness rates, and receive criminally inadequate treatment for PTSD. It does not take a military strategist to see that sending an additional 1,400 Marines to a war with over 100,000 soldiers is a desperate and hopeless action. Even General Petraeus says, "I don't think you win this war . . . This is the kind of fight we're in for the rest of our lives and probably our kids' lives." The former British commander in Afghanistan has stated that the war cannot be won, and that "American strategy is doomed to fail." So, between these admissions and the absolute criminal negligence resulting in the mass homelessness and suicides of our returning veterans, it becomes crystal clear that we are being sent to these occupations by people who admittedly do not have our best interests, or the Afghan peoples' interests, at heart.

As with the Iraq war, it has become obvious that we are giving our lives, our limbs, and our minds—not for freedom, not for liberation, but for profit. Like Iraq, Afghanistan is just another resource-rich region of the world that is not yet in the grip of Wall Street. As the months pass and more active-duty troops die as a result of suicide than in combat, it is now time for the veterans of this country to take a stand. If I could turn the hands of time back to February 2005, I would have refused to deploy to the criminal occupation of Iraq. In doing so, I would have been truly fulfilling the oath I took when I raised my right hand and swore to defend the people of this country. When we swore our oath, we swore to protect the people of this country against all enemies foreign and domestic. And today, it has become undeniably clear that the biggest enemy of the people of this country is not poor people in Iraq or Afghanistan, but the millionaire politicians, the Wall Street bankers, oil tycoons, and defense weapons contractors who throw our lives away for their own gain. It is not the poor Iraqi or Afghan who is struggling to feed his family who threatens our families in the states. It is the corporate CEOs who lay off hundreds of thousands of workers to protect their multi-million dollar bonuses. Our enemies are the bankers who take our houses and the government officials who slash our social services and our opportunity to get a decent education. The real enemies of the veterans are not found in the farmlands of Afghanistan, but in the halls of Congress. The members of Congress sleep well at night in their million dollar mansions, while the veterans who risk their lives following orders sleep on the streets. The war in Afghanistan is far from over. We will be sent over and over, on increasingly bloody deployments, to a war that is lost, a war that we have no reason to fight. It is up to us, as the veterans of the U.S., to stand up and fight back. It is not just our right, but also our sworn duty. It is our sworn duty to stand up against oppression, imperialism, and colonialism. As Marines, we are supposed to live our lives with honor, courage, and commitment, and being sent to our deaths for colonial conquest is neither honorable nor courageous. However, standing up and refusing to deploy to a war for profit is both. The most honorable and courageous act you can do is lay down your arms and refuse to fight.

Semper Fidelis,

Corporal Ryan Endicott

Quantico Marine Corps base during a protest over treatment of Bradley Manning, who allegedly released secret documents to WikiLeaks. Front Row (L to R): Elliott Adams, President of Veterans for Peace; Elaine Brower, mother of a thrice-deployed Marine; Ret. Colonel Mary A. Wright; and Daniel Ellsberg.

Colonel Mary A. Wright

The following is a copy of Mary (Ann) Wright's letter of resignation to Secretary of State Colin Powell. Wright was most recently the Deputy Chief of Mission at the U.S. embassy in Ulaanbaatar, Mongolia. She helped open the U.S. embassy in Kabul, Afghanistan, in January 2002.

U.S. Embassy
Ulaanbaatar, Mongolia
March 19, 2003
Secretary of State Colin Powell
U.S. Department of State Washington, DC 20521
Dear Secretary Powell:

When I last saw you in Kabul in January, 2002 you arrived to officially open the U.S. Embassy that I had helped reestablish in December 2001 as the first political officer. At that time, I could not have imagined I would be writing a year later to resign from the Foreign Service because of U.S. policies. All my adult life I have been in service to the United States. I have been a diplomat for fifteen years and the Deputy Chief of Mission in our Embassies in Sierra Leone, Micronesia, Afghanistan (briefly), and Mongolia. I have also had assignments in Somalia, Uzbekistan, Kyrgyzstan, Grenada, and Nicaragua. I received the State Department's Award for Heroism as Charge d'Affaires during the evacuation of Sierra Leone in 1997. I was twenty-six years in the U.S. Army/Army Reserves and participated in civil reconstruction projects after military operations in Grenada, Panama, and Somalia. I attained the rank of Colonel during my military service.

This is the only time in my many years serving America that I have felt I cannot represent the policies of an Administration of the United States. I disagree with the Administration's policies on Iraq, the Israeli-Palestinian conflict, North Korea, and curtailment of civil liberties in the U.S. itself. I believe the Administration's policies are making the world more dangerous, not a safer place. I feel obligated morally and professionally to set out my very deep and firm concerns on these policies and to resign from government service, as I cannot defend or implement them.

I hope you will bear with my explanation of why I must resign. After thirty years of service to my country, my decision to resign is a huge step, and I want to be clear in my reasons why I must do so.

I disagree with the Administration's policies on Iraq.

I wrote this letter five weeks ago and held it, hoping the Administration would not go to war against Iraq at this time without United Nations Security Council agreement. I strongly believe that going to war now will make the world more dangerous, not safer.

There is no doubt that Saddam Hussein is a despicable dictator and has done incredible damage to the Iraqi people and others of the region. I totally support the international community's demand that Saddam's regime destroy weapons of mass destruction.

However, I believe we should not use U.S. military force without UNSC agreement to ensure compliance. In our press for military action now, we have created deep chasms in the international community and in important international organizations. Our policies have alienated many of our allies and created ill will in much of the world.

Countries of the world supported America's action in Afghanistan as a response to the September 11th Al Qaida attacks on America. Since then, America has lost the incredible sympathy of most of the world because of our policy toward Iraq. Much of the world considers our statements about Iraq arrogant, untruthful, and masking a hidden agenda. Leaders of moderate Muslim/Arab countries warn us about predicable outrage and anger of the youth of their countries if America enters an Arab country with the purpose of attacking Muslims/Arabs, not defending them. Attacking the Saddam regime in Iraq now is very different than expelling the same regime from Kuwait, as we did ten years ago.

I strongly believe the probable response of many Arabs of the region and Muslims of the world if the U.S. enters Iraq without UNSC agreement will result in actions extraordinarily dangerous to America and Americans. Military action now without UNSC agreement is much more dangerous for America and the world than allowing the UN weapons inspections to proceed and subsequently taking UNSC authorized action if warranted.

I firmly believe the probability of Saddam using weapons of mass destruction is low, as he knows that using those weapons will trigger an immediate, strong, and justified international response. There will be no question of action against Saddam in that case. I strongly disagree with the use of a "preemptive attack" against Iraq and believe that this preemptive attack policy will be used against us, and provide justification for individuals and groups to "preemptively attack" America and American citizens.

The international military build-up is providing pressure on the regime that is resulting in a slow but steady disclosure of Weapons of Mass Destruction (WMD). We should give the weapons inspectors time to do their job. We should not give extremist Muslims/Arabs a further cause to hate America, or give moderate Muslims a reason to join the extremists. Additionally, we must reevaluate keeping our military forces in the Middle East, particularly in Saudi Arabia. Their presence on the Islamic "holy soil" of Saudi Arabia will be an anti-American rally cry for Muslims as long as the U.S. military remains and a strong reason, in their opinion, for actions against the U.S. government and American citizens.

Although I strongly believe the time is not yet right for military action in Iraq, as a soldier who has been in several military operations, I hope General Franks and U.S. and coalition forces can accomplish the missions they will be ordered do without loss of civilian or military life, and without destruction of the Iraqi peoples' homes and livelihood.

I strongly urge the Department of State to attempt again to stop the policy that is leading us to military action in Iraq without UNSC agreement. Timing is everything, and this is not yet the time for military action.

I disagree with the Administration's lack of effort in resolving the Israeli-Palestinian conflict.

Likewise, I cannot support the lack of effort by the Administration to use its influence to resurrect the Israeli-Palestinian peace process. As Palestinian suicide bombers kill Israelis and Israeli military operations kill Palestinians and destroy Palestinian towns and cities, the Administration has done little to end the violence. We must exert our considerable financial influence on the Israelis to stop destroying cities and on the Palestinians to curb their youth suicide bombers. I hope the Administration's long-needed "Roadmap for Peace" will have the human resources and political capital needed to finally make some progress toward peace.

I disagree with the Administration's lack of policy on North Korea.

Additionally, I cannot support the Administration's position on North Korea. With weapons, bombs, and missiles, the risks that North Korea poses are too great to ignore. I strongly believe the Administration's lack of substantive discussion, dialogue, and engagement over the last two years has jeopardized security on the peninsula and the region. The situation with North Korea is too dangerous for us to continue to neglect.

I disagree with the Administration's policies on Unnecessary Curtailment of Rights in America.

Further, I cannot support the Administration's unnecessary curtailment of civil rights following September 11th. The investigation of those suspected of ties with terrorist organizations is critical, but the legal system of America for 200 years has been based on standards that provide protections for persons during the investigation period. Solitary confinement without access to legal counsel cuts the heart out of the legal foundation on which our country stands. Additionally, I believe the Administration's secrecy in the judicial process has created an atmosphere of fear to speak out against the gutting of the protections on which America was built and the protections we encourage other countries to provide to their citizens.

Resignation

I have served my country for almost thirty years in some of the most isolated and dangerous parts of the world. I want to continue to serve America. However, I do not believe in the policies of this Administration and cannot defend or implement them. It is with heavy heart that I must end my service to America and therefore resign due to the Administration's policies.

Mr. Secretary—to end on a personal note, under your leadership, we have made great progress in improving the organization and administration of the Foreign Service and the Department of State. I want to thank you for your extraordinary efforts to that end. I hate to leave the Foreign Service, and I wish you and our colleagues well.

Very Respectfully,

Mary A. Wright, FO-01

Deputy Chief of Mission U.S. Embassy Ulaanbaatar, Mongolia

Lelyn Masters at deCleyre Cooperative in Memphis, TN. The collective is named after Voltairine de Cleyre, one of the most popular and renowned anarchists in the United States from 1890 to 1910. She was a prolific writer and lecturer on such issues as religion, secularist free thought, marriage, women's sexuality during the Victorian age, the role of crime and punishment in society, prison abolition, anarchist thought and its relationship to American traditions, anti-capitalism and class struggle, and suffrage and women's liberation.

Lelyn Masters

I learned philosophy [illegible] my parents' generation. The people I studied [illegible] public policy—the makers of public policy w[illegible] ools. It is as if my country were dreaming in [illegible] ions in another.

This is what I want [illegible] war in Afghanistan that we are waging now is not th[illegible] er the events of 9/11.

The day we took Kabul, [illegible] We Americans are finally acting responsibly towards the rest of the world. We are trying to put back together a country we dismantled." I hoped the conflict in Afghanistan would be the end of Americans meddling with other countries' domestic affairs.

I joined the Navy three months after I got my undergraduate degree in philosophy. This was after 9/11 and before the invasion of Iraq. I wouldn't say I joined because of 9/11, but it made my joining possible. I had also gone through a spiritual crisis. I didn't think I could address ultimate questions without a little life experience.

I didn't think we would go to war with Iraq, because I didn't think there was any way the Iraqis had weapons of mass destruction (WMDs). I took our government at its word that we would not go to war with Iraq unless the United Nations inspectors actually found WMDs there. War seemed too high a risk if there was the slightest doubt. I cannot express how disappointed I was that we went to war without good evidence of WMDs in Iraq.

After joining the Navy, I was sent to train as an Arabic linguist at the Defense Language Institute. I was there when we invaded Iraq. I saw the war unfold on Al Jazeera. I saw the whole insane, terrifying absurdity as it unrolled, uncensored. I saw Western "civilization" through the eyes of the Other.

I am convinced that the present military is nothing more than a conscripted army. The authorities would have you believe the military is essentially a volunteer force. It is not. If you look at how our military is led, you will immediately perceive it as a mercenary force. Mercenaries have only two motivations: greed and fear. If their fear of their officers is greater than their fear of the enemy, then they will fight.

People join the military not to fight wars, but for all of the benefits. It's the closest thing any of us ever had to real socialism. Most of the people I met in the Navy weren't patriots; they were just trying to pay their child support and mortgage. They joined because they couldn't get health care. They joined because they were working jobs in food service or retail that didn't challenge them or seem to be helping anyone. They joined when they didn't have options. I served with them. I know them. They don't want to be in the Persian Gulf cleaning up America's bad decisions.

There are officers in our military that believe that Islam is inherently violent and that we are fighting a holy war. What I am describing is the inner workings of an ethnocentrism of unbelievable proportions, going all the way up to the highest branches of our government. George W. Bush believed that he was doing God's will, and he was not the only one. This cult within the military is fairly widespread. They have their own experts; former Muslims who invent lies to pander to a Western market.

Looking back, I don't regret my time served. I was awfully proud of the job I did. I just wasn't proud of what our military was being ordered to do overseas. After a lot of turmoil, I chose to stay true to my promise to serve and to finish out the term I had agreed to.

I tend to feel guilty when I hear about someone's son or daughter dying over there. That guilt is totally irrational, but it's real. I lent my hand to it. Clearly, I have got a lot of karma to pay off. The orders I followed came from a democratically elected (at least the second time) official, President George W. Bush. He's the guy with the real karma to pay off. I was just an enlisted man.

2005/02/17

AREA

2005/02/18

ST DITKA
LONG LIVE "DA COACH"!!

John Fett after a month-long stay at a VA hospital. I drove John to the VA clinic to pick up his meds.

John Oswald Fett IV

Both times before I went to Iraq, we took out like three thousand dollar loans and went to Vegas and just partied it away in a weekend. The significance of that really didn't hit me until not too long ago, but basically, I was living my life like I had no tomorrow.

I started talking about joining the Marines before 9/11. It seemed like a good direction to go with my life, to do something with myself. I enlisted after 9/11. I went into the Marines in 2002, when I was twenty-two. In less than a year I was in Iraq for my first time—in '03—the very beginning of the war. I did my next deployment from September '04 to March '05.

Both times, before I went to Iraq, we took out like three thousand dollar loans and went to Vegas and just partied it away in a weekend. The significance of that really didn't hit me until not too long ago, but basically, I was living my life like I had no tomorrow. Who the hell cared if I took out a loan; I was going to die while I was over there anyway. I think the problem for most vets, and for me, was that when I came back from war I still lived my life like I had no tomorrow. I didn't care if I paid my bills. I didn't care what I said to my family, or to my friends, because tomorrow I may not be there. At the time, there were no consequences for these actions, and I'm smart enough to realize that I didn't think of it in exactly those terms, but I really was living my life like I had no tomorrow. It's just that when tomorrow does get here, it's a pretty painful way to go about things. Now it's really important for me to try to live my life like I do have a tomorrow, and try to clean up the messes that I've made, and make amends with my family and friends and the people that I've hurt through living that way, because we do have a tomorrow. (Note: John's war experience is described in "An Open letter to three Iraq women" written by his mother, Mary Geddry, p 199.)

After I got home, I definitely had some issues with avoidance and PTSD. You don't want to think about the problems; you don't want to deal with the intensity of these emotions or legal problems. I had a "failure to appear." I wouldn't open my mail; I would just avoid all of it. I was living like I had no tomorrow, I couldn't deal with it. I mean, I just couldn't. I really feel bad for the hardships I have put my family through. My father, my stepmother, my mother, my brothers and sisters—I had no understanding of how to be a human being again, and my actions affected my family. I really hurt a lot of them and I thank them very much, and I'm very grateful that they are still with me, and that they still love me and are understanding.

My mother has been very politically active. I believe it started when I was over in Iraq. I love her for feeling the way she does, but it just kind of adds fuel to the fire, I guess. I respect all that, but it's difficult for me to deal with in a lot of ways. The last thing you want to know when you are in war is that what you are doing is wrong. I just chose to not be aware of that, and in some ways I still choose to not be aware of that. When you are over there, you are making these hard choices and you are put in these hard places and you are doing all this stuff . . . the absolute last thing you want to know is that what you are doing is wrong. It's very tough. While I was over there, I wouldn't even entertain thoughts that what we were doing was wrong. I wouldn't even listen for a second when someone talked to me about it, and that's kind of my way of dealing with it.

Even now, I tend to avoid news of the war. That's why I drink so much. It's to avoid having to think about all these things and having to deal with it. I walked by a TV, and on the news the bottom line was, "Marines died in Ramadi," which is where I was, and I mean, it just pissed me off. I can't walk by a TV for a two second blip without being reminded of this. It's tough.

I'm going to AA and working out almost every day. I try to avoid the alcohol and the rage and the drama. What helps me is trying to do good for others. It is one of the biggest things. In one of my AA books they say, just for today, do something nice for somebody else and don't tell anyone about it. I try to do that every day. Doing a good deed for somebody helps you lay your head down at night and be happy with yourself.

I never believed in God before. The second time I went to Iraq, I was scared and I started to pray. I would pray for my family, and I would actually pray for the Iraqis. I didn't understand that it was a good or healthy thing to do. To pray for one's enemy is kind of a healthy way of going about stuff, but nobody told me that, I just kind of did it. Then I could finally feel like I could pray for myself, and I really did. It helped me sleep at night over there. Since I've been back I haven't forgotten that. For me to have that in my life is pretty big. Believing in God is a good thing and a powerful thing, and to pray for something really lets you know what is important. To pray for others is a very powerful thing as well. If you want to be a good man, you need to live your life that way. I need to fill my life with all these positive things. I just want to love myself. I want to be worthy of having a good life and feel that I am worthy.

When I really think about it, the hardcore alcoholism goes back to my first tour. The second tour just made it worse. I was going through a PTSD program, which was a really good program. I made it through about three weeks the first time, and then I got caught drinking. I went to another alcohol program, and then went back recently to do the PTSD program. It was a great program, and I got caught drinking again.

AA is a spiritual program, and whether you take that to mean Christian or whatever, it has spiritual values. You treat others well, you take care of others, you do selfless things, and you are going to be a happier and more spiritual person. You're being honest, not only to other people, but to yourself too.

I have been treated with nothing but respect from people, and that's really good. I feel pretty bad for the Vietnam guys and I don't know how they dealt with it.

I never believed in God before. The second time I went to Iraq, I was scared and I started to pray. I would pray for my family, and I would actually pray for the Iraqis.

Mary Geddry and son, John, at their home. Mary said: "Before we as a people send our youth into war, we have a responsibility and an obligation to fully understand the enormity of what it is we ask them to do. We are asking them to die. We are sending them into horrible situations in which they face horrible decisions and partake in horrible acts. To truly honor the warrior, every patriotic American must bear witness to their stories and their pain."

Mary Geddry

An open letter to three Iraqi women

The steam has dissipated from my coffee cup as I strain to write this letter to the three of you. You don't know me, and one of you will never have an opportunity to read this letter, but you have each left your mark upon my soul. Though I do not know your names, you will recognize who you are, and I speak to you woman to woman, mother to mother, and mother to child.

If you don't already know it, the U.S. military can train a man to kill, but cannot train that man how to handle it when he does. For this reason, amongst many others, my Marine son, John, who touched your lives in Iraq is in treatment, along with other veterans of this and earlier wars. They are ten wounded warriors: five from the Iraq War and five from that earlier American fiasco, Vietnam.

John has bonded with one of these older Vietnam vets. "Old Man," he calls him. The reason I am telling you about Old Man is that it took him thousands of bottles of alcohol, dozens of jobs, seven marriages, and forty years to accept that he had never recovered from his wartime experiences. They never recover, really; I want you to know that. Our paths have crossed, tragically, and we are connected now. This connection has provided me with certain details about your lives that I feel I have to share, if only that some small light may be shed on dark places.

There was a firefight in Baghdad, a 360-degree battle with the Marines taking fire from all around and overhead. You were there—not as a participant, just a civilian—and you are my first connection, though I learned of you last.

Training had the Marines firing back reflexively at anything that moved: vehicles, stray dogs, a blur of a shirtsleeve. The Marine who fired upon your husband and two children was almost 100 yards away and he jerked his weapon up in horror at the end of the burst as he watched your family fall.

You didn't know, but he watched you run out to your family. He saw you in your light blue wrap as you went from one body to the other. He tried to avert his eyes as you picked up your dead child and then the other and wailed in grief. He tried to look away, but that light blue color was always in his peripheral vision, pulling at him, drawing him back.

It might have been five, seven, or even ten minutes when, unable to bear your grief any longer, he swung the barrel around and fired. So, you see, we are connected because my son saw you die.

Does it matter to you about this man who killed you and your family? Perhaps not, but he hailed from what we call the Deep South. John called him a friend, and at 6′5″ and solid muscle he looked the perfect Marine, but he has not fared well since that day in Baghdad. Within months of returning stateside he amassed multiple alcohol-related assault charges.

Finally, he plunged over a beachside cliff and lay in a coma for months. Karma, John calls it, or self-imposed penance, but he is only now relearning how to speak.

. . . .

Not long ago, I met a Lance Corporal who had determined during the siege on Fallujah that he must enter your home in search of combatants. He prepared and set a timed charge to blow a new doorway in the side of your building. He gathered intelligence, assessed the situation, and finally gave the order to blow the charge. His men darted through the newly-opened breach and he followed closely behind.

You will remember him, because when he entered to find your husband and children dead from the blast you were crying out, "lemad'a, lemad'a" (why, why?). You will remember him, because when he saw what he had done, his knees buckled and the blood drained from his twenty-two-year-old face. You will remember him, because he fell back against the wall and clutched at his chest and gasped for breath.

You saw his reaction. You watched him try and shoulder the enormity of the order he had given, and when his eyes finally met yours, you placed your hand on his cheek and said, "masha, Allah" (God's will). Your compassion, your understanding, and your forgiveness that day destroyed him.

He would give his life to undo what he did. Today, he works hard to end our occupation of your country. I have thought of you every day since he told me your story.

. . . .

You cannot be more than six now, if that. With luck, you do not remember that October '04 day in Ramadi when your parents died. With luck, you are far away from Iraq now.

To you I feel the closest connection, the greatest responsibility, and the deepest agony. You see, your father wanted only to rescue you. He wanted only to grab you from your dead mother's arms, and he gave his life trying because he loved you so much.

My son and his Sergeant did not understand. They mistook your father's actions as a threat to their comrades, and fired upon and killed him. So, you see, we are connected because my son killed your father.

When the weapons platoon found you, scared and crying, many of them, including John, fell apart. You undid them. You and your scared, wide brown eyes and dark curls brought some of them to their knees.

They took your picture that day. You are a tiny bundle of pink and blue flowers and puffy sleeves set against the digital camouflage jacket of John's Sergeant, who did not set you down for hours. Please know that John keeps your picture, though he looks at it rarely because it hurts so much to remember.

What can I say to you? That I am sorry goes without saying. Does it help that my son suffers because of that day? Does it matter to your life that he will carry your image with him forever? No, I don't see how it can, but I will tell you I love you.

None of you can welcome this connection, but I feel it nonetheless. Taking your families from each of you has also lost my son to me, for he will never be the same. To each of you, Assalamu alaikum, peace be upon you.

—A Marine Mom

IRAQ IS THE
AMARCANS
GRAVEYIRED
HI
Mom
+
DAD
FUCK
ME

11/14/2003
10/19/2003
11/13/2
10/19/2

Author of *Jarhead: A Marine's Chronicle of the Gulf War and Other Battles* and *Hotels, Hospitals, and Jails: A Memoir*. He lives in Santa Monica, CA.

Afterword

by Anthony Swofford

If your first experience with *Exit Wounds* was anything like mine, right now you are a little bit angry, a little bit sad, a great bit proud of the young men and women in these pages, and achingly grateful to Jim Lommasson for training his thoughtful and humble eye on these soldiers, sailors, and Marines.

We civilians want to know *what it was like.* Eddie Black says, "Please do not ask us if we've killed anybody." But still, some people will ask that boring question. The only questions we should be asking are: *What is it like now that you are home? How might we help you?*

There are as many war stories as men and women who fought these wars and every other. Lommasson is an expert at allowing his camera to speak and then allowing the soldier or a proxy to speak beyond the image. What is the old cliché? A picture is worth a thousand words. These photos are worth ten thousand hours of sweat, 5,000 plus dead soldiers, a million sleepless nights, a trillion plus in national treasure—and every word spoken about the horror, the ecstasy, and the drudgery of combat and coming home.

The image-text combination in *Exit Wounds* is a rare and enduring piece of art that is a documentary, an essay, and a testament; testament to the all-encompassing and destructive power of war and the more powerful and sacred virtue of the human spirit.

Most soldiers hate being thanked for their service. I know I do. It's like being thanked for not running a red light. *Did what I was supposed to*, most men and women say.

Lommasson, I think, ran a bit of an end-around on his subjects. He thanked them quietly, from behind his camera, so that they might not object to his attention and care.

Many hundreds of thousands of words and images have been gathered about the brutality of the wars in Iraq and Afghanistan. *Exit Wounds* is as strong a rebuke to the horror and punishment of war that I know. Now that you have read and experienced this book once, go tell a friend or family member about the all-encompassing and powerful experience. And in a few days or a few weeks, or whenever you are able to handle it again, re-experience the magic and the light.

Appendix

Mosaic Multicultural Foundation

Mosaic Multicultural Foundation incorporated as a nonprofit, tax-exempt organization in 1990. Mosaic's mission is to create networks of artists, community activists, and spiritual teachers who can work in ground-breaking ways to create cross-cultural alliances and mentoring relationships for personal growth, spiritual awakening, leadership development, and vital community healing. For more than two decades, Mosaic has created unifying events and innovative projects that support and educate at-risk youth, refugees, combat veterans, and communities under stress. Mosaic seeks to find dynamic remedies for the alienation, spiritual dislocation, and personal isolation that increasingly characterize modern life for youth and elders alike.

One of our core projects, Voices of Veterans, began when Vietnam era veterans participating in discussions at a Mosaic mentoring event considered how they might help soldiers returning from current wars in Iraq and Afghanistan find their "civil feet" again and rejoin their communities as valuable, functioning members. This conversation quickly led to the development of Voices of Veterans which utilizes a retreat and community ceremony format to support veterans in the process of learning to use poetic soul-based expression to share their stories and mentor one another. In the retreat phase, Veterans returning from the current wars work with veterans of previous wars, as well as specialists who treat battle trauma and Post Traumatic Stress Disorders (PTSD). The deeply moving and revelatory personal stories of veterans are woven into mythic tales that help make sense of otherwise bewildering and tragic experiences. The public ceremonies that occur after the retreats allow fellow citizens to become compassionate witnesses to the stories of war and the necessity of creating a conscious and genuine return for veterans.**Voices of Veterans, Voices of War** began when Vietnam-era Veterans participating in Mosaic mentoring events proposed that the Mosaic's Creative Mentoring process would be helpful to soldiers returning from current wars in Iraq and Afghanistan. Older veterans help younger ones find their "civilian feet" again and rejoin their communities as valuable, functioning members. In the retreat phase, Veterans returning from the current wars work with Veterans of previous wars, as well as specialists who treat battle trauma and Post Traumatic Stress Disorders (PTSD). Spouses and family members of vets can also participate and receive help dealing with "secondary PTSD" issues.

The deeply moving and revelatory personal stories of Veterans are converted into poetry and narratives that help make sense of otherwise bewildering and tragic experiences. The public ceremonies that occur after the retreats allow fellow citizens to become compassionate witnesses to the stories of war and the necessity of creating a conscious and genuine return for Veterans.

The Telling Project

As the number of American men and women serving in uniform continues to dwindle (less than one percent of the population in the last eleven years of war, as compared to 39% of the population during WWII), connection between civilian and military populations becomes more tenuous, and real understanding on the part of the vast majority of Americans of what our military has been undertaking on their behalf diminishes. Veterans' transitions back to civil society are made more difficult through a pervasive lack of understanding of their circumstances, and civilian populations become ever more naive and disconnected from the extended implications of their day-to-day lives. As we transition toward a post-conflict society, it is critically important that we learn from the wars of the last decade, and our military legacy in general, so that we can continue to evolve as a society.

The Telling Project addresses this need on a community level through the creation of performances in which military Veterans and military family members, after interview, performance training, and rehearsal, stage the "telling" of their stories of life and the military for their communities. These performances catalyze meaningful conversation between fellow community members, rendering what might otherwise be divisive and polemical experiences and issues—war and military service—local, shared, and human. Simply put, *The Telling Project* offers Veterans and military family members the opportunity to speak and their communities the chance to listen.

"What is a soldier when you wash the Hollywood away? What is a warrior when you dispel the mythology surrounding their nobility? Everyone needs to know the answer to that question. The voices of those who have relevant experiences must make their struggles known, for their own healing and for the dream of peace."

– Jan Critchfield

Notes

An Open Letter from a Marine:

1. Homer. *The Iliad: The Fitzgerald Translation*, Translated by Robert Fitzgerald (Farrar, Straus and Giroux, 2004
2. William Manchester. *Goodbye, Darkness: A Memoir of the Pacific War* (Little, Brown, 1980)
3. Elton E. Mackin, *Suddenly We Didn't Want to Die*, (Presidio Press (November 1, 1993)
4. Richard A. Gabriel, *No More Heroes: Madness and Psychiatry In War*, (Hill and Wang 1987)

Lucas Wilson

1. Gary Mortensen: Director, *This is War-Memories of Iraq* (2007)

Edward Jewell

1. *Operation Homecoming: Iraq, Afghanistan, and the Home Front, in the Words of U.S. Troops and Their Families*, (National Endowment for the Arts, 2006)

1. Garrett Anderson:

Edward Tick, Ph. D., *War and the Soul: Healing Our Nation's Veterans from Post-tramatic Stress Disorder* (Quest Books 2005)

Vincent Emanuele:

1. General Smedley D. Butler, *War Is A Racket* (Round Table Press 1935)

Michael Campbell:

1. Cesare Pavese, "We do not remember days, we remember moments." (September 9, 1908 – August 27, 1950)

FRANCO,
THERE'S STILL TIME TO
RE-UP. JUST KIDDING!
KEEP IT REAL.
SGT.

11th platoon

Postscript

I want to thank all of the veterans, spouses, and parents who have participated in this book. Traveling across America, meeting so many wonderful and hospitable people has been an honor and a profoundly humbling experience. Mothers and spouses have privately told me that their veteran has opened up since our interviews. Vets have thanked me for listening to their stories. As I mentioned earlier, this book has taught me to listen.

The interviews have been difficult. There have been tears. The stories in this book are comprised of interviews done in homes, coffee shops, on the phone, at Veterans Day events, war protests, and long walks. Some interviews are done over several days and some are shorter because of logistics. The interviews are non-linear rambles. I have done my best to distill the stories and maintain each veteran's story and voice. Their stories are their truth.

The portraits have often been done on the fly, before, during, or after the interview. I hope the photographs help tell the story. The photographs were taken months and years after homecoming; they represent who they are today. Out of respect, I have not asked vets to "dress up like soldiers" or perform for the camera. *Exit Wounds* is a book about fifty veterans' stories of war and homecoming.

When I asked vets to talk about homecoming and they quickly returned to their war experience, it was clear they all wanted to convey a cautionary message to the reader. In so many words and in so many ways, they repeated the message that we've heard so many times from those who have fought our wars, "War is Hell." Have we become numb to this message?

After interviewing, I have asked some vets to write their own stories. At times, I have included public testimony and posts from social media. I hope the aggregate of the fifty stories will help us better understand that we all have an obligation to listen and become engaged. I hope our leaders on both sides of the aisle will read this book. As the drums of war continue to beat, I hope they will consider not their political career, but what is good for America and the world. We must listen to the honorable men and women who fight our wars.

2004